P R A T T   J O U R N A L   O F   A R C H I T E C T U R E

On Making

RIZZOLI
NEW YORK

Editorial Board
Zophonias Bjorgvinsson
Doug Childers
Anita Cooney
Akis Ioannides

Production Editor
Maura Grant

Assistant Editors
Alan Cohl
Giuseppe Provenzano

Faculty Advisor
Dan Bucsescu

Advisory Board
Keller Easterling
Elliot Feingold
Deborah Gans
John Knesl
Sol Yurick

Design/Production
Akis Ioannides
Zophonias Bjorgvinsson

Editor/Production Coordinator
Michelle Kerr

The *PRATT JOURNAL OF ARCHITECTURE* was produced by undergraduate students of the School of Architecture. Among our colleagues, we are particularly grateful for the time and talents of Danny Colvin, Margaret Flynn, Buddy Giddings, Avery Howe, Irena Ivanovich, Matthew Jelaçic, Georgetta Lascu, Perry Neuhaus, Rebecca Pugh, Warren Shaw and Caroline Umphlett.

For their generous contribution of time, consultation and advice, we thank Lisa Curtiss, James Fulton, Jack Nessel, Raleigh Perkins.

We would like to acknowledge the support of Steve Guttman from Adobe Systems Inc.

The *Pratt Journal* was produced by BLACK BOX. Type was set in in Univers and Times type families. Layouts were done on a Macintosh IIfx, using QuarkXPress, Adobe Photoshop, Adobe Illustrator and Microsoft Word. Images were scanned on the HP ScanJet IIc and Barneyscan slide scanner. Proofs were printed on an Apple LaserWriter IIg.
The Courier Connection produced film negatives at 2400 dpi and 150 lpi on an Optitek imagesetter and printed the journal on 80 lb. Recovery Matte recycled paper. The cover is 12 point Cls.

The *PRATT JOURNAL OF ARCHITECTURE* is published by the School of Architecture, Pratt Institute.

Warren F. Ilchman, President, Pratt Institute
Frances Halsband, Dean, Architecture
Donald Cromley, Chair, Undergraduate Architecture
Judith Aaron, Dean of Admissions
Isaac Kerlow, Chairperson, Computer Graphics
Michelle Kerr, Director of Publications

For unfailing encouragement and consistent support, special thanks to Sidney Shelov.

We gratefully acknowledge the generous support we have received from the administrative staff at Pratt Institute, particularly Phil Avanzato, Lillian Chasin, Alma Delany, Tim Dempsey, Loretta Edwards, Arlene Friedman, Imani Griszell, and Beverly Parker.

Distributed by:
Rizzoli International Publications, Inc.
300 Park Avenue South
New York, N.Y. 10010

Address editorial correspondence to:
Pratt Journal of Architecture
200 Willoughby Avenue
Brooklyn, N.Y. 11205

It may be oxymoronic to be theoretical about something very practical. The "making of things" is so commonplace as an activity that to discuss the subject one must be very abstract. Yet, there is nothing so practical as being abstract about practice — about praxis, about action in the construction of objects to be used by others in everyday life. Without putting words to such an activity — an exercise in conceptualization — one is left inarticulate, unable to instruct except by demonstration.

Let me explain. For some decades, we have been very untheoretical, very "down-to-earth" about the very abstract idea of "modernism." Freed from that we have begun to see in the constructing of objects in the world not only a pedagogy that is superior to other approaches to learning, but we have in this activity an opportunity to heal the separation we have all felt from the world we use and on which we depend. To once more give dignity to the act of making — even though we do so here abstractly — is to help us all to design buildings, settlements and objects that are more habitable, more pleasing and more useful. "Making" can "make" us whole again.

It is appropriate that this Journal and its subject originate at a place like Pratt Institute. By conviction and necessity, Pratt has championed for a century the importance of "making" things as a way to learn and to improve the world. To that tradition, this issue is ultimately dedicated.

Warren F. Ilchman
President, Pratt Institute

C O N T E N T S

Absence Seeks Contingency:
Architecture After Ideology

Contingency remains, however, the "Menetekel"* of lordship. This is always covert, though lordship eventually openly confesses it; totalitarianism. It subsumes as chance whatever is not like it, the slightest non-homonymy. One has no power over what occurs by chance. No matter where contingency arises, it gives the lie to the universal mastery of spirit, its identity with matter. It is the mutilated abstract shape of the in-itself from which the subject has usurped everything commensurable. The more recklessly the subject insists upon identity and the more purely it strives to establish its mastery the more threateningly looms the shadow of non-identity. The threat of contingency is simply advanced by the pure a priori which is its enemy and should allay it.

Theodor Adorno, *Against Epistemology*

The topic for this volume was born of a wariness of the role words have come to play in the production and legitimation of architecture. Architects, theorists, critics and historians seem compelled to map and speculate on where we have been, where we are, where we are going and what it all means.

* The writing on the wall. From Daniel, Chapter 5, trans.

Those of us who read some measure of this production can only conclude that the interpretations are many, the paths are multiplying and the meanings are abundant and multivalent. Our reticence expanded beyond the realm of discourse to include the ways in which the architectural object is represented. In varying degrees, both of these forms of mediation, images and words, serve the goal of fetishization and commodification at the expense of other potential values. The contingencies of making are often obscured by the proliferation of meanings, interpretations and products. Thus, *On Making* emerged as an attempt to re-found a discourse in the activities and contingencies of life and making.

Making, as an act of engagement, is invisible. It is a matter of experience, of knowing from the inside. It is what we do, whether making dinner, making a drawing or making a building. Words and objects have their own life. They may or may not reveal the conditions of their making. We believe that acts of making are the site where choices are made and knowledge is constructed — a locus where familiar distinctions such as theory/practice, mind/body, subject/object can be both sharpened and blurred.

Inevitably, making involves an adjustment of familiar assumptions. We find ourselves wanting to see *things* in a context that identifies their meaning or likeness. Frequently, when we travel, we take snapshots of the monuments and sites that we have seen most often in books. Yet, what we remember involuntarily are the intangibles: the smell of a particular street or an accidental encounter. Even with respect to specific places, sights or objects, it is the unanticipated reality that we value — the actual scale of a familiar building, the quality of light or stone, the souvenir hawkers. Similarly, making involves encounters with tangible and intangible realities, contingencies, that remain invisible when the made object is the central focus of discourse. This is not to connote the absence of a willful subject, but the presence of overlooked possibilities.

The works collected here, images and words all, were selected for their capacity to evoke aspects of making which might otherwise remain hidden. In general, they embody an appeal for, or an activation of a shift in emphasis from the ends to the means of making architecture, and making in general. Directly or indirectly, they address the nature of the object within such a realignment of priorities.

What is the object of architectural practice? On the one hand we make drawings, devise programs, construct simulations of objects. We generate words and images aimed at explaining, representing, and legally or theoretically legitimizing objects, usually made by others. Within this description of what many architects do, architecture as a practice is removed from the object of practice. This is not to minimize a material involvement or prerogative, but rather to establish a certain distance within which making takes place. Several strategies for negotiating this distance emerge. They range from redefining the object of practice such that object and practice are coincidental, to a suggestion that the distance and lack of closure be elevated to ritual.

The works are loosely organized around three themes established by symposia held in conjunction with our editorial work. The first theme comprises those articles and the symposium directly concerned with the act of making and addresses issues of representation and its relationship to making and production. The second theme challenges the dominance of theoretical models and presents the works from the maker's point of view. The third theme focuses on the issue of tools, in particular, the effect of new information and simulation technologies on our understanding and perception of the object of making.

As a whole this volume resists definitive framing. It is more appropriately seen and understood as a series of windows on an unguided tour. No map is available for this tour. There are, however, landmarks.

In her article, "Releasing the Form to the Making: Womenswork Is Never Done," Kim Tanzer argues for embracing this distance between making and its object, and suggests a "thingifying" of the process as a theoretical counter to the commodification and idealization of the object. The lack of closure, which is an inherent aspect of the daily making of architecture, is seen as an opportunity to engage certain technical and social contingencies of making. Tanzer's is an explicit argument for intervention on a local rather than a universal scale, but with larger ramifications for society and culture implied. The architectural object, the building, the drawing or the text, recedes to the less reified, slightly ambiguous position of an artifact or fossil of a thing *well made*.

In "Un-Making and the Possibility of Critical Work," Dan Hoffman exemplifies "various strategies of un-making or negation" as manifestations of critical practice. He suggests an interdependence between the notions of affirmation and negation while focusing on the capacity of negation to open the door to readings and possibilities beyond the material reality of the object, but not in contradistinction to it. The object is viewed as a record or recording device of critically engaged action.

In "Meditations on a Media Field," Hani Rashid reports that traditional conceptions of space and form have been torn asunder by technologies of communication and simulation. Architecture and its making are subjected to an unpredictable and constantly shifting terrain brought on by the facile permutation of reality vis-à-vis television, computers, fax machines and so on. He simultaneously condemns and embraces these contemporary "facts" of life. A recognizable architectural object is precluded by the rupture between intention and result, and making emerges as a form of liberation from the constraints and "tedium" of a determining past or a prescribed future.

"Broken Angel," an in-progress work by Arthur and Cynthia Wood, confounds the distance between architectural practice, its tools or media, and the object of practice. Here they merge in the *delirium of making*. The tools of construction and labor are more directly engaged as the means and ends of transformation and invention. The contingencies of making are simultaneous with the lives and personalities of the makers who are also the users. This is arguably a marginal position vis-à-vis the current state of architectural practice and discourse. However, it provokes the question of how a greater proximity between maker, user and object can be attained within the boundaries of conventional practice. Here, the object resists representation and reproduction because of its continuous making and its inextricable relationship to the maker/user.

Until recently, the activity of making has been understood (rendered meaningful) and activated primarily with respect to some overriding belief system and a corresponding structure of power: Making in the belief of God; making in the belief of man; making in the belief of art and technological progress; and now, deconstructivism's belief in the omnipresence of power itself, in particular, the insinuation of power into language and the means of representation. This latest theoretical construct renders suspect ideological and philosophical formulations that seek universal application and has led to a reassertion or emphasis on the local condition where the overly determinant mechanisms of power and ideology can be deconstructed or avoided. With respect to architecture, this has opened up the process on a representational level and led to a new formal vocabulary. However, it has yet to seriously challenge the rule of commodity and address a range of social or programmatic contingencies. Rather, poststructuralist theory applied to architectural practice is frequently reduced to a legitimizing text, and open-ended process has become merely the means to yet another stylistic and theoretical orthodoxy.

This is perhaps an inevitable result of architecture's presence in two worlds: the phenomenal and the permanent. Its existence at the tense boundary between art and utility renders architecture a particularly relevant venue in which to explore making. We propose making not as a new or neccessarily different theoretical platform, but as a notion valued for its incapacity to sustain a fixed ideological position. We have not sought to redefine architecture or its current milieu, so much as to evoke a revised scope of parameters. We believe these parameters to be neither completely predetermined nor universal (as in the notions of ideal form or essence), but specific to individual acts of making. Making is a site whose form takes shape in the construction and discovery of its boundaries. The objects that result might be understood as traces of active engagement or as catalysts to further engagement.

Doug Childers

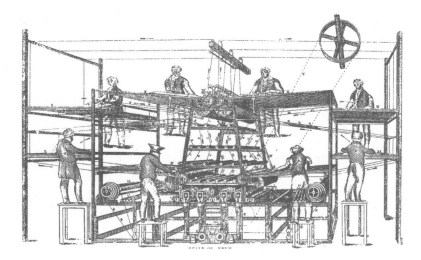

This symposium was held at
Pratt Institute's Higgins Hall
on December 12, 1990.

Moderator

John Knesl

Panelists

Kenneth Frampton
John Johansen
Ed Levine
Taeg Nishimoto

We want to explore our architectural landscape in the spirit of Gulliver, who in Jonathan Swift's tale of an incredible frolic, is both a witness and a participant in imaginary nations. The satire inspired us with its playful inquiry into tangible worlds of shifting perceptions. Swift rotates the parameters of space and gravitational pull so that Gulliver not only bursts through the horizontal x-y travel, but is also hoisted onto the z-axis in an extension outside of normal experience. Conditions of scale are shifted to a degree that transports the reader into a different state of knowing. *Gulliver's Travels* is an inspiring reminder of architecture's inherent strengths. Like Gulliver, we embark upon a journey. Ours is a journey in, around, about, through and for the notion of making. We hope, as Swift did with his novel, to illuminate and comment upon our situation by redirecting our focus. We are concerned with architecture which is tangible, which reaches into three dimensions to touch, to shift the ground, to reorient and to direct. We find reassurance in Vico's proposition that we only know that which we have made or are capable of making.

Making is a cognitive act and a mode of knowing through direct intervention and participation in the world, as opposed to an act of distancing. Thus, we propose to exchange the word design for the word make, a mainly symbolic exchange, but nevertheless important. Design describes the activity of architecture with an implicit bias: cognitive modelling is favored and physical qualities minimized. In contrast, making refers to the realms of mental and physical construction, acknowledging the dialectic quality of the process. Meaning and ideas are shifted, mixed, cut, tailored and introduced in a manner which is simultaneously both in and out of our hands. We do not want to disregard the distinctions between mental and physical activities, rather this emphasis on making more accurately describes our relationship to that which we make.

While perhaps self-evident, it is important to note that making is as significant for other areas of human endeavor as it is for architecture. Making involves such diverse fields as writing, philosophy, science, theater, politics.... Making can serve as a common ground, allowing for the intersubjectivity of those who share intimate knowledge of an act, skill or experience.

On Making

John Knesl

Many people think "making" is not much different from thinking, constructing, shaping, or even assembling – and some of the questions we would like to pose in this symposium are: Is making fundamentally different from other activities? If so, how? Who is the author of something – the individual? an organization? Is making architecture primarily, or should it be primarily, limited to a material object or situation? Or is this notion, even if it once seemed true, fast becoming obsolete in view of our ability to evoke a totally simulated electronic environment that is much more manipulable, cheaper and, perhaps, a lot more interesting?

I would like Kenneth to begin by saying a few words about how he sees the act of making – in theory and practice.

Kenneth Frampton

You can't really separate theory from practice: each influences the other. Perhaps a useful way of discriminating between the two is to introduce the idea of time. A certain reciprocity takes place in time between theory and practice. Theory after all emerges not only from other theory, but also from practice. Theory put into practice also involves transformation across time. This is evident whether it's a very elaborate construction or whether it's a very simple enterprise. Theory is situated between the model of an action and the intentionality that's involved in the

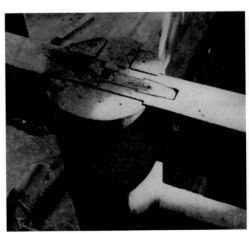

Japanese joint detail
(reprinted from *Architecture in Japan*)

action, and the anticipation of the procedures to be passed through in achieving the action. The theoretical scheme then is validated by the practice, by putting it into action.

Even over quite short spans of time I think it's often necessary to modify the procedure. Frequently, the initial intent proves to be ludicrous, as in a Buster Keaton movie. Material brings about unanticipated obstacles and difficulties, which have to then be modified in light of the original intention, and so on.

Knesl

For instance, if one were to observe a craftsman teaching an apprentice, there would be explicit instructions given as to how and why to perform something in a certain way.

Frampton

We're talking about the fact that all sorts of crafts and procedures can't be learned in an academic sense. They have to be practiced in order to be acquired as skills. This process, however, does entail a theoretical idea of how one should proceed. One doesn't enter it completely innocently, since practice is usually proceeded by some instruction. In the process of making, however, one finds that there is a gap between theoretical procedure and the actual procedure, which can only be filled through revisions or through inspection of the previous assumption.

Knesl

So if I understand correctly, making requires physical involvement.

Do you want to respond, Ed?

Ed Levine

Well, I'd like to make a point first about the relationship between theory and practice. I think this relationship and the meaning of those terms has changed, and it's changed because of the institutionalization of the education of the artist and, indeed, the architect. Not long ago, the idea of getting a degree was ludicrous. Now if you look at artists' resumés, you'll see that all the artists have gone to university and have gotten either BFA's or MFA's. That's a change in both theory and practice, and it changes the nature of that relationship. Because the ability to intellectualize is one of the primary, highly valued activities at the university, the arts have shifted to a more intellectual approach to their disciplines.

It seems to me not fortuitous that the model of linguistics is one of the major models used in dealing with, describing and thinking about the visual arts. And so one clearly is going to adopt the linguistic context in order to survive and also because it has some value. It really redefines the nature of making or doing. There are two forms of knowing: knowing by acquaintance and knowing by doing. I think Kenneth was referring to craft as knowing by doing. One doesn't know how to play chess because one knows the theory or rules of chess. By actually playing chess, one learns more about the nature of the process than any theory can teach. Just as the would-be carver cannot apprehend the nature of his materials from theory. But today the shift has been to knowing by acquaintance. One thinks that because one knows the theory of these things, one can make interesting, imaginative, moving, important art or architecture. It seems to me that this is a radical change from the way things used to be and I think it's not going to be unchanged because of the way society is dealing with education in the arts.

Knesl

At this point it might be useful if John could discuss his way of thinking about how to make a building.

John Johansen

I think that I have a very different point of view from anyone else here, having had buildings of my design built and having been very much involved in the making of them.

"Making" is a specific word and also a very general word. It could mean building in the old sense, or it could mean assembly of parts in the new sense. It would be of great importance, at a time when we are too concerned with analysis and intellectualizing, to go back to perhaps the very basics of architecture as "making." Architecture, separate and distinct from all the arts, is a service and, ipso facto, structure art. The only way to achieve architecture as an art is not to cleave closer to the pure arts, but to understand its intention, which is the performance of a service, for the satisfaction of a need. I believe design must start with this. This is where

the motivation always comes from. There can be no shortcut through this process of building.

If I were then to tell you about my process, it would be: understanding the program and the purpose of the building, analyzing the conditions of the site, respecting the limitations of the budget and understanding the client we're working with. Only by knowing the limitations do you know the latitude of your freedom. I always hold back from any solution, any vision of the image until the elements are in place. In designing the Oklahoma Theater, for example, I took the program, the functional elements, putting them visually in my mind as though they were hanging in space with no support whatsoever. Secondly supporting them, thirdly connecting them. This is a totally different approach. I would say one more thing – that many architects have great uncertainty in them-

selves in the creative process. An architect will impose an image or a solution on the work, fearing that he or she can never come out of the creative process with a successful piece of architecture or a compelling image. Now the image, of course, is important, but it must be the result of the building process. You must let the program develop, by itself, in space – I like to use the word "preside." I preside while this assemblage somehow finds its own way.

Knesl

Nevertheless, there remains a question – the programs these days for most buildings are not usually defined by users themselves. Even where they are, an argument could be made that the users don't actually know what they want. Or what they might want, if they had a real choice, could have all sorts of ramifications. So there appears to be a need for continuing intellectualization, and what we're looking for is a way of making this critical and theoretical work somehow more creative, more relevant perhaps. I think you were distinguishing between making and assembling, because much of the act of putting a building together these days is, in fact, assembly. It's putting together what are largely pre-formed pieces – not only for reasons of economy, but also because of the way our minds operate.

What do you think, Taeg?

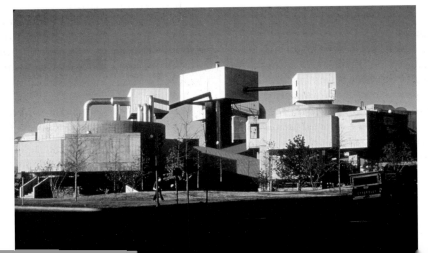

Oklahoma Theater, John Johansen

Taeg Nishimoto

I think that there are two basic ways to conceive of the notion of making. One way occurs within the context of efforts to define what architecture is, and the other occurs when one tries to define what architects actually do in the process of conceiving architecture. It is within the context of the latter activity that I am thinking of John's question.

I am constantly amazed when I consider what I actually do in my own work – I cannot touch the hammer to the nail. What I do instead is to draw certain lines, or an assembly of lines, that are to dictate the physical substance that will constitute the architecture. For that process, I use certain types of paper, certain devices to draw lines; maybe, at times, I make do with something else simply because it is available on my desk. Then I start questioning how much these simple lines, these traces, or even the availability of the paper, actually influence my thought process.

I think now, especially after postmodernism, we can see that we went through an age where what the thing itself was really didn't matter, what was signified mattered. I think there is a way to think of architecture as a physical substance. There is a well-known proposition that I can bring up: a hammer is sitting on the table, and I'm looking at this hammer, and somebody says this hammer is too heavy, and I have to respond to his indication. What does he mean? It's not about how it looks, obviously, or how expensive it is, but some kind of physical quality about the weight is determining if this hammer is usable or not. I constantly refer to this way of thinking when I'm thinking of the line or anything that is happening on my desk. The exact thing that I'm doing does eventually, somehow, get translated into the physical environment. I think it would be interesting to start thinking of making from the viewpoint that the architect's activities are really limited. I guess if you're a sculptor, you make something; it's there and it's your work. But in architectural discourse, it can never be that way. And I think that's exactly why this notion of making interests me.

Knesl

Taeg, you have used scores by John Cage to help us understand architecture. Some people might say music is a different discipline and we should not superimpose it on architecture. Other people, however, might say it's quite useful to be looking out to other disciplines.

Nishimoto

As I said, there is the architectural sketch I'm making with a pen, and this image that I'm supposed to read as a music score – what is the difference between those two images? I am a trained architect and any line that I draw is supposed to be read as the physical manifestation of something that happens where my line is drawn. And the same thing happens in Cage's score and some other musical notations. So we are doing something similar, very similar.

At the same time, the way I draw the lines is not the automatic, logical consequence of other conditions, such as some programmatic resolution. There is simply a desire for the line to be there. My effort is to find a way where a visual operation evolves into something in architecture – a process that I would concede happens in other creative discourses.

Knesl

I would now like to move on to a short reading from *MicroCAD News*, which I think has some bearing on the idea of making and its relevance for architecture today. This is from an article on virtual reality called "The Next Way":

Reality encompasses the projection of simulation and emphasizes the perfection of the interface between the user and the simulation. Today that interface through its sight, sound, communication and the ability to thrust and manipulate objects in the simulated world, allows you to interact visually with a virtual object.

The interface will eventually be one like the Enterprise's, a holodeck in which you become an active part of the simulation.

For me this "reality" is threatening or questioning the relevance of making a material environment or material object today because it clearly does away with that. Whatever you can do out there – if it's real – is probably less than what you can do in virtual reality in a fairly short amount of time. Should we be talking about cheaper, more efficient and more exciting ways of making artificial, totally simulated environments?

Levine

I just had this thought that is a little frightening. I don't know how many of you have seen the Woody Allen movie, *Sleeper*, but in it the guy goes into an orgasmatron to have an orgasm. Frankly, I'd much rather have the woman in my arms than have her in virtual reality. So my answer is obviously that virtual reality just perpetuates living in the world of the hyperrealist – not dealing with the tactility and physicality of life.

The notion that you can think through the computer is not the same as thinking with materials. One of the things that I've noticed in

architectural studios is that students work basically with just two or three materials – cardboard, styrofoam and sometimes a little bit of plexiglass, odds and ends. That's interesting, but the world is not made of cardboard and plexiglass and styrofoam. It's made of other things, which can help you think about the world in ways that you can't with cardboard and the like.

Knesl

The simulation enterprise is all about making yet better simulations and more exciting simulations. And if you are still missing this sense of touch, well, next year that can be simulated too. I don't know whether you will agree, but my answer is that when you are in actual contact with what used to be called the material, there is always something that you cannot calculate, there is something that you cannot figure out, there is something that you cannot anticipate, and I would submit that the sense of risk makes a critical difference.

Johansen

When we are threatened by certain experiences imposed by the electronic image, I think that we find

in nature certain balancing factors. Our perceptive habits have been retrained – we receive the impact of images at twice the speed our parents did, but even though we can learn to tolerate them, we have to escape and find a balancing factor in material reality. Our concern for ecology is, I believe, such a balancing factor, and we shouldn't forget current physical fitness, an extensively popular pastime, is another. Applied to architecture specifically, then simulation and illusion must be counterbalanced by actual physical experiences of moving through spaces and the tactile value of various materials.

Knesl

You can call this a counterbalancing when, in fact, I believe it's a consumption of nature. Some have asked why we can't prove, as architects, that there is something really important always missing from any kind of simulation. Personally, I don't see the culture in general turning and saying, oh yes, we forgot about this little thing called "being embodied and being involved."

I suspect that Kenneth might have a different perspective on this.

Frampton

The more I think about the word "making," and the unfolding discussion, the more I think it is difficult to exclude the political from the issue. It is the one factor that would make any sense of the topic from the widest point of view. Within the political, it is possible to situate the whole problem of making. Particularly when that is self-consciously preceded by questions about theory and practice, and the possibility of a theory that is in excess of practice or to one side of practice, or that even exists instead of practice.

When these proceedings began, I wrote down three words just as a way of starting to try to think about this. Each one began with 'm.' The first was the word "metropolis," the second was the word "marginal" and the third was the word "making." I think we really kid ourselves if we think that architecture is not a problematic endeavor. It is marginal to the production and consumption cycle that dominates the late megalopolitan–industrial reality. This is very much borne out by the fact that in this country 20 percent or less of built production entails any involvement by architects at all.

I think that recognizing the marginality of the field leads to a certain impulse to escape, escape into art, or escape into theory. This unaired question of what is the boundary between art and architecture is one of the big issues plaguing architectural schools today and the entire architectural discourse. There is a great deal of production which, in the end, presents itself as architecture, but is, in fact, really art, or would wish to be fine art – that is

to say, seeks to escape from the marginality of the field by entering the discourse of art.

Then there is this problem of the limit of the field. Prior to the division of labor and the proliferation of objects, architecture was not so problematic; the making of things in relation to the culture was less ambiguous. The question of what is the "nature" of the theoretical paradigm that informs the act of making of objects is obviously an issue or otherwise we wouldn't be talking about it. It seems to me, and I think John has this fear as well, that the recent attempt at limiting the discourse of objects and practice to a discussion of type is much too rigid and exclusionary. Typology is very limited in its capacity to give full access to the real situation.

Knesl

One of the things about making that is very important to me is that it is always related to an other, be that another person, other people, or be it nature as such. It's always related to an other that is somewhat unpredictable and has a right to be other. I think that's implied in the term. Even the most escapist and reductivist acts of making have some of that quality. One goes away to make something all by oneself, but it's always done somehow in preparation of returning it to the world.

Ed, your response to this would be important to this because it

would be coming from what is usually considered a different field, and the question has to do with the limitations of fields and disciplines.

Levine

First of all, we get caught in these dichotomies which are typical of Western thinking but, I believe, are fallacious. We know that in actuality one cannot separate theory from practice, one cannot separate mind from body, although Descartes did a very good job of trying. Abstraction can only be done with an undynamic view of the world; the intellect is really the ability to cut things apart. We often speak as if the personal and the social are distinct, but in fact, you're correct, you are aware when you make something that it will be put out there in the world and that people will respond to it.

From my point of view, all making in the arts is also a way of knowing or understanding. In other words, without making one cannot understand certain things. One cannot know in the most profound sense without making and that knowing has first to be a personal knowing. What are you making architecture for? What are you making art for? Is it to know something about art and architecture? Or is it to realize your vision and understanding, what you feel, what you think? You don't always know what you feel and what you think without either saying something or doing something. Isn't it nice that sometimes after you say something you think: I really can't believe I said that. We all have that experience. We don't know what we think until we think it. We don't know what our thoughts are until we say them. In a profound sense, it is only through the embodiment, the physicality, the materiality of what you do, that you can know something about the world.

That is why for me, at least in the arts, the first act of knowing has to be a personal knowing. And the gift is to give that act of knowing to other people so they may know, or refute, or whatever, but the gift is to make it public. So there is no separation in my mind between the personal and the social. The gaze of others makes you feel your own personality, your own individuality. It's a very profound dialectic, fluid interaction between one's sense of the boundaries of oneself and the boundaries of the other.

Johansen

Sort of a paradox in that the creative act, altogether private, has to be individual or it won't happen at all; yet, it has to be objectified, as you said, to be made known to society.

Knesl

I think that's another interesting point because there is a tendency today that arises from the conjunction of the way in which post-mod-

ern society turns us into consumers, that become more and more powerful, if only in terms of the privileged act of consumption.

Frampton

Television is surely the simulation machine par excellence, and its implications are apocalyptic. If you took television out of Western society tomorrow, you would induce states of severe psychological and political disturbance. It's quite obvious that TV serves as a pacifying somatic device.

There is a link between simulation and the formation of the self. After all, we are embodied by language from childhood and without language we can't even begin to be ourselves and that applies to almost every cultural situation. This may explain the stress placed upon originality, this desperation to be original. Originality will not come from

within, but has to be willfully, desperately, sought for – otherwise it is not possible to make it in this competitive society. You can feel this in architectural schools.

Knesl

Well, of course, I would agree with this. The more simulation, the more signs replace actual goods, the more powerless, in "real" terms, we become in society. This occurs in stages. The first stage is where you just identify with something happening on a television screen. The next stage is where they give you more and more simulated control over the world. Simulation is so seductive that I really think it's a big threat. Because as Ed said, when you are there in your body, being embodied, you're never in total control. Somehow, you always have to answer to another. You can try to avoid it, but ultimately you must. To me, that's where the true potential, the real importance, of architecture lies today. Depending on how you structure the physical world, a sense of the self can be reinforced or weakened or changed. I think that there are ways in which architecture can become relevant in this sense. (I'm not saying that we should become social engineers again, or that form can actually "do" something directly.)

But I'd like to return to the question of education and how our respective ideas about making might relate to education.

Johansen

We ought to work in our schools toward an assumption that our students should be knowledgeable about building processes, the purpose of architecture, and architecture as a service art, among other things. And we should bring together the theoretical and the practical. I insist that they can be brought together.

Knesl

On your slides, Ed, I saw some images of people lying down....

Levine

Sure. Those slides are actually of architecture students doing work in a class called "Dimensions of the Body." We started with the idea that the first pieces would be made with our bodies lying down. We wanted to explore the meaning and experience of verticality by exploring what it is to make an architecture or structure based on the idea that gravity had a different relationship to your body. The hidden assumption here is that our conception of humanness is tied to our embodiment of verticality, that our humanness is tied to our bodies and not to its disappearance.

There are certain things that I realize now by watching my students that are indigenous to the problem of being an architect, which is different from the problem of being an artist. Artists make work, architects make models.

Students in Ed Levine's class, "Dimensions of the Body"

Architecture, then, is a conceptual, abstract discipline in the educational field because you can't build. Architects are also disembodied, and that to me is very significant. If you're making a built structure, you're shaping your own body, you're shaping the body of others, you're shaping the body of the world. And not to be aware of how your body feels in space, how it's reacted on by mass and the environment seems to me a contradiction, a problem at least. So the question then is, what do you do about this? My feeling is that somewhere in the studio you have to become embodied again. There have to be projects where you're doing things which are no longer abstractions, but are realizations from the abstractions.

Drawing is a form of abstraction. It's a form of thinking too, but you're thinking about something else which is the material object. You also make models. You make collages. You're making things to help you to become better architects, as tools for understanding something about the world of architecture. It is important to know what those tools tell you and what they do not tell you. It seems that it would be important for you to have experiences where you go through the whole arc, and go back again, from being outside your body, to inside your body, to outside your body again, and then you take a critical look at what you've done. I don't think you have that opportunity until you build something, and then you get out there and you have to deal with all the things you have to deal with. When I do public art, I appreciate some of the problems that you have to deal with. It makes me want to go back to the studio every time I get out in the public arena.

Nishimoto

I agree with what Ed brought out and that is my studio's aim too. The critical point here is the relationship between the body and abstraction or representation. We often assume that when we do things intuitively, they become more arbitrary, because it's the person who is engaged as opposed to certain ideas. However, these intuitions, reactions to our sensory experience of physical reality, do not remain within the realm of private secrets. We do find a certain collective sense that we can effectively use to understand that physical reality.

For instance, to me poetry is ultimately the most effective way to create this kind of discourse. We have many vocabularies in our language, and we know basically what they mean when we use them. But somehow the combination of a set of words, or their placement, or even their utterance, begins to capture the poetic moment. There is a very physical aspect to poetic lan-

guage. In the making of architecture, I think similar things are happening on many levels. In order to understand the physical qualities of these poetic moments, we have to rely on the intuitive moment or the physical observation, which we start integrating into our work.

In my studio, we discuss the student's works, drawings or objects, as a physical substance, not as the representation of certain ideas. We look for interesting conditions in the works that are supposed to be interesting in the representation. Some students find it difficult because they are used to explaining instead of observing the actual conditions. Finally, there is a moment when our discussion of the works starts to make sense to everybody in a collective way. I think it's because there is very little sense of representation. They are not talking about borrowed reality or brought-in reality, which we can't define. The drawings and the objects begin to embody the whole discourse, the program, the site, scale and so on. Thus, the process focuses on those moments of discovery, the discovery of intentions that reveal themselves in the process.

Knesl

Much of the discussion as I see it has involved a provisional idea of reality and materiality. We have accepted making as something different from simulation, or theory, but that kind of separation could

raise questions from the deconstructivists or other post-structural quarters. I think it's important to make further headway with those terms. I think it is critical to force the issue of a bodily involvement of some kind into the world. To me this is one of the most critical things, but it is difficult to do. My sense from your description of what you're doing in the studio is that you seem to be going that way, but somebody else might argue differently. What might have happened at the end of the semester is that you all joined into one paradigm and now you have a common story.

Kenneth, what should we do, what can we do, to relate the studio in a meaningful way to this thing called reality, political and otherwise?

Frampton

The issue of consciousness is always with us, although there is the understandable feeling that too much consciousness will render the subject impotent. I wasn't entirely convinced by that question of how consciousness is developed and exercised. And vis-a-vis the reality in which we live, it seems to me that tradition and continuity are both important issues that have particular sharpness in a world in which references are extremely unstable. One of the things we find hard to accept is our intrinsic lateness vis-a-vis the idea of the new.

This question of what the building wants to be or what it can be is the question that should concern us. "What is the intrinsic nature of a work?" can only be entered through consciousness, for how else can it be approached? This brings me back to the question of the visual versus the tactile in late twentieth-century, and this has an impact on architecture schools and on everything else as well. Obviously, the visual is directly connected to the idea of competitive images and the phenomenon of compulsion to arrive at a compelling image, as opposed to a consciousness that seeks through the tactile means a redefinition of the tradition.

Knesl

If anyone from the audience wants to ask questions, now is the time, and I would ask you to address them directly to the participants.

Question

This is addressed to Kenneth. You said that the architect, in the context of making/metropolis, ordinarily would be considered marginal. I would like you to repeat why you think so. Why do architects as a profession have this unfortunate self-conscious view that they are somehow responsible for the situation, in spite of all those other things that contribute to it? They make themselves responsible, whereas they might, if they adopted another attitude, work toward the

whole culture becoming concerned about the act of making.

Let me just add one other comment about making. We come into the world already made and we embrace it, already made. It existed, in form, before us. How it has been already made is of great importance if architecture is to be successful in de-marginalizing itself. I don't think they need to recycle everything. They should understand how we are involved, how we evolved as a system of skilled beings, and ultimately how we evolved ourselves.

Frampton

The architecture profession seems to oscillate in many ways between megalomania and mea culpa. You touched on many issues, but I would like to respond to this question of permanence. I think one of the things we suffer from is our preoccupation with the production/consumption cycle. Everything falls under the sway of amortization. The idea that anything should be durable is seen in a negative light. But, of course, this presupposes grotesque dimensions of waste. The question of the relationship between the species and the natural environment is raised right here, and this clearly transcends architecture by a wide margin. So I think in a way architects don't respect material enough and, in this sense, making is of fundamental importance. The quality of

the made thing is what's at stake and what difference it makes whether the thing is made this way or that way. Of course, this is difficult to talk about, perhaps it is easier to demonstrate the point by pointing at things that have been made.

The problem with the profession is an image issue which actually runs away from the made thing. What is sold is the image, and the architect is sold as an image. The image is bought, but the thing is left in limbo; no one takes any responsibility for it anywhere. Neither the client nor the architect accept responsibility, because what was at stake in both cases was the marketing of a personality and an image.

Question

This is addressed to Taeg. I was wondering – what do you do when technology, this synthetic technology, has changed everything so much? How should we deal with this?

Nishimoto

As Kenneth was just saying, architecture has become imagery that's bought and sold. The latest phenomenon in Tokyo is a clear example of this. In Japan today, the structure of the relationship between clients and architects is changing due to the evolving presence of "producers." The producers, as in the moviemaking industry, are the people clients consult about the conception of the building, with much concern about the final image of the building and its reflection upon themselves. The producers then approach the architect from this rather pre-packaged point of view. It is undeniable that, in this situation, there is a danger of being preoccupied with the economics of imagery. And while the technological capability, including synthetic aspects, suggests so much potential in opening up the way we perceive things, we seem to feel ambivalent about this processed information. It is probably a transitional kind of reality, but this reality has to carry our own cultural heritage. If we are to integrate this new phenomenon, we need to develop a strategy that deals with more fundamental issues of life and reality. The procedure would be something of a fight for which you have to be prepared, because the technological changes are radical and occurring so rapidly.

The Seagrams Building, image presented by Taeg Nishimoto.
(Reprinted from Verna Blazer, *Mies van der Rohe, Furniture and Interiors*, Barron's, Woodbury, N.Y., 1982.)

D A N   H O F F M A N

Un-Making and the Possibility of Critical Work

In his work *The One Dimensional Man*, Herbert Marcuse addresses what he saw as the paralysis of criticism of contemporary technological society. He argues that this paralysis is due to the dominance of a singular rationalizing discourse that has effectively transformed thinking about society to a condition "without opposition." Marcuse explains further that the techniques of production which are the driving forces behind contemporary society also extend into and determine "the universe of discourse and action" that make up society itself. This reflexive collapse of discourse effectively eliminates the oppositions (or opposing ways of thinking) that have informed the history of discourse to date.

> Thus emerges a pattern of one dimensional thought and behavior in which ideas, aspirations and objectives that, by their content, transcend the established universe of discourse and action, and are either repelled or reduced to terms of this universe. They are redeemed by the rationality of the given system and are its quantitative extension.[1]

The implications of this historical development are evident in all aspects of our lives. We no longer consider the world as "antagonistic in itself, a world informed

Opposite
9119 St. Cyril. Azar, Cathcart, Fantauzzi, Van Elslander, William

1. Herbert Marcuse, *The One Dimensional Man*, Beacon Press, Boston, 1964, p.12.

by the dualisms of appearance and reality, untruth and truth, unfreedom and freedom."[2] These dualisms, which have informed Western thought since the Greeks, have been progressively leveled. Marcuse contends that a corollary to this development has been the leveling of the possibility of critique. Without the distance that opposition in thought affords, how are we to judge the value or meaning of a particular phenomenon or action? Marcuse gives as an example the modern occupation of airline pilot. The actions of the pilot are highly prescribed. A judgement can only occur in the form of an execution of an operation within the flight system (the closed set of all possible actions). The proper functioning of the system should be the pilot's only concern and becomes, in effect, the very life of the pilot. The pilot cannot afford a flaw. The understanding of the pilot cannot be burdened by the consideration of opposing ideas that are resolved within the context of a struggle. What sustains the pilot in the air are certainties, not regrets.

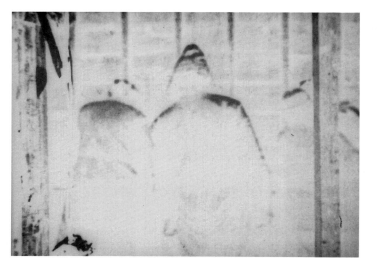

Architects at work

The question remains, however, whether this leveling has been complete. Has the "established universe of discourse" successfully eliminated the condition of meaningful opposition and the processes of negation that are its methodology? I would agree that in the context of the "established discourse" referred to by Marcuse, critical difference has been dispersed and marginalized. For example, in architecture we have witnessed a succession of "critical" positions with reference to the modernist ideology in the early part of this century. The manifestations of these positions into building, however, have had little effect upon the structure of the building industry and its products. At best, they have been able to frame an appearance for architecture, and at worst, they have simply been apologies for the on-going economic concerns of the building industry. Yet, it is at the margins that we continue to find, in various ways, the possibility of ideas and aspirations that may transcend, however briefly, the seemingly infinite embrace of technological society and its monolithic discourse. Herein lies the furtive but necessary possibility of art.

2. Marcuse, p. 125.

For in its pursuit remains the invigorating idea of negation that gives rise to possibilities other than those found within the given discourse.

A negation is not simply a cancellation of an affirmation. Rather it suggests a certain complexity that simultaneously incorporates an affirmation and the qualification of that affirmation. Bergson states that negation differs from affirmation "in that it is an affirmation of the second degree: it affirms something of an affirmation which itself affirms something of an object."[3] The inherent complexity of a term that both affirms and qualifies an object opens a space in a discourse that would otherwise close down upon itself. The nothingness that positivism attempts to supplant by its rational activity is not devoid of meaning, but is rather an expectant field of possibilities. Again, Bergson finds a complexity in the "one dimensional" term when he describes nothingness of the void as "the idea, distinct or confused, of a substitution, and the feeling, experienced or ingrained, of a desire or regret."[4] It is the possibility of **feeling** that nothingness can admit to. As a process towards nothingness, negation creates a space of absence within which the expectant grain of our emotions may rise.

The following will be a discussion of works that I feel have engaged these conditions or possibilities of negation. This is not an attempt to establish another theory of artistic work, but is rather a gathering of works that are significant in the manner in which they have critically examined their discipline and culture. The critical positions in the work are maintained through the use of various strategies of un-making or negation to produce new possibilities, aspirations, anticipations or regrets.

In these works, the production or making of the work is paralleled by a corresponding movement towards the un-making of previously held assumptions about that discipline or framework within which the work is understood. However, un-making is not limited to this contemplative aspect. It can also become the program of actions of the work itself. These two approaches should not be considered simply as opposites, but as a pair of related terms or activities that can inform and bind an artistic work to its context.

The culture without criticism that Marcuse speaks of should be understood as a monolithic circumstance that these works seek to transcend. It is a circumstance that must be challenged at every turn, for the oppositions that once found themselves within the very structure of thinking are now dispersed to its margins. It is there that we must endeavor to sustain a critical work.

The *Black Square* by Malevich remains as a silent observer to much of twentieth century artistic and architectural work. Much has been said about the *Black Square*, except for the simple observation that it is a painting over, or blacking-out, of a previous work by Malevich – a fact confirmed by a recent x-ray analysis of the

Black Square, Kasimir Malevich

3. Henri Bergson, *Creative Evolution*, Arthur Mitchell, trans., Henry Holt & Co., New York, 1931, p. 288.   4. Bergson, p. 283.

painting.[5] In a symbolic way the *Black Square* is a blacking-out of the history of painting. The black-out erases the possibility of a construction in depth upon the canvas, thereby frustrating our "hunger for images."[6] Yet, by placing the square on the canvas so that a frame of white remains on the periphery, the conditions of canvas and frame are retained. (The white is actually an off-white like that of the canvas.) The frame, then, frames a void, or nothing, but as was indicated above, this "nothing" is tempered by the first reading of the square as a blacking-out or painting-over in its resistance to representational depth and imagery. What the *Black Square* offers is a deflection of the subject of the painting towards the circumstantial conditions of the periphery. The flatness of the image is a reiteration of the wall upon which the painting hangs and by implication, the other walls and floor of the

9119 St. Cyril, in Willis Gallery

room itself. The negation or un-making of representational depth is displaced by the simultaneous construction of the phenomenal depth peripheral to and in front of the painting. What begins as a negation through concealment evolves into an affirmation of experiential depth before the painting, the small size of the painting encouraging an engagement with the surround, not its domination. The *Black Square* is an absent gaze from the dark, mirrored "other" upon the wall, making one conscious of the conditions of one's own being before the painting.

The reduction of the painting to make the image or symbol of the square raises the question of the meaning of the square itself. Though the title implies a geometric construction, Malevich is careful to point out that the square is not geometrically constructed, it being an approximation, by eye and hand, of a square, drawn within the frame of a canvas. Is not Malevich considering the square as an "approximation" accepting the inevitable split in geometry between its idea in thought and its construction in material, that within geometry there is an essential distance that technology can never transcend, that no square is ever ideal in its applied construction? By labelling the painting a square and constructing it by eye

5. Milda Vikturina and Alla Lukanova, "A Study of Technique, Ten Paintings by Malevich in the Tretiakov Gallery," *Malevich*, Armand Hammer Museum of Art and Cultural Center, Los Angeles, 1990, pp. 193-195.

6. Luise Hurn, "About the Ars Multplicata of Gunther Forg," *Gunther Forg, The Complete Edition, 1974-1988*, Museum Boymans-van Beuningen, Rotterdam, 1989, p. 13.

rather than geometry, Malevich finds a space of opposition within the hermetic assumptions of technology. Its negation (as a qualified affirmation) both confirms and denies the significance of the square in painting and in technological culture. Its metaphorical reading does not go unnoticed, for in the name *Black Square* we have the ambivalence that the word "black" suggests in a title: the aura of a dark void and the sign for the opacities of its "other" life.

The condition of witness surfaces again in a work by Joseph Beuys entitled *Vacuum ⟷ Mass*. The work involves an "action" that was performed in a cellar over a six-hour period in the presence of a "crowd of people." At the end of the action, certain objects used in the action, such as bicycle pumps and pieces of fat, were sealed in an iron chest that had been placed in the room. The chest is all that remains of the action, the witnesses having departed when the photographic documentation of the sealed chest was made.

The double negative in the work (the empty room and the sealed chest) results in a presence that draws in the feelings of the viewer. Here we are presented with a chain of circumstance that binds the scene back towards its (now imaginary) past. The emptiness of the room is qualified by the projected memory of the "crowd of people," a lingering absence that haunts our vision. In *Being and Nothingness*, Sartre demonstrates how absence is felt as a palpable condition of consciousness by describing a visit to a cafe where he was to have met his friend Pierre, but Pierre is not there in his accustomed place:

> His absence fixes the cafe in its evanescence; the cafe remains ground; it persists in offering itself as an undifferentiated totality to my only marginal attention; it slips into the background...this figure which slips constantly between my look and the solid, real objects of the cafe is precisely a perpetual disappearance; it is Pierre raising himself as nothingness on the ground of the nihilation of the cafe.[7]

Vacuum ⟷ Mass., Joseph Beuys

Beuys's empty room is charged with the phantom of Pierre's nothingness. Its emptiness is not the absolute emptiness of a void, but is rather the active potential of a "vacuum" that draws us into the workings of the piece. The solidity of the half-cross is also qualified by the projective memory of its function during the six-hour action. This memory is given a material and temporal grain with the thought of the grease decomposing within the sealed vessel of the chest. All of these mnemonic projections prevent the chest from being considered as an absolute solid. Beuys uses the term "mass" because of its relational nature (it being linked in physics to other terms such as momentum and the constant of acceleration due to gravity). The designation ⟷ is not an equation, but a continuous relation where one term is penetrated by the other. The visibility of the chest is haunted by the decomposing

7. Jean-Paul Sartre, *Being And Nothingness*, Simon and Schuster, New York, 1956, p.42.

engine of its own interior which, when recalled, opens the chest to the room itself and the memory of its past inhabitations. The extension of the mass of the chest is absorbed in the memory of the room, for as Beuys states, "Mass and its endless extension makes it invisible."[8] The solidity of the traditional, sculptural object is negated through its transformation into a mass "of endless extension." The medium of this extension is no longer space but the materially charged flux of time. The absolute location of an object in space is made relative by a memory permeated by anticipations and regrets. Here the phenomenological implications of the *Black Square* are enriched; the space of the room is temporalized as bearing witness to the actions that have occurred or will occur within it.

Because our understanding of the piece is permeated by memory, a symbolic reading of the work becomes inevitable. The half-cross is a cipher between the conditions of history and the psyche "...this half or divided cross symbolizes the divided state of the world: the tension between East and West, the Berlin Wall and the inner divisions of the human personality."[9] The figure of the cross is present as an inspiration in the whole that it promises and as a regret in the division that manifests. The volatility of its un-making is the silent text of the work. In a postcard-multiple done in the same period, the half-cross is seen stamped upon a photograph of the Cathedral of Cologne, the location of the action – a black tear in the Christian fabric of the city. Is this the sign of the death of the Christian era or the mark of its transformation into the a-historical condition of shamanic visions?

9119 St. Cyril, plan

The discussion of Malevich and Beuys establishes a territory from which one can begin to assess a recent work by the architects Jean Claude Azar, James Cathcart, Frank Fantauzzi, Terry Van Elslander and Michael Williams entitled *9119 St. Cyril*. The work involves the dismantling of a one-story house in Detroit, Michigan over a period of a week and the subsequent displacement of the house into a gallery, also located in Detroit. The circumstances surrounding the work are

8. Joseph Beuys, Caroline Tisdal, *Joseph Beuys*,
The Solomon R. Guggenheim Museum,
New York, 1979, p. 114.

9. Beuys, Tisdal, p. 114.

important to review, for they have played an important role in determining the nature of the architects' work. As was mentioned, the work occurred in Detroit, a city where un-building has exceeded building for many years. The painful evidence of this activity is apparent in land use maps that are blackened out to record the growth of empty land parcels in the city. This filling in of the city by its absence is not a figure field exercise of opened and closed space, but evidence of the inexorable spread of economic decay. The blacking-out of Malevich has been transformed into a virtual erasure of building and a reduction down to the base-level city plan of streets and utilities. The architects' decision to work within this context of un-building, or un-making, was certainly a difficult one, for so much of the ideology of the discipline concerns the progressive organization of materials and energies towards an idealization of building, however temporary this might be. The reversal, or un-making, of the assumptions of architectural practice becomes the actual value in the work. This can be understood in a number of ways. To begin with, the architects did not wait for a site upon which to apply a program. Instead, they began their work by finding a site themselves and deriving a program from it. The house, or site, was worked upon from the top down rather than from the ground up. In this way the plan was achieved through the **removal** of successive layers of material. The making of the plan in this case becomes an act of compression to a planar surface. The density of the plan is revealed through the weighing and sorting of all that it holds. The idea of the plan is now found through an un-building activity rather than projected through building. Along the way, the ordering of the construction is made manifest to the architects through their proximity to the work:

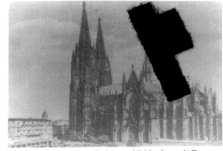

Cologne 1968, Joseph Beuys

> ...the house transformed itself into successive states...at one point the house was entirely plaster, at another, all wood. Our labor was confined to splitting the house, loosening its fastenings and overcoming the forces of friction which kept the house in an unrequited relationship to the forces of gravity.[10]

The project is documented in a series of "construction photographs" showing the various "successive states" of the house. But these are more than construction photographs of the work, they are a privileged view of a process that has become part of the background activity of the city, a silent lament that recalls the ritual slow-motion torture of children that ends Passolini's *Salo*. By extending this process in time (the house could have been demolished in less than a day by heavy machinery), the architects have succeeded in delaying the inevitable, producing a window through which we gain a brief, critical distance from the contemporary "universe of discourse" that blinds us to these acts of erasure of our cities and lives.

In their work the architects have revealed to us the persistent assumptions

10. Azar, Cathcart, Fantauzzi,
Van Elslander, Williams,
9119 St. Cyril,
Willis Gallery, Detroit, 1989.

upon which our culture builds. For building always assumes un-building in some way, either through the displacement of resources in the industrial process or through the displacement of populations due to shifts in capital. Building always occurs at a "cost," but it is rare that this cost is considered as a sacrifice. The building of the Tower of Babel can be understood as an attempt by mankind to reach the infinite point of God, the place from which all constructions are seen in their ideal way as plans. The destruction of the Tower is a metaphor for the sacredness of the plan, its invisibility. In their way, these architects have given us a view of the plan while retaining the aura of its presence as a building, as a home. The collapse from the ideal to the real is played out in this work in the painful economic context within which the work occurred. The poignance of the act of un-making is brought

9119 St Cyril, elevation

home, as it were, in the gallery where the house remained for a time condensed into piles of material. In a corner of the gallery, away from the piles, was a small metal box filled with photographs and letters found in the walls of the house. Here was the true memory of the house, the collapse of the lives that once filled its rooms, a box filled with "anticipations and regrets."

The significance of these works is that they occur against the background of a universe of discourse that refuses to accept opposition and critical thinking. Yet despite its monolithic nature, the rationalization of the discourse does not succeed in eliminating the idea of negation and the opportunities and aspirations or ideas that it offers. The uses of un-making and negation that these works employ remain as points of resistance from which we can gain a critical position. Works of art and architecture are important for their attempts to unite thought and action. The marginalization of artistic activity should not be understood as a step towards its elimination, but as an indication of its capacity for resistance, the need for a counter-activity that is a repository for thought and feeling. There always remains a difference, for as Beckett has observed, nothing is "almost nothing."

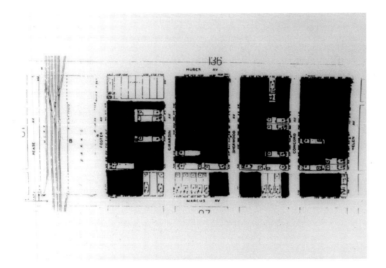

Detroit vacant land map

A N D R E A   **K** A H N

Moving Forward, Looking Sideways

These reflections on the relationship of theory to design consider how, like design, theoretical production is a process of making. The paper contends that a certain kind of theoretical production, the making of conceptual structures with the material of language, can project a critical perspective that transcends the pragmatics of design and the exigencies of the profession as presently constituted.

Theories, which constitute an already available discourse, used to answer specific questions of how to design or what to make in a given instance are here set aside to address theoretical production as an interpretive endeavor. Instead of contemplating theory as a discourse responsible for legitimating practice, or one that directly supplies procedural models and methods for design solutions, theory is presumed indirectly connected to design practice. At once imaginative and critical, the work of theory as critical praxis[1] is regarded as analogous to that of design as a process of critical inquiry.

Failing to confront practice, theoretical work [mis] construed to meet pragmatic needs (the fate of instrumentalized theory) risks becoming epistemologically enclosed by them. For architecture, this enclosure implies, first, a theoretical production likely to be considered commensurate with the work of design and, second, a movement of knowledge from theory to practice idealized as clear and

Sites sighted from a train traveling from Washington, D.C. to New York City, recorded at regular intervals.

1.   The value of the term "praxis" is twofold. "From the side of the theoreticians, our familiar word *practice* is too often understood as mere practice, the simple application of all too pure and contextless theories. From the side of the practitioners, practice can become a desperate cry for an illusory freedom from the interpretations and theories that all practice consciously or unconsciously involves. The word *praxis,* however, by its very strangeness in English, reminds us that every worthwhile practice is informed by some theory. *Praxis* can also remind us that theoretical activity is itself a praxis – and one to be tested by the practice it serves." David Tracy, *Plurality and Ambiguity,* Harper & Row, San Francisco, 1987, p.10.

unobstructed. The supposed commensurability and idealization sets theoretical production in a supporting role, and depends on an assumed transparency, or translatability, between words and things. The measure of the value of such theoretical work in turn becomes tied to the ease of its application as either design methodology or criteria of legitimation. The tendency of architecture to instrumentalize the work of theory appears to be directly related to the professional nature of architectural culture. It may also, at least in part, be a function of the large number of architectural theorists who have been practitioners as well: Rossi, Scott-Brown & Venturi, Le Corbusier, Viollet-le-Duc, Alberti, to name just a few. In light of this, professionalism can impact strongly upon theoretical production. If tied to an existing image of the discipline, architectural theories can have difficulty extending, altering or reevaluating this image. They will lose their speculative capacity and concentrate instead on maintaining a status quo which tends to devalue theoretical production by according to the practice of building a greater prestige. Further, by encouraging the habitual responses characteristic of professionalism, theoretical production will steer away from issues that do not have immediate application to practice.[2] If developed in conformance with the context and existing concerns of praxis, theory as commentary will be expected to have a clear and direct connection to action, adopting, rather than questioning, the accepted limits of architectural activity.

The fundamental differences between theoretical discourse and design practice – the former being primarily verbal and the latter being primarily material – are sufficient to question the possibility of a direct transfer of information from one to the other. These differences also make the hierarchical alignment of practice over theory, or equally theory over practice, difficult to sustain. When theoretical production is assumed to be translatable into material form, or equally, when it is intended to fit into professionally defined political structures, it must slip easily into a space whose limits are already determined. The idea of such a comfortable association is anathema to the work of architecture, work initiated by a tension between things, a "problem" born of the need for multivalent connections.

It is possible, however, to imagine a more vital affiliation between theory and practice. This revised conception depends upon recognizing both theoretical production and design production as distinct modes of interpretation which touch tangentially at a point but fail to translate directly one to the other. Their connection can be likened to the kinship posited by Walter Benjamin in *The Task of the Translator*. For Benjamin, bad translation mistakenly strives for likeness to the original through direct transmission of subject matter. Good translation, on the

2.   According to Samuel Weber, "Professionalism is construed not merely as 'a set of learned values,' as an integrated system, but more to the point, as a set of habitual responses...[the professional] has undergone a lengthy period of training in a recognized institution (professional school), which certifies him [sic] as being competent in a specialized area; such competence derives from...mastery of a particular discipline, an esoteric body of useful knowledge involving systematic theory and resting on general principles." Samuel Weber, "The Limits of Professionalism" in *Instituton and Interpretation, Theory and History of Literature,* Volume 31, University of Minnesota Press, 1987, p. 25.

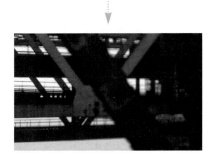

other hand, "is so far removed from being the sterile equation of two dead languages that of all literary forms, it is the one charged with the special mission of watching over the maturing process of the original language and the birth pangs of its own."[3] According to Benjamin, genuine translation "extends the boundaries of language" by forming an elusive and oblique connection to an original based on a "kinship" that "does not necessarily involve likeness."[4] This kinship permits translations to follow their own trajectories, expressing the intended effect of the original through an oblique affiliation that does not deny the integrity of either text.

If movements of knowledge from theory to practice subscribe to this model of good translation—elusive, tangential, and possibly even errant—theoretical production can substantially affect the growth of the discipline by following its own line of questioning. However, the expectations of architectural culture must change before speculative theoretical production fully develops its own path. First, architectural culture needs to acknowledge the criticality of a difficult and oblique theory/praxis relationship. In turn, architects must credit theoretical work as a productive and constructive activity in its own right, a building process analogous to design in critical operation and intention, different in physical operation and choice of materials.

To propose that theoretical production is akin to the process of design is to admit a more profound affiliation between theory and practice than simple instrumentality. Here, the work of theory is no longer to project formulae that inform the artifact. It is used instead to inform the maker by calling upon creative and critical skills. Working with materials having little apparent affiliation to architecture, both apart and in conjunction with specifically architectural texts, the maker is provoked to build conceptual constructs out of diverse ideas and positions. By revealing affinities between material and conceptual production, it is the very engagement in theoretical production which ultimately influences design thinking. Theory and practice begin to interact through a processive affinity. The relationship of theory to practice is here analogous to relationships marking the act of design itself; from program to building, from drawing to construction, architecture is about interpretive transactions which are rarely, if ever, direct translations. As the act of constructing ideas, theoretical production demonstrates and demands a thought process equally essential to design. It builds interpretations.

The kinship of theory and practice originates in interpretation; not theory as an interpretation of practice, but interpretation as a condition of making common to both. As a form of construction independent of the material aspect of architecture,

3.   Walter Benjamin, "The Task of the Translator," *Illuminations*, Harry Zohn, trans., Hannah Arendt, ed., Schocken Books, New York, 1969, p.75.

4.   For an interesting coda to Benjamin, see Paul de Man, "Conclusions: Walter Benjamin's 'The Task of the Translator,' " in *The Resistance to Theory, Theory and History of Literature*, Volume 33, University of Minnesota Press, 1986.

theory is not a handmaiden to practice, and conversely, practice cannot rely on theory for justification or legitimation. Instead, theoretical production and design production proceed along tangential trajectories. As a function of their different paths a critical distance emerges, freeing theoretical work to disclose the assumptions upon which the authority of practice and the profession are based. Liberated from its second-order status as commentary, theoretical production disrupts a singular conception of architecture. It is able to reassess the knowledge-base of practice; by drawing from diverse sources, the work of theory can challenge the premises of architecture. This challenge both resists the subordination of theory to practice and confronts the notion of architecture as warranted by a single set of validating criteria, the legitimacy of which remains unquestioned. While a univalent position may seem preferable to those who want the certainty of one hierarchically superior interpretation, by suppressing conflict it severely constrains the potential growth of the discipline.

In architecture, and in architecture schools, it is possible to consider the problem of multiple interpretations in a nonhierarchical light. The question "Which is the authoritative interpretation?" can be rephrased to address how different interpretations are constructed, how they supplement one another, complement one another, reveal one another's underlying assumptions. If architecture is a body of knowledge and action based upon manifold relations, it is well-suited to take up the challenge of contesting and contested interpretations, particularly since the resulting battles, negotiations and terms of settlement are precisely what allow the architectural community to surpass its own limits to think of architecture in an expansive way. This approach challenges a unique set of legitimating criteria defining what is and is not architecture. In addition, it projects theoretical work as a simultaneous speculation upon and demonstration of architecture as a field acknowledging the mutual rights of multiple authorities. What remains to be figured are the dynamics of this field.

To exploit the architectural condition of theoretical work—a building project in the realm of ideas–one cannot teach it as a systematic method of producing answers nor as a simple body of historical knowledge. Rather, theoretical work entails engagement in the process of building questions. When theory is taught as engaged acts of conceptual construction, a reevaluated theory/praxis relationship is advocated, eschewing instrumentalization and diverging from the dictates of professionalism. The question, or perhaps more to the point, the quest facing the academic institution, is to demonstrate, first, how a complicity between theory and practice makes for certain exclusions organizing the field known as architecture,

and then, second, to include a self-reflective critique upon the nature of reasons for these exclusions. This work may well involve exploiting materials apparently beyond architecture as professionally defined, exploring how they reconfigure our assumptions about the limits of the discipline. As the construction of indirect connections, looking sideways to move forward, creative theoretical work invokes its kinship to other modes of architectural production—built, drawn, modeled, designed. It informs praxis through interlinear movements and at the same time reveals the inherently speculative and interpretive condition of all making. The call to arms of theoretical praxis as a legitimate (rather than a legitimating) discourse is in large part an effort to question the presumed autonomy of a particular body of ideas within architectural discourse. By exposing tacit assumptions that rule the discipline, theoretical work holds forth the opportunity to rechart and expand architecture's territory. Rather than remain beholden to an exclusive image of architecture, theoretical production with indirect affiliation to design practice contributes to an architectural conception of architecture. Emphasizing that its affinity to design is built on difference and contingent upon interpretation, such theory thinks architecture as a discipline whose constituent aspects contribute to the shape of the whole but need not be wholly determined by one another. The critical question today is whether the voice of theory has reconfigured the shape of the discipline, or simply claimed the seat of power for itself.

Note: This article is based on a paper originally delivered at the national ACSA conference, Chicago, March 1989.

K I M T A N Z E R

Releasing the Form to the Making:
Womenswork Is Never Done

In 1966 Richard Feynman, the Nobel Prize winning physicist, gave a lecture to the American Association of Teachers of Physics. He said:

> When I was at Cornell, I was rather fascinated by the student body, which it seems to me was a dilute mixture of some sensible people in a big mass of dumb people studying home economics.... I used to sit in the cafeteria with the students and eat and try to overhear their conversations and see if there was one intelligent word coming out. You can imagine my surprise when I discovered a tremendous thing, it seemed to me.
>
> I listened to a conversation between two girls, and one was explaining that if you want to make a straight line, you see, you go over a certain number to the right for each row you go up, that is, if you go over each time the same amount when you go up a row, you make a straight line. A deep principle of analytic geometry!
>
> She went on and said, "Suppose you have another line coming in from the other side, and you want to figure out where they are going to intersect. Suppose on one line you go over two to the right for every one you go up, and the other line goes over three to the right for every one that goes up, and they start twenty steps apart," etc.– I was flabbergasted. She figured out where the intersection was! It turned out that one girl was explaining to the other how to knit argyle socks.[1]

1. Josue V. Harari, David Bell, "Journal a Plusieurs Voies," in Michel Serres, *Hermes*, Johns Hopkins University Press, Baltimore, 1983, pp. ix-x.

Womenswork Is Never Done

Shuck and silk the corn, removing any damaged portion.

1. The length of a temple is adjusted so that its width may be half its length, and the actual cella one-fourth greater in length than in width, including the wall in which the folding doors are placed.

1. Given ink, pen and sheets of transparent paper of determined dimensions, a master page (without notations) is made, having four total systems.

First select the number of sheets and apply the margins and title blocks.

Use a short needle especially made for quilting to speed the work.

Wash in cold water and drain.

Let the remaining three parts, constituting the pronaos, extend to the antae terminating the walls, which antae ought to be of the same thickness as the columns.

"Total" here means having enough space above and below each staff to permit its being either bass or treble.

All title information should be filled in at this time to assure that preliminary prints with partial information will be positively identified.

Also use quilting thread; it is strong and smooth and less likely to knot.

"Men work from sun to sun, but women's work is never done."
Traditional saying

This is a paper about womenswork. Please note that I have spelled womenswork without an apostrophe, that is, without possession. I have taken the property out of the work. This is not work that belongs exclusively to women.[2] Rather, I will discuss an attitude about work that has often been done by women. I want to focus on the notion that this kind of work is never finished. For most of us this phrase holds some frustration, resignation, and perhaps, even bitterness. The reasons many people feel this way about homemaking are similar to the reasons many architects, myself among them, feel frustration with the practice of architecture.

Twentieth-century womenswork is formless. It continues without beginning or end and therefore lacks closure, lacks punctuation. "The absence of required tasks and the formlessness of the housewife's day can ... be problematic features

2. In the early days of the American economy it was assumed that work around the house would be done by both sexes, and housework manuals at that time were addressed to both sexes. "Another early household guide was John Aikin's *The Arts of Life*, first published in 1803. It consists of a series of letters addressed to 'my dear boy' and provides information on food, agriculture, manufacturing, and architecture. Aikin's manual advises his readers on 'The Arts of Life' because he considers it 'unworthy of a man...to rely upon the exertions of others.' " Maxine Margolis, *Mothers and Such*, University of California Press, Berkeley, 1984, p. 118.

of housework .... A housewife's work may also lack a sense of completion because the same chores must be done over and over again, day in and day out."[3] It is repetitious. It is invisible. One of the major problems with homemaking is that no one notices it unless it is done wrong. "The housewife, working alone in her own home, lacks an audience. No one is there to judge or appreciate what she is doing.... Almost the only time a woman's domestic activities are noticed is when they are not done."[4]

This description may resonate among practicing architects. What we do day-to-day is largely invisible – we negotiate our way through a constellation of telephone calls, memos, letters, meetings, and changes and additions to drawings. Our days lack closure. There are few moments when we feel a sense of completion – perhaps finishing a punch list or meeting a schematic design deadline – but in between, hundreds of days may go by without objectifiable accomplishment. Architectural practice is largely repetitive. Much of what is done in offices is done many, many times. There is monotony involved in putting sticky-backs on drawings, redrafting typical details, writing specifications, meeting with sales reps. And, especially in today's litigious climate, many of the things we do go unnoticed unless they are done wrong.

It is important to note a divergence between two kinds of womenswork. Both have the characteristics of formlessness, invisibility, repetition, and lack of closure. However, earlier in America's history, this kind of work was not separated from life. "In pre-industrial societies there is no distinction between 'life' and 'work'; work is not something done outside of and separate from the home....The colonial housewife performed her work in the midst of life, and in this sense housework did not exist as separate activity. Women were not isolated from the work-a-day world – they were part of it."[5] This type of work was also more product oriented. Things were produced for the home – soap, foodstuffs, clothing. Finally, the act of doing these tasks, the process of making these products was an integral and important part of the product produced. Quilting bees, women talking while they spin, or raising children while they weave, parties at which people put up canned foods, are examples of these processes. These are group activities in which people work toward a common goal which is a part of their everyday life. In contrast, twentieth-century housework might be seen as something which separates people from each other and from their product.

The Industrial Age changed the role of womenswork. Margolis argues that industrialization took the production of goods – clothing, soap, canned foods, candles – out of the home and into the factory and replaced these tasks with cleaning and childrearing taken to new extremes. "The objection can be raised that domes-

3. Margolis, p. 145.   4. Margolis, pp. 145-146.   5. Margolis, pp. 112-113.

tic chores have always been without a sense of closure. Still in the pre-industrial era the seasonal organization of life must have given women some feeling of specific accomplishment. The fall canning and the spring housecleaning were major undertakings that stayed done for the whole year."[6] In the industrial world, "the tasks that remain in the home can less and less be described as making goods; the better descriptive term is making goods available at the time and in the place and combinations desired."[7]

I will let my subject, the production of architecture, slip, to remind myself and you that this discussion applies not just to people who design architecture, but also to people who build architecture. I think the frustrations and dissatisfactions that architects feel in terms of the formlessness, invisibility, repetition, and lack of closure in their work, are also felt by other people in the construction industry, and probably by many people working in the industrialized world. Author Studs Terkel interviewed a steelworker:

> I'm a dying breed. A laborer. Strictly muscle work...pick it up, put it down, pick it up, put it down. We handle between forty and fifty thousand pounds of steel a day.... You can't take pride any more. You remember when a guy could point to a house he built, how many logs he stacked. He built it and he was proud of it.... It's hard to take pride in a bridge you're never gonna cross, or a door you're never gonna open. You're mass producing things and you never see the end result of it.... There's hard work behind it. I would like to see a building, say, the Empire State, I would like to see on one side of it a foot-wide strip from top to bottom with the name of every bricklayer, the name of every electrician, with all the names. So when a guy walked by, he could take his son and say, "See, that's me over there on the forty-fifth floor. I put the steel beam in." Picasso can point to a painting. What can I point to? A writer can point to a book. Everybody should have something to point to.[8]

The Thingification of Technique

With a sharp knife cut down the center of each row of kernels, holding the knife blade parallel to the cob.

If the temple is to be more than twenty feet in width, let two columns be placed between the two antae, to separate the pteroma from the pronaos.

6. Margolis, p. 146.

7. Margolis, p. 131. Quotation by Hazel Kyrk, *Economic Problems of the Family*, New York, 1933, p. 52.

8. Studs Terkel, *Working*, Pantheon Books, New York, 1974, p. xxxi.

Thus, there being the conventional two staves (one for each hand), each has enough space above it to accommodate nine ledger lines (as equidistant as those of the staves) and below it to accommodate six ledger lines plus (leaving room for the extreme low piano key and string).

The date, job title and legal description should be identical.

Use a short length of thread and pull the knot through to the batting so it will not show.

Turn the blade horizontally and shave the kernels into a large mixing bowl.

The three intercolumniations between the antae and the columns should be closed by low walls made of marble or of joiner's work, with doors in them to afford passages into the pronaos.

Between the two there is a narrow space, bisected by a line, allowing for the notation of noises produced by hand or beater upon the interior (above the line) or exterior (below the line) piano construction.

If the title blocks are completed in the beginning, you avoid the need to do them hastily at the end, when time is always short because of last-minute coordination.

Place the forefinger of left hand over the spot where the needle should come through.

> "The idea becomes a machine to make art."
> Sol LeWitt

The "thing" made and the process by which it is made define a dialectic couplet. To begin I hope to establish the making process as the "figure," reversing its position relative to the thing made, which becomes the ground. I realize I am simply reversing the polarity, with its contingent theoretical limitations. However, I think it is important to foreground the practice, the making of architecture, its technique, explicitly, in order to begin a more profound realignment.

Walter Benjamin's discussion of technique begins, "In bringing up technique I have named a concept that makes literary products directly accessible to a social, and therefore, a materialist analysis. At the same time, the concept of technique provides the dialectic starting point from which the unfruitful antithesis of form and content can be surpassed."[9] I will first discuss practice in its conventional formulation, and then suggest that technique might be a starting pointing for changes which are, in Benjamin's argument, politically correct.[10]

A technique is a method of performance.[11] Because it is a method of performance, it has the ability to straddle the fence between form and content (re:

9. Walter Benjamin, "The Author as Producer," in *Art After Modernism: Rethinking Representation,* Brian Wallis, ed., The New Museum of Contemporary Art, New York, 1984, p. 298.

10. Some theorists hold that technology, as a systematic treatment or method of work, is a strategy to displace grief, to fill the gap between Self and Other. I hope that by the end of this paper I will have presented a convincing alternative formulation.

11. Frances Yates, *The Art of Memory,* University of Chicago Press, Chicago, 1987. Yates describes the history of memory systems as an evolving methodology. She suggests these methodologies became performative and predictive with the advent of science.

Benjamin) and also, I hope, between production and product. It is the invisible filler, or web, between these sets of opposites, these things.

Technique, read as a figure, might be understood as ritual in architectural practice. For instance, Cesar Pelli's office dedicates Friday afternoons at 4:00 to the application of presstype to working drawings. The ritual involves pulling the presstype out of the drawers and rubbing it down communally, celebrating the end of the week while at the same time working, in the manner of a quilting bee. Bohm-NBBJ applies all of the seals and the last set of titles to the title blocks of working drawings after the set is complete because the sticky-backs would get dog-eared if they were affixed earlier. So the end of each set of working drawings is celebrated by laying all the sheets out very neatly, having various titles each in its own neat stack, and methodically and systematically applying the last bit of information before the drawings are printed and sent out to bid. I.M. Pei's office pins up portions of each completed set of working drawings, sheet by sheet, and serves tea, before sending them to the printer.

In the schematic design portion of practice (in the linear way those terms are currently configured), Peter Eisenman has explicitly designed methods which produced forms. For him, the performance of the method is as important as the form produced. I think specifically of the scaling operations in the Wexner Center and the Romeo and Juliet project, and the shifting of figural solids in the Guardiola House. Many of Eisenman's drawings physically demonstrate the method of the production of the object.

One reason I would like to thingify the method of production, the technique of the practice of architecture, is to recover the joy of the everyday. Another is to loosen our collective fixation on a fetishized end form. Fixation on a particular goal, call it a style or an ideology, may become an obsession or a fetish. Artist Robert Morris: "Form is not perpetuated by means, but by preservation of separable, idealized ends. This is an anti-entropic and conservative enterprise. It accounts for Greek architecture changing from wood to marble and looking the same, or for the look of Cubist bronzes, with their fragmented, faceted planes. The perpetuation of form is functioning idealism."[12] Fixation on ideals, at least the current set, is not helping us, as a profession, as a society, as a race. We might benefit by relinquishing the desire to control the end, to appreciate the process of getting there, to accept changes beyond the boundaries of our own figural condition. This may be what Benjamin means when he talks about making something which is literarily correct because it is politically correct.[13]

The machine model as a method of working is certainly very common, both in

12. Robert Morris, "Anti-Form," *Artforum*, April 1968, p. 33.

13. Walter Benjamin discounts the use of ritual and the resultant ritualized objects as remnants of a desire for authenticity which is inappropriate in a mechanized world, and suggests artistic production can be based instead on the practice of politics. Refer to "The Work of Art in the Age of Mechanical Reproduction," *Illuminations*, Harry Zohn, trans., Hannah Arendt, ed., Harcourt, Brace, & World, Inc., New York.

our profession and in our teaching. Benjamin describes the technique of making art objects in the mechanical age: "The technique of reproduction detaches the reproduced object from the domain of tradition. By making many reproductions, it substitutes a plurality of copies for a unique existence. And in permitting the reproduction to meet the beholder or the listener in his own particular situation, it reactivates the object reproduced."[14] I believe it is possible to reactivate the object produced through a focus on the technique of reproduction. A reactivated object is one which is resistant to consumption. It is important that Benjamin theorizes reproduction rather than production, since both the womenswork and the processes of making architecture are processes of reproduction rather than of invention.

If the process is thingified, the end form might become a fossil rather than a fetish. Daniel Libeskind describes this relationship: "The purpose of the equipment (his Reading, Writing, and Memory Machines) is to release the end to itself, not to take the end, but to release the end to itself. I think the objects in architecture are only residues of something which is truly important: the participatory experience (the emblem of reality which goes into their making). You could say that everything we have is that kind of residue. It is this experience that I would like to retrieve, not the object."[15]

This process requires an acceptance of nonideal conditions, the conditions evident in the practice of architecture. The end form which occurs might be viewed as a fossil, a nonideal resultant form, rather than an idealized fetish object. Paradoxically, releasing the end to the making may reactivate the object produced.

Technique as Work/Technique as Dilemma

In a separate bowl, beat the three eggs, adding the milk and half-and-half slowly.

2. If the width is to be more than forty feet, let columns be placed inside and opposite to the columns between the antae.

Measurements are such that the entire sheet (within the margins) is potentially useful.

Then assign each element of the drawings to a specific page by notations in pencil at one corner of each sheet.

Push needle through with right hand until it touches finger.

14. Benjamin, p. 223.

15. Daniel Libeskind, "Architecture Intermundium," in *Threshold*, Marco Diani and Catherine Ingraham, eds., Rizzoli, New York, 1988, p. 251.

Beat in the salt, pepper, nutmeg and basil or parsley, and add the mixture to the corn kernels.

They should have the same height as the columns in front of them, but their thickness should be proportionately reduced: thus, if the columns in front are in thickness one-eighth of their height, these should be one-tenth; if the former are one-ninth or one-tenth, these should be reduced in the same proportion.

2. Laying the master page aside, chance operations derived from the I-Ching and channeled within certain limits (1-128 for 21-36; 1-32 for 37-52; which are established in relation to relative difficulty of performance) are employed to determine the number of sounds per page.

Elements which relate to one another should be located in close proximity so workmen in the field can coordinate them.

Change hands and pull through with right hand.

I hope I have been able to objectify or thingify the process of making architecture, that it has become a figure in your thinking, relative to the ground of the thing made. My next move is to suggest that, rather than making a new idealized condition, this process may become changeable. Rather than completing the thingification of the process, I would like to suggest a move from, in Roland Barthes's terms, architectural technique as work to architectural technique as text. For Barthes, "the work is a fragment of substance, occupying a portion of the space of books (in a library, for example); the Text on the other hand is a methodological field...the work can be seen...the text is a process of demonstration, speaks according to certain rules (or against certain rules). The Text is experienced only as an activity of production."[16]

I began the last section with Sol LeWitt's quote, "the idea becomes a machine to make art." To reconfigure Sol LeWitt's statement and work, Krauss says, "To get inside the systems of this work, whether LeWitt's or Judd's or Morris's, is precisely to enter a world without center, a world of substitutions and transpositions nowhere legitimated by the revelation of a transcendental subject.... Aporia is a far more legitimate model for LeWitt's work than Mind, if only because aporia is a dilemma rather than a thing."[17] Dilemmas are difficult, unsolvable. Dilemma means "two propositions" and Aristotle tells us two contradictory propositions cannot both be true. Robert Smithson, writing about LeWitt's work says, "LeWitt is concerned with enervating 'concepts' of paradox. Everything LeWitt thinks, writes or has made is inconsistent and contradictory. The 'original idea' of his art is lost in a mess of drawings, figurings, and other ideas. Nothing is where it seems

16. Roland Barthes, "From Work to Text," in *Art After Modernism: Rethinking Representation*, Brian Wallis, ed., The New Museum of Contemporary Art, New York, 1988, p. 170.

17. Rosalind Krauss, "LeWitt in Progress," *The Originality of the Avant Garde and Other Modernist Myths*, MIT Press, Cambridge, Mass., 1988, p. 251.

to be. His concepts are prisons devoid of reason."[18] If we view a process as a dilemma, a paradox, we explode the black box and confront the messiness, the many pieces out of place.

Benjamin's ideas about the technique of production, particularly in film, suggest several strategies which may enable architectural techniques to become a text, a dilemma. These strategies involve a reconsideration of what is "natural" or "real," and attempt to undercut outdated presumptions of legitimacy. In film, says Benjamin, one characteristic of montage "constantly counteracts an illusion in the audience.... Epic theater...does not reproduce situations; rather it discovers them. This discovery is accomplished by means of the interruption of sequences. Only interruption here has not the character of a stimulant but an organizing function. It arrests the action in its course, and thereby compels the listener to adopt an attitude vis-a-vis the process, the actor vis-a-vis his role."[19] If a method of architectural production is not considered natural, transcendental, inevitable, but rather discoverable, an architecture of calculated interruptions may become a Text. The conventional practice of architecture is already a study in interruptions which could be conceived as organizational. However, since we have not foregrounded those interruptions, we tend to deny their creative potential.

In contrast to the theater where both actor and spectator see action in its "natural" sequence, films are shot "out of order." Episodes are shot according to other organizing principles: all outdoor scenes may be shot at once, then all scenes of the female lead, or all stunt scenes, so the narrative "picture" emerges only in the editing room. The production of the film is much like the production of architecture. An architect doesn't go out and build a building. All the disparate parts of the design of a building have a logic of their own which is not the natural logic of the end form. "The shooting of a film, especially of a sound film, affords a spectacle unimaginable anywhere at anytime before this period. It presents a process in which it is impossible to assign to a spectator a viewpoint which would exclude from the actual scene such extraneous accessories as camera equipment, lighting machinery, staff assistance, etc. – unless his eye were on a line parallel with the lens."[20] Architects might benefit from a comparison with film producers. The innovations we look towards, and the rewards we hope to find in our work have as much to do with production techniques as with the final "natural" product. "The stage actor identifies himself with the character of his role. The film actor very often is denied this opportunity. His creation is by no means all of a piece; it is composed of many separate performances."[21]

One further strategy for turning architectural technique into text involves col-

18. Robert Smithson, "A Museum of Language in the Vicinity of Art," *Art International*, March 1968, p. 21.

19. Benjamin, "The Author as Producer," p. 307.

20. Benjamin, "The Work of Art...," pp. 234-235.

21. Benjamin, "The Work of Art...," p. 232.

laboration. Again, Benjamin, "it is inherent in the technique of the film, as well as that of sports, that everybody who witnesses its accomplishments is somewhat of an expert."[22] In addition "[t]he distinction between author and public is about to lose its basic character. The difference becomes merely functional; it may vary from case to case. At any moment the reader is ready to turn into a writer."[23] This is happening, or has happened, in architecture. Everyone I meet eagerly tells me about the building he or she wants to design. Perhaps rather than stifling these responses, we might look at the architectural text in a way which allows the consumer of architecture to become a co-producer, reframing for ourselves our role as producers. "An author who teaches writers nothing teaches no one. What matters, therefore, is the exemplary character of production, which is able first to induce other producers to produce, and second to put an improved apparatus at their disposal. And this apparatus is better the more consumers it is able to turn into producers – that is, readers or spectators into collaborators."[24]

Technique as Error: Gossip

Melt one tablespoon of the butter in the skillet or saute pan.

For their reduction will not be discernible, as the air has not free play about them.

A blank sheet of transparent paper is then placed so that its pointal imperfections may readily be observed.

The layout guide that follows is provided for assistance.

Forefinger of left hand should now be underneath.

Add the scallions and saute very gently, taking care only to wilt them.

Still, in case they look too slender, when the outer columns have twenty or twenty-four flutes, these may have twenty-eight or thirty-two.

That number of imperfections corresponding to the determined number of sounds is intensified with pencil.

Next, sketch the outlines of the elements to scale, spacing them as desired on their respective sheets.

With right hand push needle down through the three layers to touch forefinger.

22. Benjamin, "The Work of Art...," p. 233.

23. Benjamin, "The Work of Art...," p. 234.

24. Benjamin, "The Author as Producer," p. 306.

I want my signature on it too. Sometimes, out of pure meanness, when I make something, I put a little dent in it. I like to do something to make it really unique. Hit it with a hammer. I deliberately (screw) it up to see if it'll get by, just so I can say I did it. It could be anything.... A mistake, mine. Let's say the whole building is nothing but red bricks. I'd like to have just the black one or the white one or the purple one. Deliberately (screw) it up.[25]

Mike LeFevre, Steelworker

Gossip is idle talk about the affairs of others. A gossip is also a person, especially a woman, given to tattling or idle talk. And, as anyone who has been involved in gossip knows, it is very subject to errors. Errors get reconfigured as they get retold, rumors start. But gossip has a very interesting history. The word is from the Old English word godsibb, which means a godparent, and comes from god and sibb, as in sibling. Perhaps gossip was once talk among people who saw themselves as relatives through God. "Enlightened gossip is a sort of communal novel writing. It can suggest motives and delineate characters as well as describe events."[26] It is a kind of talk that involves the creations of errors and the making of mistakes and imprints. Gossip is communal, as cities are communal, as architecture, is communal. It is that invisible, light, formless stuff that moves between person and person and between person and form. As a model for the making of architecture it is (initially) well-intentioned and nonheroic. Through repetition, it is collaborative and generative. It lacks closure. Through the introduction of calculated interruptions it creates dilemmas, makes text. Its organizing strategies are complex; it lacks a "natural," linear, logical order. It defies truth. As an enabling process, it may be responsible for many of the environmental fossils we love most.

Add the sauteed vegetables to the corn and eggs, stirring to mix thoroughly.

Thus the additional number of flutes will make up proportionately for the loss in the body of the shaft, preventing it from being seen, and so in a different way the columns will be made to look equally thick.

4. Placing the penciled sheet in a registered way upon the master page, first the staves and interline and then the ledger lines where necessary are inscribed in ink.

Allow space for titles and dimensions by penciling in guide lines.

Pull through with right hand.

Preheat oven to 325 degrees.[27]

25. Terkel, p. xxxviii.

26. Quintin Crisp, *Lear's,* June 1990.

27. Bill Neal, "Green Corn Pudding," *Bill Neal's Southern Cooking,* The University of North Carolina Press, Chapel Hill, 1985, p. 74.

3. The reason for this result is that the eye, touching thus upon a greater number of points, set closer together, has a larger compass to cover with its range of vision.[28]

Secondly, conventional whole notes are written in ink wherever a penciled point falls within the area of staves or ledger lines, inked-in notes (crotchets without stems) being written wherever such a point falls within the space between the two staves.[29]

Adjustments will have to be made before each sheet is designed to satisfaction.[30]

Work alternately in this fashion.[31]

Postscript: The Object of Technique

What is the object of technique? The question can be answered two ways. The object of technique is to choreograph, design, give form to the repressed half of the production/product dialectic. Or again, the object of technique is the material embodiment of a series of techniques. It is a physical thing, well produced.

Taking the latter first, I'd like to note that the physical object most readers call to mind, the building, is once-removed from the objects produced by architects. Architects seldom make buildings. Rather, they make drawings, models, specifications, and other kinds of written agreements which refer to buildings in quite specific yet varied ways. These two scales of physical objects, architectural notations and buildings, enfold and unfold through production.

The object made through a considered manipulation of techniques is one which records, responds to a technique of gossip, and thereby generates a textual reading. I would say that, due to the physical imprint of errors and mistakes, much of Palladio's architecture is textual. For example, the Palazzo Chiericati has been written about exhaustively, yet no "truth" is forthcoming. It is a rich methodological field for inquiry, continually confounding urban and architectural analysis. A comparison of Palladio's built works with their documentation in his *Four Books* produces not one univocal understanding, but a blurring of the utopian and the distopian. These projects, particularly the unfinished Loggia del Capitaniato or Palazzo Barbarano, are in almost literal flux, while the built Basillica Palladiana accommodates the quirky geometry of the existing medieval Palazzo della Ragione, in contrast to the purified version Palladio presented in his own promo-

28. Vitruvius, "The Cella and Pronaos," *The Ten Books on Architecture,* Dover Publications, New York, 1960, pp. 114-116.

29. John Cage, "To Describe the Process of Composition Used in Music for Piano 21-52," *Silence,* Wesleyan University Press, Middletown, Conn.,1961, pp. 60-61.

30 Roberrt C. McHugh, *Working Drawing Handbook. A Guide for Architects and Builders,* Van Nostrand Reinhold, New York, 1982, p. 9.

31. Vera P. Guild, "Quilting," *Good Housekeeping's Complete Book of Needlecraft.* Doubleday, New York, 1959, p 183.

tional documentation. Which is the "real" architecture, the drawn, the built, or both? The same conceptual oscillation occurs through his collage of the temple facade on the vernacular type in his villa projects, or of several temple facades in his Venetian churches and villas.

A shuttling back and forth (a considered manipulation of technique) between drawings and buildings is evident in the production of Carlo Scarpa. Both his drawings and buildings are precisely inconclusive. He makes the vagaries of construction, the variability of human habitation, the imperfection of materials, into a constructive aporia.

What is the object of making technique figural? The production of every object involves technique, involves process. They are inseparable. It is said that advanced yogis will get violently ill if they eat foods cooked by people with bad intentions. That is, not only the objective food, but its method of preparation is harmful to these people of refined physical/spiritual awareness. I feel that in some way the same is true with architecture. We have, of course, all heard of the sick building syndrome, but I think this is a pathological version of a more pervasive problem. Here I am thinking of "lifeless" buildings, buildings which don't inspire us, and probably didn't inspire their builders, designers, or owners, either. These are the objects whose making techniques were repressed in favor of the finish, perhaps a tax advantage, or the lowest possible bottom line. Ironically, in focusing on the end, it is what is most acutely lost.

Marxists allege that capitalism is responsible for the emphasis of product at the expense of production. The human cost of labor is repressed. This may be true, but other factors must also be implicated. Production is invisible, especially in architecture schools. While carpenters' apprentices learn to square foundations using string, and Zen archers learn to make arrows before shooting them, students of architecture are praised solely for their products. Things invisible are often forgotten.

How can I capture a textual architecture, the object of a technique of errors? How can I document the feeling I get in my stomach, knowing as I walk along Mussolini's approach to St. Peters of the winding medieval route it replaced? Harwell Harris says of Rudolf Schindler's temporary buildings, "Such architectural flowers Wright called 'ephemera.' They were not made to endure. They charmed as nothing permanent could." Adolf Loos says proudly that his interiors cannot be adequately photographed. It may be that the aspects of architecture which are most textual are invisible to documentation. And perhaps, precisely because they cannot be captured, they cannot be consumed.

Note: This paper was previously presented at the ACSA conference, Washington, D.C., Spring 1991.

A few hundred feet from the Pyramid,

I bent down, scooped a handful of sand and then, let it spill.

Under my breath I said: I am modifying the Sahara.

The deed was minimal but the words

that were scarcely ingenious were exact and

I considered that I had needed an entire life to say them.

Jorge Luis Borges

A L V A R O   M A L O

The Hand: Organ of Knowledge

I start to write with hesitation. The doubt is provoked by the fact that the proclamation of the rights and virtues of the hand may not be done properly in language. I think that this advocacy must be done by presenting the evidence of the hand's own making. Yet, as the writing progresses, I sense the proof beginning to appear on the movement of the hands across the keyboard, the shape of the script, and the precise rectangle of whiteness of the paper. Still indecisive and seeking support, it is my hands that open a book and I read, "through his hands man establishes contact with the austerity of thought."[1] I close the book and set it on the table. I open another and I read:

> Thinking is too easy. The mind in its flight rarely meets with resistance. Hence the vital importance for the intellectual of touching concrete objects and of learning discipline in his intercourse with them. Bodies are the mentors of the spirit, as Chiron, the centaur, was the mentor of Greek heroes. [2]

My project now is the pursuit of this paradox (and I will continue writing), that there are two kinds of knowledge: One is the knowledge of matter, which belongs to the notion of instinct, and is encoded as a system in the sensor-motor memory of the body; the other is the knowledge of form, which belongs to the notion of intelligence, and has a seat in the affective-imaginative memory of the mind. [3]

1. Henri Focillon, *The Life of Forms in Art*, Zone Books, New York, 1989, p.157.

2. Jose Ortega y Gasset, "Man the Technician," *History as a System*. W.W. Norton, New York, 1941, p.160.

3. Henri Bergson, *Matter and Memory*, Zone Books, New York, 1988, p.78-131.

The knowledge of matter is instinctive, it is part of the natural order. It is the awareness of the world by which every living organism, plant and animal, is in continuous exchange with its surroundings. It rises spontaneously out of physical necessity and has an effect on matter by integrating it into the body, or arranging it as a direct extension of it. In this order, time is not a separate category of awareness, but it is a mode of simultaneous coexistence of matter, a presence forever certain in the present. The knowledge of form is intelligent, operating within the datum of nature, deliberately rearranging matter to set up a new kind of order, the artificial order. Intelligence, which gains complete instrumentality in the human being, fabricates by abstraction, and is separable from the physical act of making. The sense of time as pure possibility, as a reversible category of representation, and as an abstract measure of virtual or real work, is the transcendental sign of intelligence. [4]

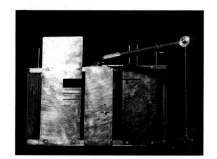

Intelligence and instinct, if highly specialized, may represent two divergent solutions of the same problem: the problem of being aware in the world. But in the human being they are necessarily cooperative capacities: "There are things that intelligence alone is able to seek, but which, by itself, it will never find. These things instinct alone could find; but it will never seek them." [5] The cooperation between intelligence and instinct is best represented not in *Homo sapiens*, but in *Homo faber*, who is the being in complete self-possession of his own instrumentality. The project of the *Homo faber* is the reform of nature by the construction of the artificial world, a supernature interposed between the human being and original nature. Because the human being is made of such paradox as to be natural and extranatural, his whole being is fulfilled only in the *Homo faber*, "a kind of ontological centaur, half immersed in nature, half transcending it." [6] Because he lacks all the necessary instruments to satisfy his extranatural being, to earn his life metaphysically, he fabricates them out of outlying matter in order to become a master of his own destiny. The dialectical project of the *Homo faber* is found in "the concept of nature as 'the inorganic body of man': the naturalization of man and the humanization of nature." [7]

When I consider the system of things which I call the natural world, my body is one of them. But the distinction is not so simple. My body is also the boundary, perhaps shifting, between what is interior and what is exterior to myself. It is the ever advancing boundary between the future and the past, the exact position of the present. It is the place of passage between intention and extension, "a hyphen, a connecting link between the things that act upon me and the things upon which I act." [8] In the *Homo faber,* the body has a tendency, a favorable disposition

4. Immanuel Kant, *Critique of Pure Reason*, St. Martin's Press, New York, 1965, p.74-91.

5. Henri Bergson, *Creative Evolution*, Henry Holt, New York, 1911, p.151.

6. Ortega y Gasset, p.111.

7. Jean Baudrillard, "The Mirror of Production," *Selected Writings*, Stanford University Press, Stanford, 1988, p.106.

8. Bergson, *Matter and Memory*, p.151.

towards action. Already sensing the weight of earthly gravity, it must play its mus-
cles and joints and direct its movements to the task of surmounting the resistance
of materials, making them malleable, pliable, and carvable at will. It is most effectively in the hand where energy converges and leaves the body in the process of
fabrication. All kinds of fabrication must be at the beginning, essentially, manufacture: that is, they must start with the intentionally directed movement of the hand.
Initially, the hand may move across materials by direct contact, such may be the
rudimentary movement that leaves on the sand the drawing of a circle, imprecise
though it may be. If the movement must become more precisely measured, or if
the hand is by itself insufficient for the task, the hand must then manufacture an
artificial instrument to make its action more efficient. The manufactured instrument, the tool, multiplies the capacity and efficiency of the hand that constructs it.
In one sense, the tool is the "congealed outline of an operation," and the objective
memory of movements already executed. In another sense, it is a "finality without
end," soliciting the free and ordered play of the mind in its project of fabrication. [9]
Tools are occasions for further work of the hand; they are the precise locus of a
dialectical experiment of knowledge that neither mind nor sight can conduct
alone. The human being patiently creates his own hands by gradually freeing
them from the animal world. "The hand that is in his mind is at work," liberating
the human being from animal bondage and turning him into recognition of his
own aspiration, his own project of life. Like the Centaur, he has transferred into
reality the program that is his own transcendental self. Though my hands make
other things, they can also make that 'thing' which is myself: "They are the instrument of creation, but even before that they are an organ of knowledge." [10]

   Holding a compass, and supported by it, the hand can bring its movement into
greater control and draw the outline of a more precise circle. Here is the beginning
of a systematic geometry, which records the abstract choreography of movements, as lines constructing the basic scaffolding of space. In this ordered space,
subtending and reflecting the conceptual capacity of the mind, the hand may continue the production of measured work. In the act of drawing itself, we can establish a gradual passage from intention to extension, identifying at least three
stages: first, conceptual drawing as a precise abstract of a form in space, without
regard for material; second, pictorial drawing, displaying in light and shadows an
object capable of embodying such form with articulation and detail; and third, construction drawing as a mode of transfer of the object into its material stereoscopic
body, reciprocally measuring the object and a possible material, and their coherence, in anticipation of manufacture. Representation or imagination is the evoca-

9. Jean-Paul
Sartre, *What Is
Literature?*
Harvard University
Press, Cambridge,
1988.. p.55.   10. Focillon, p.166.

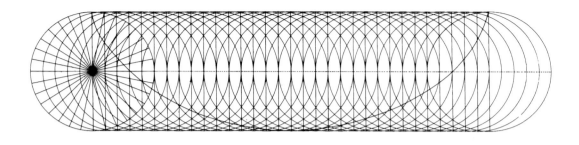

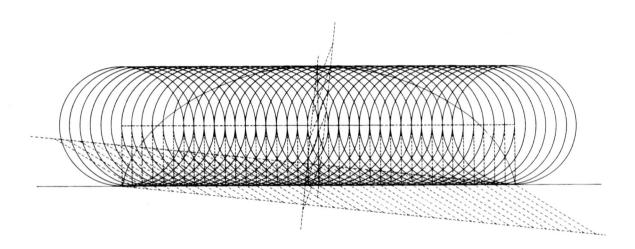

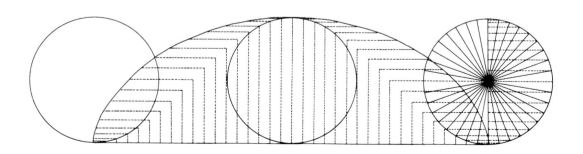

tion of objects in their absence. Distinct from that, perception is the knowledge of objects resulting from direct contact with them, through the manifold of the senses. In the act of drawing, both intelligence and instinct are brought into a precise oscillation and correspondence, making the opening on a plane through which the perception-image going towards the mind, and the imagination-image launched into space, rebound from each other in proper synchrony. Writing is a peculiar kind of drawing that does not aspire to become a material object. It is rather the drawing of words, or calligraphy, which in themselves may be abstract representations of things. Yet, calligraphy itself has a particular kind of materiality that is lodged in the widening gap between words and things. In the calligram, where the arrangement of the script plays with the visible resemblance of the thing represented, the quasi-materiality of the writing is further enhanced, and the text becomes tautological, or redundant as words. [11]

While I remain intuitively skeptical of our tendency to use words to explain our understanding of things, for intuition is silence, and the name is inessential in the face of the thing which is essential, it is inevitable that we must speak. We are within language as within our body, and words are prolongations of our senses, which articulate the structure of the external world. The hand's action defines the cavity of space and the fullness of the objects that occupy it. For the poet, the movement of the hand, with the permanent mark of humanity on the inside and outside of all objects, has a metaphysical equivalence to a whole life of literary production:

> That is the kind of poetry we should be after, poetry worn away as if by acid by the labor of hands, impregnated with sweat and smoke, smelling of lilies and of urine, splashed by the variety of what we do, legally or illegally. [12]

I think that the poet would agree if I modify the proposition, and say, "I make, therefore I am." Now I am comforted and less apologetic of the fact that lately I have been frequenting hardware stores, and avoiding the local libraries.

11. Michel Foucault, *This is Not a Pipe,* University of California Press, Berkeley, 1983, p.19-31.

12. Luis Poirot, *Pablo Neruda . Absence and Presence,* W.W. Norton, New York, 1990, p.38.

CHRISTIAN XATREC

**Void
Architecture**

Quarry at Lacoste, Luberon, France

Quarry at Lacoste, Luberon, France

Quarry at Lacoste, Luberon, France

Quarry at Lacoste, Luberon, France

Quarry at Estaillades, Luberon, France

This symposium was held at
Pratt Institute's Higgins Hall
on April 27, 1989. Presented
are the moderator's introduction and excerpts from the
panelists' presentations.

Moderator

Sol Yurick

Panelists

Tom Finkelpearl
Bolek Greczynski
Pascal Quintard-Hofstein
Lee Breuer
Tibor Kalman

Volume 3 of the *Pratt Journal of Architecture* will investigate an architecture of presence: its tangibility, materiality, sensuous content and surface.

> Everywhere one seeks to produce meaning, to make the world signify, to ren-
> der it visible. We are not, however, in lack of meaning: quite to the contrary,
> we are gorged with meaning and it is killing us. As more and more things
> have fallen into the abyss of meaning, they have retained less and less of the
> charm of appearances.   (Jean Baudrillard, *The Ecstasy of Communication*)

At this stage of our investigation, we find that the dominant linguistic model currently employed to define and explain the production and interpretation of architectural
objects, as well as all other cultural artifacts, has resulted in an elevation of "ideas above
the senses." Frequently, art and architecture are only accessible through informed critical analysis. We concur with Baudrillard and find that the more architectural objects are
treated as texts and the more meaning is intended, the less form speaks. The semantic
content of form not withstanding, meaning in architecture and other visual arts originates
and exists primarily in active participation with the material world.

The Mumbler Meets the Maker

SOL YURICK

Some Notes Towards a Sociology of Theoretical Obscurity
(A Variation on the Thought of Alvin Gouldner)

We live in an age, sometimes called the information or postindustrial age, when 'words,' a maddening logocentrism, symbolicentrism, significentrism, what you will, seem, more and more, to replace and substitute for the material and sensual objects of art, architecture, literature, theater, etc. Call it the age of what Johnathan Swift called Laputa (an imaginary island floating above the earth, populated by makers of vast theoretical systems, *luftmenschen*...), or what Dickens called the Circumlocution Office.

The subpopulations of a soft and ill-defined bureaucracy are possessed by an insatiable desire to intervene between people and their direct perceptions of sensuous reality. They exhibit the propensity to 'read' the unreadable as if every thing, and every space, were a 'text,' drawing encyclopedias out of the minimally irreducible, finding vast babble-kingdoms in the interstices between nuclear particles (which are constantly proliferated), inflating, conflating, enclosing, colonizing pure nothingness itself.

I am talking about an overpopulation of semioticians, structuralists, hermeneuticians, postmodern pontificators, deconstruction experts, information theorists, encoders and decoders, analysts (takers-apart), synthesizers (putters-together of broken-apart wholes), re-analysts (takers-apart of what the putter-togethers...), public relations flacks, buyers and sellers, phenomenologists and para-phenomenologists, psychologists, accountants, discourse-spinners and proliferators, money launderers, tax evaders (the list of middlemen is endless); among whom are the Levi-Strausses, the DeMans and the Derridas, the Lacans, the Barthians, Foucaults, the Baudrillards, the Deleuzes, the Guattaries and, of course, their epigones. Even dead philosophers (Heidegger, Nietzsche, Kant, Hegel, indeed, even the so-called fathers of philosophy – Plato, Socrates and Aristotle) have been resurrected and enlisted in the word-war against the object.

This infecundation seems to be an outgrowth of the creation of an international culture/economy which, in spite of a variety of cultural and national differences, is in the process of attempting (against local resistances) to create a universal, high-level meta-culture, a new kind of catholic church.

The original church attempted to organize a universal religious, hegemonic, cultural system, with a universal language, Latin, and a universal art-and-architecture-dominating culture. Not only was the church an attempt to become a mono-organism, a theo-cultural system, but at the same time it was a hierarchical, centralized, communications system with a universal language and symbology, which sought to control the worship traffic (prayer) by making it flow through a unified switching and relay system (parish to diocese to Rome to God and back down again), striving to mediate all messages by the appropriate use of, and channeling of, words, ritualizing gestures, and to control, convert and direct emotional energy by routing the passions through icons (Freudians might call this a form of transference), statuary buildings, and so forth, by assigning appropriate meaning to a diversity of cultural verbal, material and sensual artifacts and, in the process, rewriting previous meanings and histories of those artifacts.

As then, so now. In our present age, this restructuring attempts to do the same thing, binding and shaping all communications by routing (and transforming) them through the creation of an international and fundamental language, appropriate to an international and universal 'wire-linked' marketplace in which all things (as well as words) become converted, or translatable, commodifiable (measured-against...rationalized, or put in-ratio-to) rendering all utterances controllable. The age is being made, as it were, logocentric in a variety of ways. Indeed, it must become logocentric so that, for example, a Japanese buyer can consider (share meaning), in order to acquire some artifact alien to his own now-changing culture. In short, the 'new words,' the reevaluation, the translation, not only re-means and redefines, but also tells the appreciator whether or not the object has value.

In this vast and inchoate project the Laputans, or the circumlocutioners, are tasked, frequently unconscious, and driven by what seems to be the 'spirit of the age,' of deconstructing and re-defining what has gone before, frequently asserting that the creative him- or herself not only doesn't, or didn't, understand what they were doing, but indeed, the 'originator,' the 'creator,' the artist, the builder, the materials-handler, has in fact disappeared, or is only a mechanism for expressing certain inexorable informational trends and tendencies, implying that there exists a sort of automatic universal drive which plays theme and variations on what has gone before, fitting everything into some ghostly scheme of evolution in which everything is getting better and better.

Going further, these *luftmenschen* sieze the middle ground and would have us believe that the words and word-systems can substitute for the object, so that the logo in fact becomes the icon, the cult-or-fetish object, and that the juggling of the words and images can, in some way, change the very materiality of the object itself rather than the perception of the object.

Where does all this analytic-synthetic logomatic drive originate? In the New Testament recreation of the Old Testament Creation (the Gospel according to the Gnostic-oriented St. John), we are told, "In the beginning was The Word...and The Word was made flesh." And while this statement is not, of course, the first instance of the Word, we may, until we know better, assign this as a provisional beginning of this tendency. The later Cabalists themselves viewed the Torah (the Old Testament: words) as being an organic, living body, which a babbling God created, and out of which, not only is the whole universe created, but all bodies, human and otherwise. This, of course, reverses the true sequence of events in which body, mysterious materiality, precedes all philosophical and scientific thought.

We may safely assert that without material bodies of all sorts, including human bodies, there is no sensational input and no thought and, of course, no words. To go along with Kant, the universe of things, bodies, created or given, is ultimately not understandable or knowable in itself, although we can write, talk about, represent.... The procedures we invent to represent the out-there in a variety of ways are heuristic devices enabling us to play with, or experiment with, the what's-out-there so that we may, until we know better, provisionally communicate about the out-there with one another, hoping that our descriptive languages of all varieties may point, with some degree of accuracy, at the 'out-there' in a one-to-one way in time. Thus, whether or not we are talking the languages of physics, biology, binary digits (computers), mathematics, literary or philosophical words, the jargons of sociology and psychology, finance (a sort of information), we are talking about the out-there and what we interact with.

But does anything contain meaning? Does the out-there contain information? Is it coded, encrypted? No. It is what a certain subset population of the generalized 'we' bring to it; meaning is what is assigned to the universe. When the act of assigning informational essences, meaning, is complete, when others have reperceived for us, if we are readers of architectural, art,

philosophical, or other kinds of journals, we may have been victimized by an invasion of the language-snatchers.

What then is this proliferation of thinker-talkers all about? What, if anything, do philosophical thinkers, the so-called postmoderns, all throwing out an absolute Babel of competing discourses (jargons), have to tell us about the object? Where did they all come from?

Clearly there has been an over-proliferation and overproduction of university-trained word-slingers who have to try to find some role to play in the world in order to justify their existence. And, of course, to make money and survive. In short, we are talking about a set of people who – to parallel a crude but effective statement of businessmen – never had to meet a cultural, artistic and economic payroll (payroll meant in a larger sense). Such people, in order to be effective, must first differentiate themselves from the common herd and then, by the constant invention of neologisms, of whole systems of words which product-differentiate themselves from one another. Like modern armies and modern bureaucracies, the top, logistical echelons are overloaded; how many hundreds of theoreticians to the producer in the trenches, so to speak?

What then of the maker, the creator? On what level does the maker operate and is what he, or she, or they do capturable by those who

would lyse the object in the acid of words and attempt to reconstruct it? And what of the object itself? What of the tyranny of the material (to say nothing of the economic) universe in which such considerations as gravity, wind-forces, space and time, and the obduracy of materials play an overriding part?

It is this dimension that we will address today. The mumbler meets the maker.

TOM FINKELPEARL

I'm involved in producing art on a very nontheoretical, participatory level. When I first got to New York about ten years ago, I was tired of working on a theoretical basis and working for gallery spaces and working in the studio. Directly out of school you don't usually have an opportunity to have a big show, so I went out into the streets. I found wrecked cars, and I cleaned them out completely – people thought I was crazy. Then I painted them gold and did installations in the cars. It taught me a lot about context. My pieces are all based on context and on some kind of social analysis of the position within the world that the site holds. As an artist, I have taken the position that I have to build everything that I do.

Being a curator is like using the artist's finished work as material to create an overall installation. This is a piece by an artist named Steve Gray, in an art and technology exhibition.

I organized an exhibition at P.S.1 called Out of the Studio. Each of these artists works with a group of people, outside of the art world, outside of the intellectual mainstream. In this case, Mierle Ukeles is the artist-in-residence at the Sanitation Department. This piece was a ninety-foot-long ramp made out of recyclable materials.

BOLEK GRECZYNSKI

I am working on a collaboration with mental patients at Creedmoor Psychiatric Center. And I'm for art which means something. I'm terribly bored with working alone in my studio, then exhibiting fifteen paintings in a posh gallery, and shaking hands with people who eventually might buy one. I think it's just a waste of life. It feels very natural for me to be at Creedmoor, in the center of life. It can be a struggle, not unknown in art, to retain one's sanity.

X, from I Miss the Revolution

Creedmoor Memos, from the Pattlefield Project

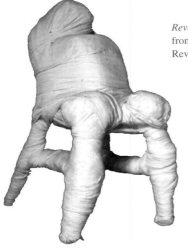

Revolution Bound, from I Miss the Revolution

PASCAL QUINTARD-HOFSTEIN

To quote the architect and teacher, Henri Ciriani, a building has to be analyzed according to the three P's: "presence, permanence and pertinence." Against all odds and fashions we must, as architects, define and qualify the notion of presence. Presence has to do with the building marking and holding a space through the invention of limits, perimeters, surfaces and the transformation of a site under the light. The idea of transformation is about the invention of an inside; its spatial integrity, its programmatic proposition, its construction, its plastic resolution.

In the framework of this symposium, it seems important to insist that composing, transforming, modifying, making architecture becomes the "concept finder." The tendency in many design studios is to find a concept first, which sounds a little pretentious. To find a concept demands work, hypothesis and development. Developing an idea has to do with the pursuit of one's own obsessions, with the discovery of one's continuity and plastic rigor. Intuition does not seem to be enough. Conceptual discovery has to be pursued according to what Le Corbusier called "the patient search," removed from fashions, style-makers, salons, etc.

Only when this is understood will we be able to detach ourselves from the idea of the architect as commodity, the architect as mere program illustrator.

The four cardinal points, the horizon, gravity, geometry ... all these are a programmatic beginning....

Study model for laboratories in Philadelphia

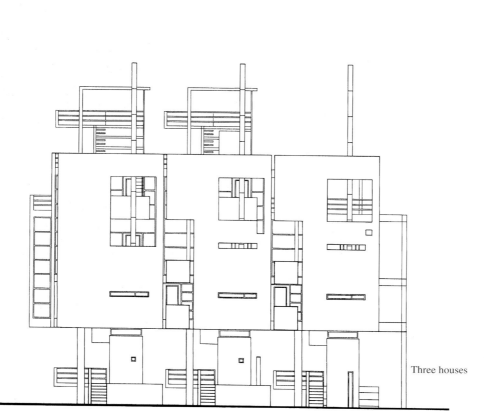

Three houses

LEE BREUER

I like it when artists and writers and singers come to see my work, and interestingly enough, they like exactly different things. I am at the precise juncture of the two streams of American culture: literary and oral culture. In the literary culture, the word, the printed word, can extend all the way back right into the image, into the picture, into architecture, into space. The spoken word can extend forward into music. And the performer takes the written word and makes it the spoken word and so he/she is at the precise juncture between the two disciplines and precise juncture between the two cultures. So architecture is part, in my mind, of literature. It's an extended phenotype and it extends into behavioral ideas, what you build is behavior. In stage terms, it's called business, stage business, but in architectural terms it's called building.

My father was an architect and he dreamed of what he was going to build to die in. It was the final statement. It had a swimming pool; it was a ranch-style house; it was really cute. I thought maybe architects are just building things to die in, because that is their final statement about how to exist in this world, basically their metaphor for immortality. Maybe the pharaohs just dreamed about what kind of pyramid . . . and it hit me: "permanence." Now why does architecture have to be permanent?

In the theater, we are often at war with architects. We go into a theater that an architect has been very architectural about and we find that we can't change the space. It's so defined and rigid and permanent that you couldn't change it if your life depended on it. You put an actor in it, you change the light and it just stays there. You dream of a good old blank wall or a black box or something like that because the architect is competing with you for domination of the space. They want their gravestone up there, their mausoleum, their "my father's house." And of course, the director wants his or her statement, the play, the changeable, destroyable artifact, the one that gets flushed away and a new one gets born. From the theatrical view, there is a war with architecture, and it's a war for domination of psychology or the so-called size and importance of the human in the space. When a culture reaches the point that it wants to say

Let's cut to a faucet and a drop of water under it. If you watch the drop of water and you play 3/4 time, that water will drop at 3/4 time. If you play 6/8 time, if you play a rhumba, the water will drop in rhumba time, because sound tells you what to think about what you see. But by the same token, words can tell you what to think about what you see even more powerfully than sound. In fact, words can tell you what to think about what you hear. It's weird because you have to be very careful about which wins. It's kind of like the rock cuts scissors deal. The word, when it's presented powerfully against the image, will tell you what to perceive. This is one of the traps of the literary level of communication.

that the idea is more important than the human being, they start making the ceilings high, like in cathedrals, and then from cathedrals to nice high lobbies. All just to say that God is bigger than you or the corporation is bigger than you. There is a war and this is just the beginning. I just wanted to make a few observations from the psychological, nonspatial, nonconceptual, emotional, oral, nonliterate, kind of, you know, what am I doing here point of view. Well, this is one man's emotional perception of space and the theatrics of space.

TIBOR KALMAN

I'm a graphic designer and I'm also a commercial artist, not a fine artist. We're a graphic design firm employing around twelve people. It's called M & Co. None of the work produced by our company is entirely mine, it's fairly collaborative. Most of our work in some way relates to words and language and we are the type of beast that Sol attacked in his opening statement.

When you do design, and I suspect that this is also true of architecture, one of the things that happens, because you are doing commercial work, is that the process of conceptualization is fairly artistic and the process of selling that to a client is very unartistic and very cerebral. Frequently, you come up with an idea, and you don't know exactly why you've come up with the idea, and then you have to invent a whole series of reasons to sell that idea. As far as the tease goes, I think that the tease, whether it is for us, whether it is in the *Talking Heads* videotape, whether it's in the graphic design, or whether it's in architecture, becomes the question of how you sell a commercial client, a sponsor, or whoever, a given idea. Part of the reason it happens is that people are selling into history, they're selling class, classicism and all of that shit.

Scenes from the video *Nothing But Flowers,* Talking Heads. (Director: **Tibor Kalman**; Design: **Alexander Islev**; Writer: **Sean Kelly**)

We have worked for a restaurant called Restaurant Florent in Manhattan. The thing about Restaurant Florent that is important to understand is that no one ever designed it, it had no architect, and as such we took the cue for the graphic design from that point of view. Now the design style that began to evolve for the restaurant was to try to use images the way one would normally use words and words the way one would normally use images.

Placemat at Resturant Florent. (Design: **Tibor Kalman, Emily Oberman**)

S C H W E T Y E   L U C H I N I   M A R I T Z

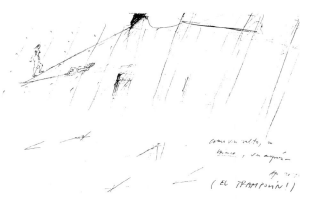

Descents

Maritz-Starek Residence

The moment when a few lines accommodate their proper weight is not sufficient. It becomes necessary to surprise them, unfolding the hidden connections
that might occur, not only among the points they connect, but the spaces they
seem (only seem) to leave untouched as well.... Ah! the persistence of the observer – now a voyeur – could actually trigger the occasion when a gesture adopts, with
precision, all the essential demands which turn echoes into experiences and
expectations into involvements. In that scenario, it is no longer possible to disen-
gage from the trajectory of a gaze, or the texture of a shadow: all matters and
everything collaborates. As such, the alchemy of architecture invokes the status of
a project and the discourse inevitably oscillates among materials, actions, dimensions. And only then can we incorporate words, draw accurately, dream. Soon a
JUMP occurs. Now we are in the middle of a text which delineates the shape of a
stair, already placed between ground and sky: steel and wood, support of stone
(white, are the wings of an angel?). But this artifact is also the diving board for a
swimming pool. If we jump, it is to extend to the surface of the water; if we walk, it
is to discover, through the frame of a window, a room which turns IT into a pointing device, occupying the horizon line ... a trajectory which, by now bounces off a
fence clad in copper that undulates, again, actively unlocking the paradox which
turns a field into a territory. Not yet ignorance, or vision, or even shame. But
rather an a priori where the thickness of your skin brushes against the texture of
the world and it's too late to come back.

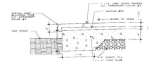

Paving edge detail

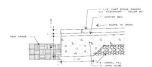

Paving edge detail

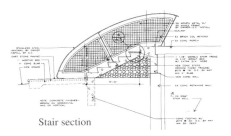

Stair section

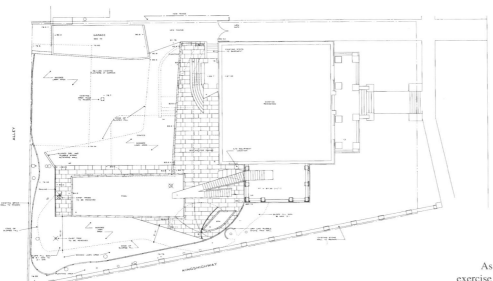

Location map

Site plan

Existing condition

As an addition, this project in fact becomes an exercise in **avoidance:** the old structure, a 1912 mansion located in the central West End (a historic neighborhood of St. Louis) is a unique case of Viennese Secession architecture.

Our project involves rebuilding the original columns and cornice (destroyed in 1931), bringing back the full sense of monumentality that the mansion had. The project also involved the inclusion of a pool, jacuzzi and deck, along with a new fence surrounding the property. In this case, we opted to establish a very clear distinction between the old and the new. Therefore, the stairs connecting the sun deck with the deck/jacuzzi are literally "jumping" over the existing walls, minimizing contact. At the same time, the landing from the stairs becomes a **diving platform** to the pool, reiterating the intention of avoiding connection to the house. By the same token, the new deck stops short of touching the walls of the house, and the new fence (ten feet high) barely connects with the sunporch on the west side.

The wall at the stairs is clad in stainless steel panels, all exposed structure is also stainless steel. The steps and landing are teak. The decking is paved with stone panels. The fence is finished with copper sheets.

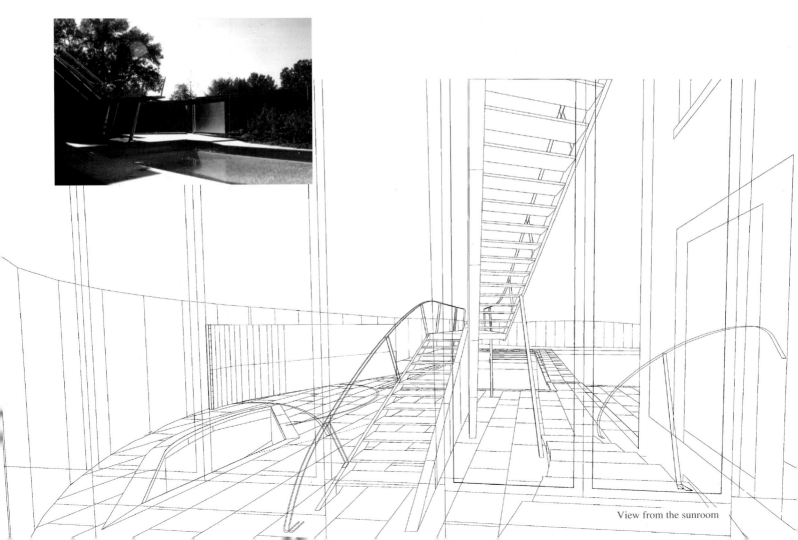

View from the sunroom

View from terrace towards pool

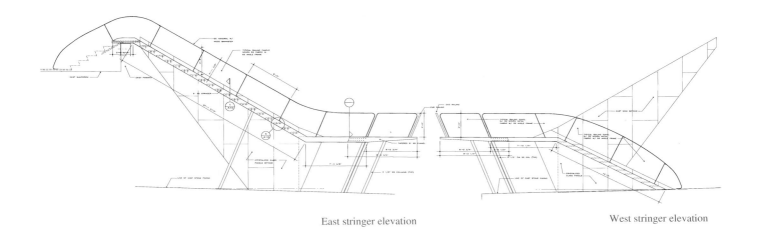

East stringer elevation   West stringer elevation

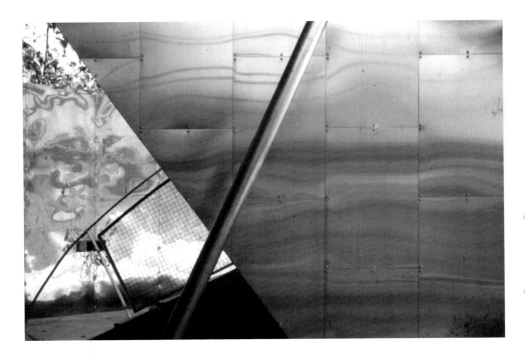

ARCHITECTS:
Adrian Luchini
Thomas Schwetye

ASSISTANTS:
Matthew Forman
Elizabeth Kincaid
Matt Read

Station Building

Site
The remaining elevated track of the New York Central Railroad, on Manhattan's lower West Side.

Process
The conditions of confrontation between the buildings and railroad track generate the images (buildings above the track, divided by the track, below the track, adjacent to the track). The "space" of the drawings is derived from these conditions of confrontation by colliding them and by compressing them into framed views.

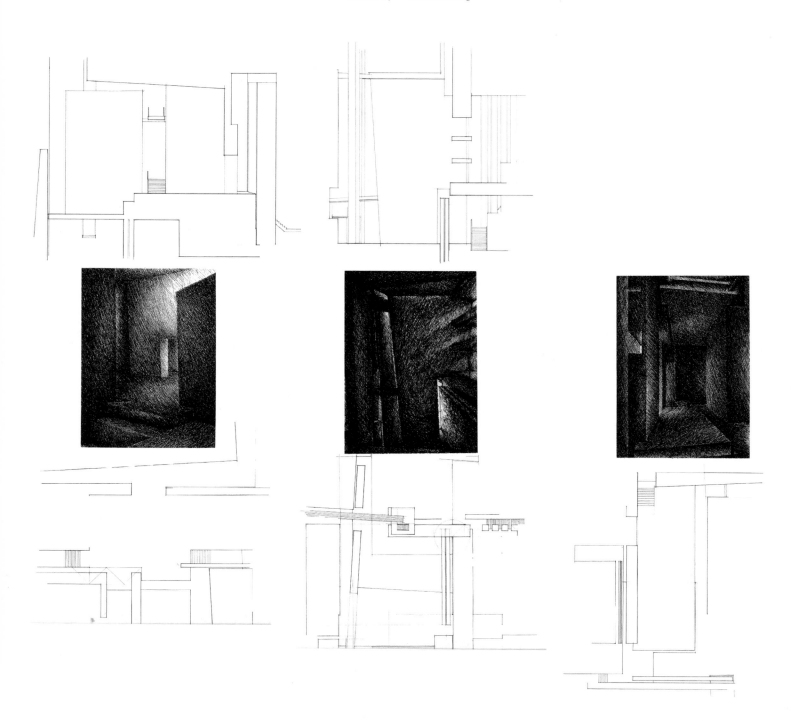

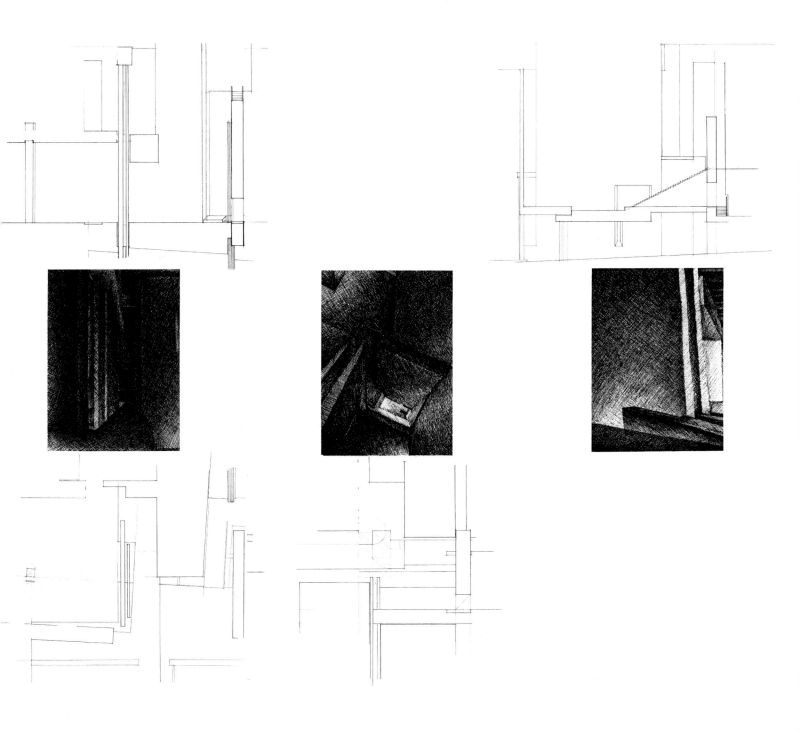

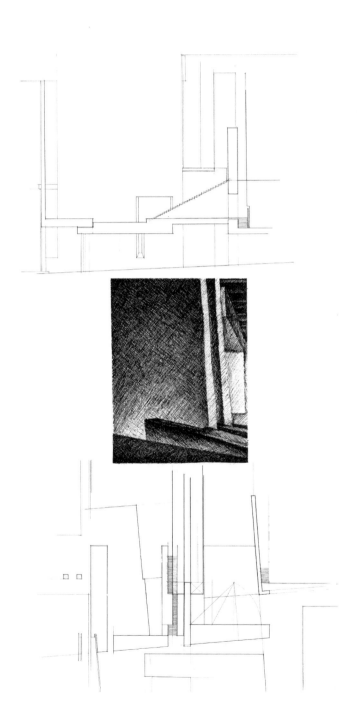

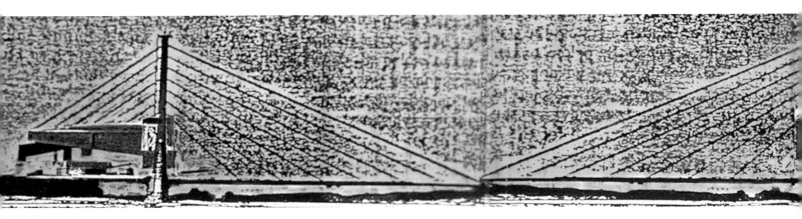

The limits of making
Sketch for the Occupied Cable-Net Bridge
Tokyo Bay

The question of making, the act itself, is best addressed by action or, at a later date, by the results of that action. It is counterproductive to substitute words for action. Authentification is possible through the sublime silence of making.

Resist simulation.

P E T E R   W I L S O N

Bridges

We no longer need to travel. Media brings the world to us, all places being today equally near.

Today we all continue to move, but rarely to travel. Today places and spaces exist only for the moving viewer. Today the sum of our movements resembles atoms in a highly charged field, frantic vectoral oscillations replace grand narratives of travel.

Objects of transition (terminals, freeways, bridges), if they are not to remain completely invisible, must today also be stoppages. That is, they must divert and interrupt the traveler's/oscillator's trajectory. These bridges are such stoppages. Each is a mechanism of transition, but each subverts the "curve of efficient transition." The need to cross is overwhelmed by the requirement to stay – to stay suspended – to occupy the bridge.

The bridge not as pure engineering, but as a complex collaboration of structure, use and meaning has become a recurring type for us, as well as a metaphor for our attitude towards architecture. These bridges are, in fact, "bridge-buildings"; like medieval bridges they all have appendages, adjacent structures, devices to cause the crosser to stop, to – even for a moment – dwell in this unique suspended state. We know from Heidegger the significance of a bridge in terms of dwelling: it gathers.

Translucent Bridge, Fort Aspern, Holland, 1989

Two converging U–steel sections that rise twenty meters are enclosed by screens of translucent greenhouse plastic. Landscape, canal, dyke and horizon are hidden on entering the bridge. In crossing, one rises slowly becoming aware of the qualities of the site.

A change in the program made crossing impossible. Appropriately, the attainment of central suspension then becomes not a transparent incident, but the principle revelatory function of the bridge.

During construction

Plan and elevation

Central suspension

Night view

Berlin Bridge

In Berlin the situation is contemporary, an incomplete and incompletable space. The appropriation of an existing bridge as ready-made and its unexpected placement exaggerate the latent surreality of the contemporary city. The influence of industrial monuments like this bridge for modernism and specifically the National Gallery by Mies becomes today a subject for architectural discourse. As architecture tackles the question of transparent and electronic technologies, a new perception and consequential new spatial formulations will emerge. Bridges and other dinosaurs of the first modernism no longer at the forefront will also require new interpretations, new mythologies. As Barthes has written, the civilized future of a function is its aesthetic enoblement.

One of a series of objects in a planning proposal for the culture corum, the Forum of Sand. It is proposed to transfer the unused nineteenth-century structure from Wedding in the north to the culture forum. It becomes the core of the forum, an active deck above the empty field of sand between the National Gallery of Mies and the Philharmonie of Scharun.

The bridge is serviced by three small additions: Cafe of the North, Cafe of the South and the Oservation Tower.

The journey of the bridge

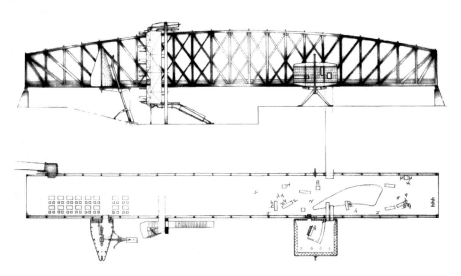

The bridge

Bridge between National Gallery and Philharmonie

Ponte Dell' Academia

A city measured by its bridges. The bridge-building type must combine occupation and traversing, figuration and abstraction; it identifies the modern condition; meanings are isolated and relative.

By the displacement of the ship-shaped truss, an unprecedented slenderness is achieved.

To one side, the bridge ramps gently; to the other it arrives dramatically. These radically different end conditions preclude the possibility of a symmetrical structure. To Campo S. Vidal, the city fabric is penetrated; the new bridge-building closes the wound.

The program for the bridge-building is both commercial and cultural.

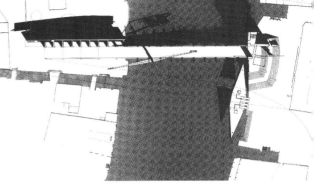

Site plan

Ponte Dell' Academia bridge

D E B O R A H G A N S

Bridging the Gaps

Display

These exhibit designs expose the way in which they were made because they were intended to be unmade. The connections do not compromise the integrity of the parts so that the parts can be reused.

Hardware is an important feature in such designs because much of it is reusable. My father owned a hardware store. I always loved the open bins of parts waiting for the ingenuity that would recognize the potential energy described in their forms and put it to use as a part of a larger order.

The process of designing such an exhibit has a lot to do with making it. Details are shopped for rather than designed. The drawings are a way of measuring pieces and the specs are a way of counting parts before final the assembly. Measure twice, cut once as the saying goes. Projects such as these suggest that the fundamental link between the processes of drawing and of building is the act of measuring. The architect measures at one scale what the maker will measure in another.

Bridging the Gaps

Deborah Gans, Architect
Anthony Webster, Engineer

Gans

In designing Bridging the Gaps, our sense that the stands were not part of the permanent architecture of Avery Hall at Columbia University determined the exposed connections to the wall and the floor via bolts, guy wires and neoprene pads. The stands have an impermanent perceptual existence in that they appear large and substantial from one side but narrow and tenuous from the other. Like the Thin Man, they can almost disappear.

Webster

The greatest irony of the exhibition stands is that, designed for a four-week show, they have lasted so long. They are used for almost every exhibition. In order to function well, the staands had to adapt to the space's diverse roles as a busy Avery thoroughfare, a grand foyer to Wood Auditorium, and an exhibition hall. The challenge was to create a foil to the hall's form and scale without creating spatial barriers. This was the motivation for the small cross sections of the legs and rafters, and the separation of the frame from the wall and from the exhibit mounted on it. The resulting transparency also stresses the continuity of the curved wall.

Between exhibits the bare stands look unfinished and give the hall a distinctly in-between feeling. The dialogue between volume and armature, space and stage set changes with the rythms of the school.

Bridging the Gaps, detail

Vacant Lots

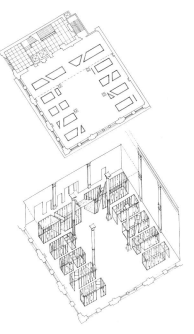

V a c a n t   L o t s

Deborah Gans
Armand Legardeur
Tibor Kalman, Graphics

The installation Vacant Lots was very tangential to the permanent architecture of the Mercantile Exchange Building with no connections to existing walls and floor. After the show's disassembly, Clark Construction reused the studs, the temporary lighting and the eye bolts. Spatially, the design played with the idea of temporality through its reference to stage design. The long front wall was like a scanae frons through which the visitors passed in order to wander among the display blocks which were a kind of urban stage set.

Vacant Lots

B R I A N   M c G R A T H

Exhibition space

Rome Exposed

An Installation from the N. J. I. T.
Summer Program in Rome

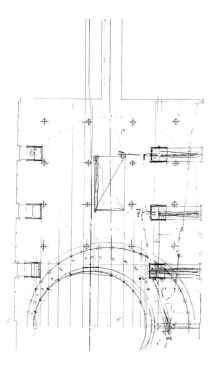

Sited in N.J.I.T.'s gallery, a former gymnasium in which was constructed a circular wooden partition which houses the architecture library, the installation Rome Exposed consisted of five elements.

1. Six study carrels for private browsing through the students' large sketch pads. The carrels were constructed by removing display panels from the side walls of the gallery exposing twenty years of dust.
2. Tar paper floor traces mark a semicircular "shadow" of the existing library partition and create a second "negative apse" in the space. Also marked are six paths leading from the exterior piers of the space to the carrrels and a rectangular mat under the central skylight, on which is displayed Nolli's map of Rome buried under sand from the New Jersey shore.
3. Four canvas screens direct light into the southern three carrels and one directs light from the skylight to the Nolli map.
4. Sixteen suspended metal lecterns for the display of each student's personal journal/sketchbook, a record of their stay in Rome.
5. Four analytical models of early Christian basilicas in Rome, constructed of wood, steel and marble, are also displayed.

The installation temporarily transformed the former gymnasium to a gallery, a library, a scriptorium, a temple and a basilica. Like the basilicas analyzed in Rome, the space reveals traces of its history.

Plan

Assistant: Christie Bruncati

Suspended metal lectern (Photo: Grant Taylor)

KELLER EASTERLING

Volume was performed in 1990 at the
Judith Andrea Theater in New York City.
Performed by a deaf man and seven
objects: a xylophone, a binoculars, a fur
hat, a part of a toy car, a triangle, a globe
and a glass of water.

Volume

BINOCULARS

[A SINGLE XYLOPHONE NOTE]

AND now faintly aware of the pop and sizzle of one's grandmother next to an okapi who converses with a prawn who lies next to a microbe all silently hinting at their kinship across the powers of ten.
Even Deaf Homer's Assorted Stories Enchanted Seven Cousins.
Now faintly aware of a vortex of sound, we arrive at the threshold of the outer ear.

[WITH HIS EAR VERY CLOSE TO THE XYLOPHONE, HOMER BRINGS THE MALLET DOWN ON A SINGLE NOTE]

Telescoping down in size into stifling warmth and diminishing light.

[HOMER PLAYS A SINGLE XYLOPHONE NOTE AND SINGS...OH]
[HOMER PLAYS A SINGLE XYLOPHONE NOTE AND SINGS...OH]
[HOMER PLAYS A SINGLE XYLOPHONE NOTE AND SINGS...OH]

Here, with thousands of messages from one's older sister distractedly making their way forward, one already gets the queasy feeling that one wants to leave.

[A WOMANS VOICE SAILS IN.]

. . . . .HOMER !

But tightening the focus of our microscopes, we take measured respectful tippy-toe steps up to the tiny membrane, the modest curtain stretched before the real laboratory of hearing – the eardrum. And miraculously, we are echoed to the other side, the middle ear, there in company with three bones left over from the bits of dinosaur jaw worth saving. **Even Deaf Homer's Assorted Stories Enchanted Seven Cousins. Even Ear Deaf Drum Homer's Hammer Assorted Arrived Stories Stirrup.**

With nothing but proximity in common, their accidental design polished and honed by the heat of a millennia of sound, of thick fugue upon fugue billowing and spiralling together through the rafters and into the vaulted domes.

This heterogeneous necklace of objects diligently extrudes more and more amplified movement through tinier and tinier dimensions. And what was once a small bird's tiny peep, becomes the dance of a giant pelican in the wilderness of Addis Ababa.

And all the attic boils with heat and vibration and all the movements of the last of all the bones are just reflection of their own movement.

[HOMER HAS ARRANGED THE XYLOPHONE NEXT TO THE FUR HAT]

F U R   H A T

Similarly, in the development of the static electric Van de Graaf generator, it was the accidental placement of objects next to each other, which caused a spark. [THE FUR HAT IS ON HOMER'S HEAD.] For instance, fur in contact with a rotating glass sphere could displace enough electrons so as to send a charge on into a metal cylinder, also in rotation, which then might, through a human body wearing a silk dress, travel from one outstretched fingertip to another outstretched fingertip, which in turn could create lively patterns of movement amongst the hairs of a hat also made of fur.

The daughter of R.J. Van de Graaf, who invented the Van de Graaf generator, was heading straight for me on College Walk and wearing a fur hat. We might have collided had she not deflected or deionized my charge, sending me into a tiny orbit, and propelling me in a parallel path beside her up to the Anton Van Leevenhoek Auditorium where her father was speaking and where she... dropped that fur hat. In the crush at the door, I retrieved it with difficulty, and as I handed it to her, received a shock that traveled throughout my body and up the antenna of

all my graying hair. I don't think she said anything. Her lips didn't move except to smile. The Van de Graaf generator, in its nascent form, was constructed of tin cans, a silk ribbon and a small motor, which by their touching...

[HOMER PLAYS A SINGLE XYLOPHONE NOTE ON THE XYLOFONE.]

I was watching her mouth at the dinner table with the Van de Graafs as I was carefully watching the mouths of all the Van de Graafs. Unable to hear their conversation, I mentioned out of the blue that I seemed to know of a wonderful fish form, sea creature, well really a burrowing sand animal, but couldn't remember the name of it. They responded by asking me if I knew the "Van Teetums." "NO..." but did know something about the Van Marum generator. (I would have them yet. I would illuminate her father's work to her and others. I found it all to be so much like the ear.) But as I met with their approval, I watched Miss Van de Graaf's mouth gradually bend over my hand and deliberately bite it. Miss Van de Graaf had undergone a change of species. It naturally follows. (We had previously known Miss Van de Graaf to be so wonderfully old-fashioned.)

[WEARING THE HAT, HOMER PLAYS A SINGLE NOTE ON THE XYLOPHONE AND SINGS...]

[HOMER'S VOICE WANDERS AS HIS FOCUS WANDERS TO THE CAR PART...]

C A R

And then of course the combustion engine can be built from household objects. One has proven this. In fact, one was able to build a miniature automobile before the age of fifteen. Someone at the science fair suggested that the auto was too advanced to use ordinary gasoline. In fact, the right fuel was never found. Quite frankly, the dogs were used to pull it. Like the summer of only playing Monopoly, one devoted one's self to the continual painting of the auto. One seemed even to affect its style in stance and in clothing which could be seen billowing and flapping with aerodynamism. And the helmet of the hair was specially combed like the bottoms of one's pants to have a flared skirt riding just above the wheels.

[HOMER LOOKS AT THE CAR PART THROUGH BINOCULARS]

Only the little cousins were small enough to ride in the auto. One tried to help the dogs overcome their awkwardness and embarrassment at having to pose as the engines of the car, but when the sky lit up with thunder and lightning, they more freely expressed their agitation threatening to upset the auto. Instantly one's older sister appeared and probably saying, "Why couldn't he just do the party

favors?" collected the seven little girls and their even tinier little brothers to the door to have cake and cumulo nimbus, and the empty little automobile (in silly

[A WOMAN'S OFFSTAGE VOICE SAILS IN. HOMER DOES NOT HEAR IT]

HOMER! HOMER!. . . HOMER, I'M ON THE FIRST STEP.

hysteria) hurled itself down the hill. **Even Deaf Homer's Assorted Stories Enchanted....** And though hundreds of times smaller than the eustachian tube – a back stairway to the rest of the body pops and squeaks and steps on the stair.

[A DOG BARKING. A DOG BARK-ING. A DOG BARKING HOMER!.]

T R I A N G L E

[HOMER IS FOCUSED ON THE POOL TRIANGLE.]

Only pool.
Pool on a gigantic pool table taller than the eye...watching the seven solid colors and black floating back and forth against each other and the seven stripes, and floating and never stopping, each with a different amplitude and wavelength.
My very educated mother just served us nine pitchers. Mercury, Venus, Earth, Mars, Jupiter, Saturn, Uranus, Neptune, Pluto. My very educated mother just served us nine pitchers.
And the balls never stopped and they never stopped because they didn't want to. From under the table, the balls were rolling and shaking the rafters like a long drumming of the thunder and lightning.

[HOMER BEGINS TO PLAY NOTES ON THE XYLOPHONE.]

And a man's hand reached under the pool table to drag you out, to get your hair and drag you out. And the pool cue reared back and swung, in orbit, down and around and back up....
...to tap you..."Break Homer," I saw Mr. Van de Graaf say.
"What?," I said.
"Both a bit touched aren't you?," he said, because he thought I couldn't hear him say, "Break Homer."
And there was a breaking crack of thunder and rolling balls.

[HE HAS LIFTED HIS HAND FROM THE XYLOPHONE AND NOW IT IS PLAYING BY ITSELF. SOMETIMES CAPRICIOUSLY DOU-BLING BACK ON IT SELF.]

G L O B E

When I came downstairs from playing pool with Mr. Van de Graaf (HE NEVER MARRIED), his daughter, Miss Van de Graaf was already gone. She later sent me a box curtly addressed simply to 44 Walker Street...(HE IS UP ARRANGING HIS BILLIARD BALLS) a box full of all of her hair to add to my nice assortments. (ALL HIS LITTLE THINGS ARE IN THE ATTIC. HE WAS ONLY ALIVE FOR JUST A FEW MOMENTS AFTER HE WAS BORN.)

[HOMER FOCUSES ON THE GLOBE. A WOMAN'S OFFSTAGE VOICE SAILS IN.]

. . . . HOMER, I'M ON THE SECOND STEP.
. . . . HOMER, I'M ON THE THIRD STEP.

The planets were rolling, dissolving into something else, all reincarnating in hopes of avoiding these calamities.

[XLYOPHNE DOG BARKING, XLYOPHNE, DOG BARKING, THUNDER AND LIGHTNING, XYLOPHONE, DOG, DOG, DOG]

W A T E R

[HOMER SINGS A SINGLE NOTE]

OH! In the last instant, through the last gasps of air, we are swallowed steaming into an inner chamber filled not with air but with water and lymph. **Even Deaf Homer's Assorted Stories Enchanted Seven Cousins.** We are hydraulically coddled and sudsed through the semicircular canals. Then, dear colleagues, with the soft pedal depressed so near to where there is finally to be sound, we arrive in the tiniest chamber of all, the spiral cochlea.

[ALL SOUND STOPS]

[HOMER DRINKS SOME WATER]

The microscopic home of a striated sea creature made of thousands of overlapping arpeggios encased in a clear gelatinous spiral diminishing in size to a point at the highest pitch–a chromosome burrowing into what now seems like a gigantic stony cave in the tiny bones of the skull.

And of course, sound is not heard, it is touched. Miss Van de Graaf understood a little something more than her father's work. She joined a wild African tribe in Addis Ababa to whistle through her nose and play spoons and dance in silk dresses at the speed of light. A perfect platonic anarchy occurring in nature and visible with the naked eye.

[HOMER DRINKS AND SPINS THE GLOBE. HE TAPS EACH OF THE OBJECTS WHICH NOW PRODUCE THE SOUNDS OF A XYLOPHONE. THEY CARRY ON A STEADY SERIES OF NOTES EVEN AFTER HE HAS STOPPED TAPPING.]

And we strain to touch or drink a sound from tears and sinuses, that is only alive for a few moments. Until there is some little trace element, one tiny little crystal of salt that is dissolved and swims directly to the brain generating a string of captivating stories and delectable impurities—spaced so that they can be surrounded by and pulled into the mouth from a mouth speaking slowly enough to see.

[HOMER DRINKS]
[HOMER STOPS]

AND

so that for an instant we are faintly aware of the pop and sizzle of one's grandmother next to an okapi who converses with a prawn who lies next to a microbe all silently hinting at their kinship....

[THE MALLET IS SUBMERGED IN THE WATER. THERE IS A SILENCE THAT HOMER CAN HEAR.]

[COMPLETE BLACK, THEN LIGHTS UP FAINTLY. HOMER IS GONE. THE GLOBE SPINS. THE HAT LIES ON THE FLOOR. OBJECTS BEGIN TO MAKE SOUNDS BY THEMSELVES.]

Just before the echo travels back.
Just ahead of the echo of my own sound.

. . . . **HOMER!**

[XLYOPHNE DOG BARKING, XLYOPHNE, DOG BARKING, THUNDER AND LIGHTNING, XYLOPHONE, DOG, DOG, DOG]

[BLACK.]

S O L   Y U R I C K

Making: The Realm of Facts vs. The Realm of the Imagination

An architectural journal is an odd place for the work of a novelist and essayist to appear. But this is an odd age. These seem to be days of grand, textualist illusion. It is almost as if pure image and words, the world as text, as signification, has seized the imagination of many intellectuals. In fact everything and everyone has become text. Everything communicates. Everything, we are told, is redolent, packed with symbol, signification and allusion in this that some call the postmodern world. What this seems to have done is to make many people lose their grip on reality. Maybe this craze for signification and communication is just another marketing device, or a way of giving those who don't actually design or build – that is to say, those who don't work with intractable materials in a world still ruled by gravity and impassible barriers – those who merely critique, a piece of the action. Note that even a simple cubical structure, for example, can be invested with magical and allusive properties by wordsmiths. Some can see the wonders of the ages in a pyramid while others see only a pile of neatly arranged stones. This rage for every shifting meaning is an age-old activity. What intellectuals have 'talked' other intellectuals into, a new generation of intellectuals will soon enough 'talk' themselves out of, as soon as the new intellectual cycle of fashions change.

And yet, architects and writers, share a certain discipline. I too have had to deal with spatial constructions, albeit in words. Being a writer of a 'naturalistic' bent, the characters I create have to move about in 'real' space. (Although I also have a penchant for ascending to the surreal from time to time.) The words I use try to give the reader the sense, indeed the illusion, that he or she, along with my fictional characters, is traversing actual space, moving in natural or humanly built, artificial landscapes. 'Traverse' in the sense of doing something as simple as getting from one room to another by some means of locomotion...walking, running or even flying. That is to say that I must construct my architecture by copying configurations out of a commonly accepted universe, or make universes never before seen on earth, sometimes out of dreams. Whether I accept the common rules that bind us all, the rules of spatiality (and thus time, for there is no movement in space without the time taken to move in it), or I construct new rules, science fiction rules, for instance, in which light-year spaces are jumped across in an instant, binds me, limits what I make and, hopefully, limits the reader so that he or she is forced not only to perceive (without, I hope, stopping to think about it), but also to feel the spaces I construct, and thus has to expend some energy, even the energy of imagination, on what it would be like to move about in what I am making. In short, even as vast and/or involuted spaces may be created in a computer by some CAD program, I try and weave mind-grappling illusions. For after all, computer 'space' as well as word driven 'space,' are at the mercy of alphanumeric 'words.'

But are words spatial constructions? Words are spoken or written, heard or seen, acts which themselves operate in space and time, for as even one reads, the planet moves. Indeed the generation of these 'words' involves a long cultural buildup, as well as an expenditure of energy and, above all, money (which can be considered to be a representation of stored-up energy). Space in which to erect real or mind edifices is a function of money which allows some part of the population to dream extravagant dreams and renders others, who don't have the money, unable to think, or even dream, of more than where the next meal is coming from and how far (say in the case of starving Ethiopians) they will have to walk in order to get something to eat and stay alive for another few hours.

(Parenthetically, let me say two things. First, when I use the phrase, 'function of,' I mean that a set of conditions accompanies another set of conditions in such a way that when considering one set of objects and actions, another set of objects and actions, no matter how apparently distant or hidden, must be taken into account. Secondly, when it comes to writing, I usually avoid the word 'structure.' I prefer the word 'arrangement.' In the case of 'structure,' where, for example, a building is concerned, there are laws and limitations. The bottom, the foundation, must be put into place before the middle or the top. Given the vast range of possibility, when seemingly unbound by the laws of gravity, the top may be presented before the bottom. Rhetorical laws do not limit: one can play infinite games. Consider *Finnegan's Wake* in which, in principle, all the elements are in theoretical simultaneity: there is no beginning or end. Even here there are problems: Joyce has to begin at a certain point and end at another point since he was bound by the laws of publication in a book and a book is a structure, a kind of housing. Ideally, to realize *Finnegan's Wake*, Joyce should have made an artifact that kept on shifting physically even as the reader read. More ideally, a technology should have been invented that would allow the 'reader' to grasp the whole novel in an instant.)

Now I will admit that while I am drawn to the concrete, the materialistic, and have a somewhat Marxist outlook on the world, I am not above playing certain games. But, above all, I remain aware of the concrete in relation to the limitations of a world in which we find ourselves. I am aware of gravity and its effects on the body, of corridors, of walls and so forth. I am also aware of the power of illusions that can be constructed in realms other than words: cinema, television, computer, graphic arts or the realms that unfold for us while under the influence of some mind-bending drug. I would like to call your attention to a little philosophical rumination in *Moby Dick*. Ishmael, the code name of the author Herman Mellville, talks about the strange effect on the mind of the limitless sea. He discusses a philosophical sailor who might be aloft on one of the masts, thinking about the 'infinite.' (Clearly, a critique of Hegelian phenomenology was on his mind.) Ishmael warns us, in a concrete illustration (an almost Marxian caveat such as is found in *The German Ideology*), that if you lose your grip on reality, as well as a good hold on the rigging, and should find yourself falling, you will be brought to yourself as you splatter on the deck. The deck concentrates the mind wonderfully.

So, from the perspective of a writer, one who deals with words, I would like to deal with a few manifestations of how authors in the past have dealt with space.

Let me begin with some peculiar spatial configurations, which are somehow connected to language in the Bible. There are many spatial problems in the Old Testament that are not fully resolved, even among those so called 'People of the Book.' (It has also been said that the Jews are time oriented, rather than space oriented. History shows that such assertions are false.) First let's take the case of Nimrod's tower. The citation is very brief. King Nimrod, a mighty hunter, decides to build a tower to the heavens. It is not given where exactly this tower was to be built: the tale probably incorporates many legends the Jews, or Hebrews, told in their wanderings of the home of their founder, Abraham, in Ur, the Babylonian or Chaldean world now known as Iraq. The Old Testament does not tell us how high heaven is, but it seems attainable by the worldly art of construction, of piling bricks upon bricks. This architectural structure is a distinct and realizable possibility. What is also told is that in those days, everyone in the world, certainly those who would work to construct the tower, spoke the same language. Nimrod is confounded by God's decision to strike linguistic confusion among the workers and make them all speak different languages. Question: Is the tower a 'real' tower or is it an imaginary tower, a constructed knowledge tower, a mystic mind tower? And what is the relationship of this piece of architecture to language? Why couldn't God have just destroyed the tower without going to the difficulty of making the builders speak different languages? Thus, on some level, the relationship of something spatial to a means of communication is established. Very postmodern, it would seem.

The second Old Testament construction is Solomon's Temple, something that has engaged the hopes and wishes of a certain segment of Judeo-Christian society through the ages. Dimensions are given, but there have been endless arguments about the way it would look, to say nothing of where it was situated. Some have asserted that the dimensions (cubits and the rest of it) are in fact mystical. This allowed Newton, for example, to state that there was a correspondence between the dimensions of the Temple and the physical, astronomical, cosmological universe. What this points to is the constant attempt to encompass the universe in a man-made construct and, on a deeper level, the perpetual activity of poets, and frequently architects, in asserting that 'this is like that,' the activity of ascribing some holy and deeper meaning, sacralizing what is indeed very ordinary activity.

Next I would like to talk about Homer's concepts of spatiality in *The Iliad*. Homer tells us how a league of Greek city-states decided to assault the "topless towers of Ilium." (Why topless?) Homer constructs, or assembles, perhaps from legends and old reports, a whole terrain, the walled city of Troy, to besiege. This terrain, in spite of Homer's poetic use of language, is very ordinary. Indeed, the city was situated in a strategic place, athwart the trade routes leading from the Mediterranean complex of seas to the Black Sea and the rich hinterland of what is now called the Ukraine and Georgia. Perforce, being real, warriors besieged a walled town, charged across ground when the armies confronted one another. Unless there is an intervention by the gods, Homer's warriors fight in very recognizable surroundings. They are subject to distance and the time required to get across it, whether by foot, or chariot or the flight of an arrow. This terrain is earthly. But there's another terrain besides the earthly terrain, a series of worlds in which the gods live. It's a barely glimpsed universe out of which they appear to exhort one side or the other in their fight. The Greek gods' other dimensional realm, their magical space, is usually on mountains (Mount Olympus, for instance), in the earth and under the sea. One notes that there is no real attempt to describe the architecture of these other-worldly realms. While those towers of Troy are described again and again as topless, they nevertheless get burned to the ground. One would think that a conflagration that would demolish a "topless" tower should, in principle, take forever.

What am I beginning to get at? That the 'other-dimensional' realm, the mystic, perhaps the 'fifth-dimensional' realm is always present. And that in our time, the effort to realize this extra earthly realm takes place in science fiction or, for that matter, in a computer.

Let's skip across the centuries and move towards the very odd construction: Dante's Hell, Purgatory and Paradiso in *The Divine Comedy*. The tale begins on earth. Dante sees a high, shining realm from his position on earth. It's called, after Augustine, the City of God. But, as Dante tries to walk towards it, he finds that it is impossible. There are various mundane barriers: a forest and three beasts who block his way. Dante realizes that he must go the long way around. The whole journey will take three days, the traditional three days which parallel the crucifixion of Christ. His descent into hell, His ascent to heaven, and His return from the dead on earth. (At the end of Dante's journey, he will re-emerge on earth.) Note that the realm of the Inferno is in the center of the earth. (A theme later to be echoed by Jules Verne; of course, in these latter days of scientific discovery, we know that we cannot construct realms in the earth, or at least not too deeply. We have cast our vision outwards towards space, if not on adjacent planets, then to the absolutely unreachable distant stars and galaxies.) Dante moves downward into and through the Inferno (the inside of a cone), and comes out at the bottom on the other side of the world, and then ascends along and around the circular cone shape of Purgatory. When Dante has reached the peak of Purgatory, he can then rise towards heaven (although the gate through which he enters is not specified), which, oddly enough, is not constructed in a cone shape, but rather in the form of a spinning set of concentric circles, and at whose center resides God. The peculiar feature of these spinning circles or disks is that the outer rings spin more slowly and the inmost ring spins with the greatest velocity. This, of course, is contrary to our present knowledge of physics in which, if you spin a set of concentric disks, the outer rings spin the fastest and the inner ring the slowest. But the interesting thing is that the architecture of the disks is such that it is not only linked to an imaginary space and to velocity, but to degrees of knowledge and love, as well as names of people who are in various degrees of excellence or blessedness. My point is that any space, even the space required to traverse a page, a set of pages, or a volume, is tied not only to perception, but to knowledge in a variety of forms: epistemology, classification and so forth. Let me reiterate: every act of knowledge has an implicit price to it, if nothing else then the intellectual investment of those who have gone before.

My fourth instance of how a writer handles space comes from Dickens's *Bleak House*, where the lawyer, Tulkinghorn, has a mysterious ability to traverse enormous spaces in an instant. He walks out the door of his chambers and, suddenly, he is miles away in another part of England, in a country mansion. The instances of such manipulations of space, manipulations tied to coincidence and mysterious abutments of places and characters, can be multiplied in Dickens's works. Through a mysterious set of folded spaces, Dickens revivifies, as it were, surrealism in an age in which science was becoming primary. And yet, he is part of an ancient tradition of miraculous constructs in heavenly or hellish spaces not bounded by the forces that we all recognize.

What lessons do we learn from these few instances, which could be multiplied? That humans, at least some humans, yearning to escape the bounds of gravity and the limitations of their bodies, long not so much for the fantastic but, in fact, for a kind of immortality. It's that kind of thing that Johnathan Swift mocks in his "Voyage to Laputa" part of *Gulliver's Travels*.

Sol Yurick — Making: The Realm of Facts vs. The Realm of the Imagination

101

Now, by no means am I immune to these longings in my own practice. I hover somewhere between two poles of attractions: the naturalistic and the fantastic. As my mind soars, I am dragged back to earth by, if nothing else, the memory of and the limitations of all those mundane things, forces and space the world is subject to, Euclido-Newtonian space, brought up short by the vicissitudes that affect us one and all. Let me give a few examples of how this conflict works itself out in my own work.

In a novel called *Fertig,* my hero, or anti-hero, is jailed. I describe the jail at great length, for I wanted this jail to be both real and a kind of antechamber to another world. When some literate corrections officers read the book, they said that I had captured the jail perfectly. They were there; they worked in jails, yet what they failed to notice was what I was literally describing. I took the architecture of my jail from two sources: from Piranesi's *Carceri* and from Jeremy Bentham's *Panopticon.* I constructed a jail that had never been built anywhere on earth. What did the readers think they were 'seeing' as they read the words? I had generated an atmosphere, an illusion, albeit an illusion with a long and illustrious secular, mystic and surrealistic history. Later on in the book, I describe an asylum for the criminally insane set up somewhere in New York state. The configuration of the asylum was such that it was a building to which additions had been made, constructions that ringed the inner original structure, which was built of stone. As one proceeded from the inside to the outside, the building became more and more modern, constructed out of more modern materials. All this was set in a bleak landscape, an icy swamp. This construct was also hailed as a masterpiece of realistic writing when, in fact, I had consciously and deliberately duplicated the structure of the bottom of Dante's *Inferno,* set in ice. Wondrous are the ways of illusion and wondrous are the desires for the impossible on the part of readers. For, if the writer comes out of a long tradition (a tradition which I shamelessly manipulated), so does the reader come out of the same tradition.

Secondly, when I was writing *The Warriors*, which involved the journey of a fighting gang into unexplored territories, from Coney Island to Woodlawn Cemetery in the Bronx (the underworld) and back. This territory is to be found in the real world. It can be traversed by subways and/or on foot, or by car. And yet, at the same time, the Bronx was terra incognito to my protagonists, the realm of the mysterious 'other,' an alien space full of terror. At another point, one of the journeys involved the tunnel between 96th Street and 110th Street, a singularly long stretch of track unrelieved by any stations, perhaps a mile in length. Now my strategy, my plotting through time and space, involved a desperate escape from 96th Street through the tunnel all the way along that frightening and unfamiliar subterrain. What to do? How to capture both the real and the frightening? I walked and timed how long it would take someone to go through it.

This is a mundane stretch of distance, amenable to very mundane calculations. To be sure that space had a history which had involved digging and moving of earth, supports, and so forth, as well as, in the background, capital investments (and also bribes and kickbacks which are part of the hidden costs of building anything in this city). And behind that history is a longer history of tunnels, of mysterious passage-ways, stretching back into antiquity. One thinks of Persian *quanats* and Roman cata-combs. The knowledge of such a history, a knowledge which would have calmed him, was unknown to my hero. But I wanted more. I wanted the sense of fear and what that did to the perception of that stretch. One: my hero was frightened. Two: he had never encountered such a structure. Three, and perhaps crucial: his shoe was coming apart, slowing his desperate need to get away and out of that frightening ambiance. So, in dealing with a space that everyone should be able to understand, I wanted to make, to create, at the same time, the sense that the tunnel was endless and was thus implicitly more than a space, it was the space which, when traversed, was also a rite (or route) of passage into manhood.

I learned several things: that the first time one traverses distance, it always seems longer; that emotion, fear, changes the perception of distance; and, finally, that a distance that one has to walk while, say, hungry, perhaps starving, is always longer.

Given the changes in perception that have been taking place in this new, so-called computer information age, I became interested in writing a novel in which I could explore the illusionary possibilities inherent in something we might call virtual space. Such a space might give one the actual feeling of moving through and living in the most various kinds of space, spaces not necessarily amenable to the laws of physics as we understand them. I tried to do this in a novel called *The King of Malaputa*. Malaputa is an island that doesn't exist and yet has reality. It is nowhere and everywhere. It is, as the financiers say, offshore, which also means out of this world.

But I didn't want this to be a mere intellectual financial exercise. How could I make it real? We are all subject to sense impressions: touch, feel, sight, hearing and so forth. Sense impressions may come from the outside, what we see, what sensa-tions we receive on our skins, and so forth. Sense impressions are also distorted by cultural expectations. Real and cultural impressions are processed through the peculiar and imprecise system of the central nervous system. The only way to make us feel this new space was to suppose that we are strapped into some sort of com-puter-mediated machine, a body suit that encompasses our entire body so that we receive various stimuli from this machine suit. If this could be done, how could we tell the difference between what is 'real' and what is 'not real'? I called this machine suit the Gerontomat. Let me quote:

> The subject was put into the Gerontomat, a sensor-filled body suit. It had
> been long recognized that each and every organ, every cell, indeed every
> organelle in every cell, even every molecule, broadcasts its own special frequen-
> cy signature, its own little tune: the totality a veritable 'symphony.' When com-

bined, processed, and totalized by the Gerontomat, the micro, mini and macro emanations could be expressed as numbers or organ topologies....

The body received nutrients, psycho- and somatherapy intravenously and intraneuronically, trailing wires and tubes in and out of every orifice...including micro cameras cathetered into veins, arteries and vital organs. Wastes were eliminated the same way: incontinence was no longer a problem. In addition...to offset boredom (for boredom led to breakdown), the Gerontomat also received (and responded to the desire, indeed the need for) entertainment: movies, video, music, conversations, melodramas, comedies and tragedies, docudramas, stories, novelizations, news reports, historical reconstructions, myths of all nations in all of their variants, folk-tales, a vast storage of psychoanalytic confessions, epics, sitcoms, and real life tales. When plugged in, the [subject] could [perceive] two sets of visions: a banal [real world] one and the other, bypassing actual eyes and ears, a window on many worlds as the entertainment feed was pumped directly into the optic and auditory nerves.... Thus, the degenerating and decrepit could participate in a fuller life than any human in the world had ever led, even as they were dying. These new developments led Mellon to wonder if there might not be another use for the Gerontomat, one that had not been thought of. Discussions indicated that even though there was a two-way traffic in signals between the patient and the virtual image stored in Jerusalem, the [subject] was essentially passive. Was it possible that the [subject] could take an interactive role and use the Gerontomat not only to receive but to send; make of it a two-way command post, use the self as a veritable console to go beyond to other environments? Filtering the information received from those diverse worlds, could that knowledge be translated into bodily terms, metabolized, so to speak? If so [the subject] could become the truly ultimate sysops (systems operator) by sensing and feeling everything and in some way regulating this omniverse instantly. How? By will! For didn't an exertion of the will change bodily and mental states, generating an electromagnetic signal? It was a way, Mellon thought, a true way, of being one with his system. What such an experience would look or feel like they couldn't say. The idea had never occurred to them.

...The first experience was exhilarating, shattering, ecstatic and terrifying. New feeling; touch and sight and smell and, yes, even sound, came not to those crude, outmoded sensors, ears, eyes, skin and nose, but was assembled directly in Mellon's brain. Vast repositories of wisdom, in a multitude of forms, everything in the diverse computer systems could be processed, combined, permutated, signified, simulated and routed into the subject's physiological portrait. The portrait gobbled up these info-viands, translating them into body-speak. When the data had been metabolized into meta-proteinic code, the feed was relayed back to the subject making his real-time body a titanic, random-access memory device. Mellon felt like his skin was dissolving. His nervous system, penis, heart and bowels, his bodily fluids, became connected to everything that was going on everywhere and everywhen in the observable and recordable universe. And that made the universe a living being because he was its core. 'Many' became 'One': 'One' was 'All.' Mellon's impulses began to affect the world's trading, buying and selling. He was the quick, unreadable flicker of changing prices, every order in every real and simulated financial market. And, as if he were there, he simultaneously experienced the collective, orgiastic, shouting frenzies of trading, which further stimulated and altered his virtual neurotransmitters, affecting his body, whose currents kept time to sudden, swift rises of financial mountains of exhilaration and depression into sloughs of despond. Contrawise, when he needed sudden outlays of money, he found he could liquidate and convert the para-flesh of his simulation's accumulated energy-knowledge into many forms of currency. Market activity began to affect his sexual impulses. After all, money in all its manifold and devious forms circulating, was translated by his simulacrum's virtual body into hormones, blood, neurotransmitters, electrical impulses. His erogenous zones were thousands of miles outside his skin.... If he could control his body, he could control his simulacrum and all the universes encapsulated in its mapping. He began to experiment with his feelings. What would a blast of hate do? Or love? Joy? A rise...a fall? He generated a feeling of sadness, of despair, of gloom and doom. Yes, the world began to sell and the markets would drop twenty-five points that day.

...Now he became aware of a new sensation. The longer he sojourned in the Gerontomat, the more the boundaries of his being and time were eroded by the invading somata-signals of other apartmented, yet conjoined lives. Hundreds of thousands of real and concocted limbs, organs, neurons, biofluids, biographies, genetic grammars, syntaxes and semantics were leaking into him, causing his personal genome to expand and dilute. And this new glut of code was changing him. He realized what was happening: becoming greater, he was becoming alien to himself. He began to have difficulty separating the memory of his own real, lived life from the input of other not-lived lives. This effect had not been instantaneous. For what seemed like a few eons, Mellon retained his unique authenticity even as his intimation of personal mortality was being mixed into a pleasant, primordial, sensual, oceanic catch basin of tranquilized recollection. He was becoming someone, or something, else. As if in a confused stupor, he realized he was undergoing a kind of death, for isn't life not only the sensations one feels at any given moment but a unique, personal memory arranged in a singular sequence? Drowning in this omniotic fluid of multiple existences, he sought to rouse what he remembered to be himself and himself alone, to escape from this universal, personality-destroying memory-glut to remember himself from this accumulation of alien appendages which was integrating him into a not-Mellon. And yet, at the same time, he wanted to lose nothing of what he was learning. He began to struggle to come back to life by seeking out some indubitable and proprietary moment, a once-in-all-time actually lived event.

Now this computer-assisted escape into infinite and convoluted space of the imagination seems very exciting, doesn't it? It would seem that what I am proposing, and indeed what people are working on at this very moment, is, finally, a way out of the very limitations of the body itself, doesn't it? I can now design a building, for instance, whose dimensions on the outside are confounded by the limitless possibilities of multi-dimensional spaces on the inside of such a construction. What's more it would appear that I could even enjoy a felt trip through such a construction. In short, we might now take Dante's journey into the triple realm of the afterlife and, indeed, feel, to some extent, the tortures of those who are in the Inferno, or Purgatory, as well as the infinite bliss of those who reside in Paradiso. Or we might

Sol Yurick — Making: The Realm of Facts vs. The Realm of the Imagination

105

no longer look to journeys to other planetary systems of other stars, or in other galaxies. To be sure, we will continue to live on this limiting earth in limited bodies, but what does that matter?

But let me bring you all down to earth again. In the first place, let us remember that whatever marvels it seems that our computer can construct, the computer is nothing more or less than an adding machine, with an extremely limited grammar, as it were. What we're talking about here is the age-old desire on the part of some thinkers to convert the totality of the natural universe into numbers, to transform the qualitative into the quantitative. In modern times, this is reflected by the assertion that the universe is mathematico-logical. This assertion is fundamentally problematical; it is an act of almost religious faith. Marxists, for instance, call this the transformation of quality into quantity. What the form of this ever-repeated desire conceals is a terror, indeed a hatred, of nature and the limitations it puts on all of us. Not only must space be conquered, but also the random, the unexpected, and the unaccounted. But has this development made life easier for us? That too is problematical. For instance, in the fifteenth or sixteenth century, Venetian printers developed a system for dealing with the multi-referential and infinitely allusive Talmud that was a conquest of space. They laid out a complex page with a central text accompanied by sidebars and underbars of commentary text. Now the wonder of this accomplishment was that the printers, working with their eyes alone, succeeded in a project of vast complexity in a very short period of time. Why bring this up? Because to do the same thing with various page-making programs on a computer involves an inordinate amount of calculation-time. Note the way newspapers, now laid out by computers, look. They are clumsy, often full of unsightly and unaesthetic gaps. Note how difficult it is to teach computers to do what humans do in an instant: pattern recognition. Yes, I know what you're going to say: neural networks of multiple processors are going to solve the problem. Let me categorically assert: they will not. The question is not only the cost of developing such a system, but where the money comes from. For our gain is someone else's loss. Is it really possible to envision some five billion people-dreamers strapped into machines, each one on an infinitely varied journey with infinite adventures? At the same time, how will all these people be fed? And what spaces will be devoted to the growing of food? That's only one problem. The implication of my little story is that the gorgeous spaces I constructed were a function of knowledge, of information or, as is held in these days, of a kind of humongous text, a text out of which we can construct variegated realms, and deconstruct them into other realms as we either grow tired of what we are experiencing or question them in order to create new realms. What of the structures that will house these dreamers? And what of the amounts of energy required to keep these machines running? Let me put it this way. Einstein has told us that $E=mc^2$ when, in reality, we must factor into this equation the question of money, something that Einstein forgot to do. How do I get to this formulation? In the first place, aside from energy in nature, not all of which is harnessable by a long shot (the energy of stars, to say nothing of black holes, if there are such things), man-made, man-used energy always, in this society, comes with a price. In the second place, energy always deploys itself in time, whether to construct a building or to write a novel (including, as it does, the history – in space and time – of the accumulation of the capital that provides for the leisure to acquire knowledge and write). And, in the third place, we have the honorable formulation that money is time (a concept not only of the medieval Church but of Benjamin Franklin), a formulation that in fact has an even more ancient history, going back to the ancient Chaldean magicians. Note then that as our so-called 'developed' society becomes enriched, has more time, and even more longevity, other societies become depleted, the life spans of their populations growing relatively shorter and shorter. Put it this way: as some in our society experience an organization of energy-money-time-knowledge in more highly ordered concentrations (negentropy), other parts of the world experience a dimunition of energy-money-time-knowledge (entropy). A moral issue arises at the threshold of our infinite possibilities, and morality can also be seen as a dialectical problem of entropy-negentropy. Or to put it another way, this is an issue of cosmic debit and credit. What is this little essay all about? To have us pause and deliberate about the limits of imagination and how much time, effort and machinery we shall put into such deliberations. Telescopes, which expand our 'knowledge' of space, space in which we can construct marvelous buildings on other planets, or in other galaxies, go in and out of black holes, are really nothing more or less than imagination machines. But this imagination can also sail forth into the infinite with nothing more than a closing of the eyes and a meditation, or a dreaming.

People have died . . . died in vast numbers. Real people, 'facts,' living in real space, if you will, are dying. Some for reasons that are quite concrete. Others for no reason whatsoever. As for those who die, disappear, they come back as numbers, as a form of memory, as credit. And a system, a world system, a theorizable system, seems to need, in the present new or old world order, these deaths even to feed those who, because of their very system of thought, ensconced in comfort, occupy continents of intellectual space, intellectual space which crowds out myriads.

Some of the ancient rabbis stated that he who kills a person, kills a whole world. Some kill directly. Some kill indirectly. Yes, they also kill, who sit and critique or invent machine-and-capital-intensive texts. How is it that they can empathize with some ancient or modern fantastical piece of text and find it impossible to empathize with something that is, after all, a living human person? What would it matter if, for the time being, we gave up our fevered inspections of these tired and ever-repeated pieces of writing? Consigned them to oblivion? Haven't we got better texts to address? Humans and where they might live?

R O B E R T   R O G E R S

Two Houses, Two Ranches

A ranch is a controlled landscape. Its operation and ownership are sustained by the ability of the rancher to extend and protect his interest in the property and its capacity. To build and to occupy is the essential cultural sign of this interest.

The two projects presented here have similar conditions of origin. Each is a new residence for a third-generation owner on ranch land that was homesteaded during the early settlement of the American West. Each is on a parcel that has been divided from the original acreage. In both cases, the original ranch buildings no longer exist.

The primary goal of these projects is to reinstate the occupancy and the presence of "owner," not just on the site, but in the surrounding physical and cultural landscape. This work seeks to understand the fundamental typology of the ranch residence and produce a contemporary architecture without relying on the obvious sentimentality of rebuilding.

These two projects are developed as a continuation of historical possession: possession through progressive and sequential acts of building. The expression of this process is based on recognizing that the initial subsistence construction of homesteading provided a source for elaboration and extension. Thus, the reconception of the ranch "compound" is the initial critical theme; the accumulation of varying structures and activities is a key typological condition in the planning of each residence.

McCarty House
Upper Diamond Bar Ranch
Cody, Wyoming
Construction 1991

The house and compound are set low in the Shoshone River Valley, in the riparian zone that stays wet and green through the summer. This is the traditional place for original homestead cabins, where water and cover were readily available. This siting of the house establishes a certain visual control over a large portion of the valley. The extension of this "control" is developed by references to local ranching practices and habits. The point of entry and length of approach are indicative of expansive boundaries. Building groupings are evidence of occupation over time. A sense of land acquisition is realized by the connective geometry of roads, trails and livestock paths.

The long bar house is flat in the landscape, contrasted to the high walls of the barn. The long south elevation is divided by a great hearth and chimney that, like early multi-stage dwellings, separates living and sleeping quarters.

A thick interior wall intersects the concrete block chimney to isolate service rooms. This wall engages the envelope of the house and extends the line of internal public/private division through the pasture to locate the working yard, barn and corral. Traditional peeled log trusses, held away from the ceiling by purlins, establish a skeletal reference for the rhythms of the house, porch and rail fences that combine the landscape and the home.

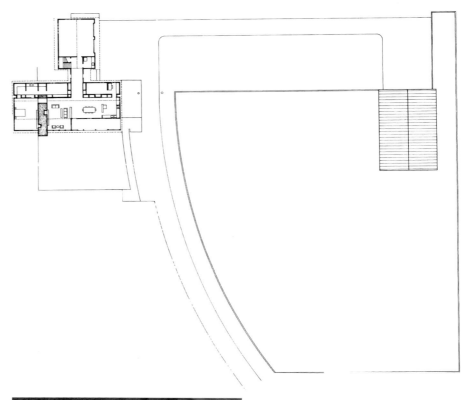

Plan

Interior view

Elevation

Site plan

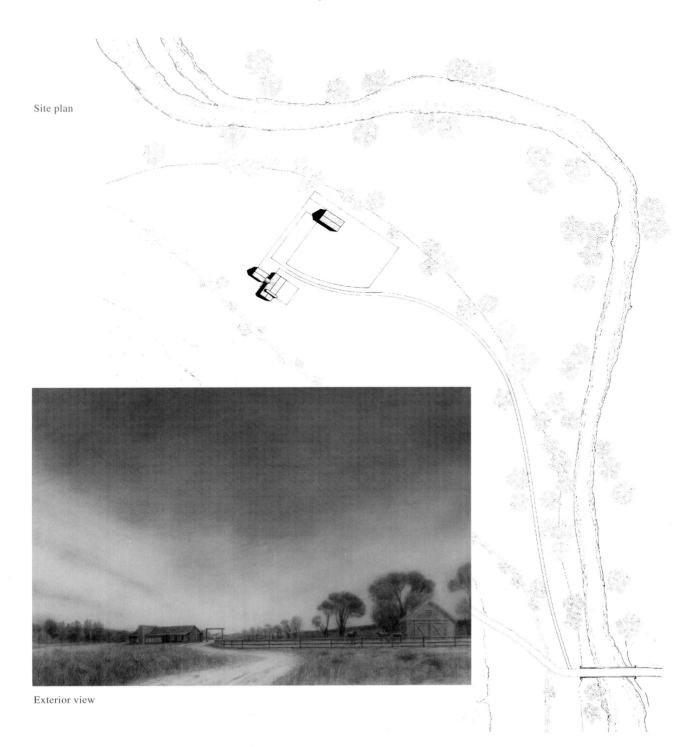

Exterior view

House at 8000'
Valleydale Ranch
Estes Park, Colorado
Project, 1990

This project is presented as a point of comparison. Here the cultural and social link to presence and ownership is formed by condensing the elements of the landscape into a tight group. This house and site overlook Rocky Mountain National Park; the area is rugged and steep. Long views, framed by identifiable geological landmarks, make the house a point of origin. The tradition of the mountain home was one of refuge. This project sought to recognize this by control of entry, by a close grouping of structures and through materials selection.

The compound is bound by the extent of the concrete plinth, which gathers both road and streambed into its boundaries. The road and stream are long ties into the mountain; in the precinct of the house they are controlled and collected.

The house is built on a short structural bay, marked by piers of local flagstone, to provide a physical density and to allow prominent openings towards the views. A lower level is buried into the hill as a foundation and deep refuge.

Credits:

Robert M. Rogers, Principal
Robert Thorpe,
Philip Drew Assistants
Mary Bucher, Renderings

Site plan

Elevations

Tomb

A columbarium for a church in Brooklyn

By a wall, the exhaust of each candle

is gathered. With fire and smoke the sorrows

lay themselves one upon the other until in

darkness they are joined.

Detail of accumulated smoke

Gates of the mourner's wall (interior view)

Mourner's wall (interior view)

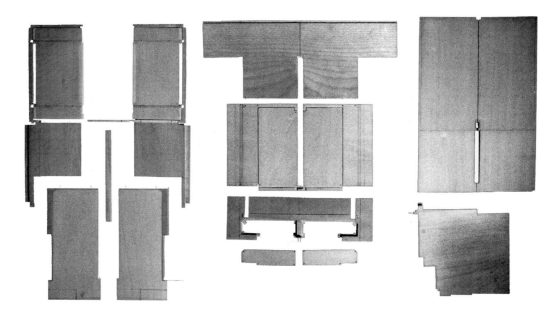

Disassembled model

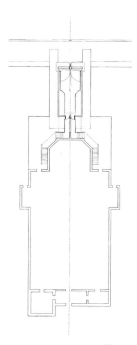

Plan

J O H N V E I K O S

Library

Site plan

In the Library of Evolutionary Knowledge, the understanding of storage and process came into form, labeled the categorical and the referential. The two operations explored the basic functions of a library.

It is the resurrection of a library.

The evolution of a program, the generation of a notion of a library, is expressed here in the context of three contiguous projects, created over the course of two years in the studio of Gamal El-Zoghby. The Library of Evolutionary Knowledge attempts to deal formally with two operations: referencing and cataloging. It is programatically the only library. The Monastery and Pantheon explore the two notions separately. The three projects aim to reinvent the notion of a library in an electronic age that has challenged the traditional use of information.

Library, detail

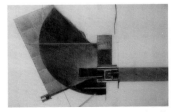

Monastery, detail

Pantheon, detail

The Monastery is also a library, but its epistemology is based on reference, in this case to light. Light is the constant measure for speed, perception and position. All measurements are a function of this value. With this single reference, simulation becomes the manipulator of what is real in the building.

It is a library of reference.

Library, detail

Monastery, detail

Pantheon, detail

Monastery, plan

Monastery, section

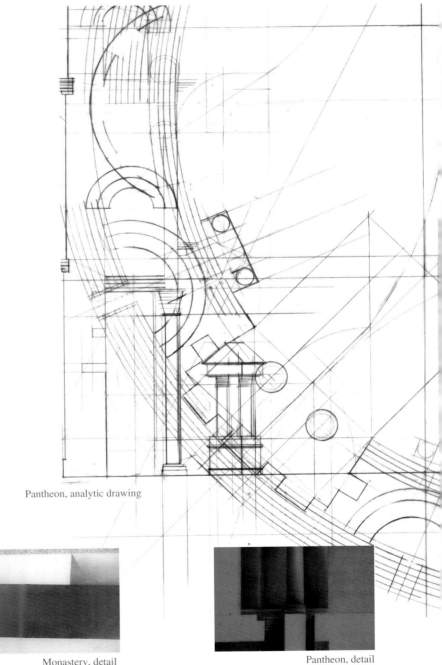

Pantheon, analytic drawing

Library, detail

Monastery, detail

Pantheon, detail

The Pantheon is, in its contemporary context, a fragment. Buried beneath Rome are the foundations that fill its taxonomy. This program is an act of excavation, identifying and cataloguing fragments, thereby inheriting them. In any notion of unity, exists subvertly, the fragment, yet it is not debris, it is particular and complete. The fragment inherits a permanent fossil iconology,[1] it has no responsibilities and is free of invention and implication. It is the severed limb, torso or head, gruesome and violent, yet seductive. Within this sinister relic is the ability to determine beyond its own physicality.

It is a library of tactility and unforeseen connections.

1.   The implication is that the language used to describe these objects is necessarily our invention, consequently "permanent" in the sense that it is uncovered not discovered.

Section elevation

Model

Model

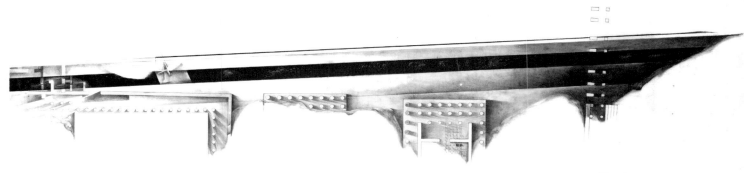

Site plan

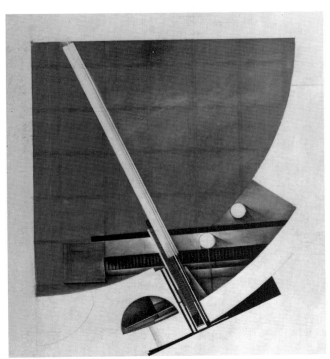

Plan

Model

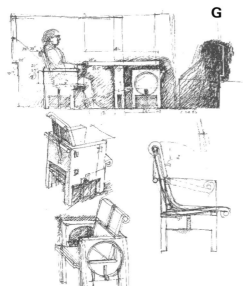

G A M A L   E L - Z O G H B Y

Nine Chairs
Report on the Making of an Ideal Object

Clarifying Statement

The made object is a medium of phenomenal power of emanation bounded by the conditions generating its concept and material. This introduction identifies the conditions and values that constitute the ideal qualities inherent in the chair as an object from its conceptualization to its materialization. The following are the conditions necessary for the ideal objectives:

1. The Object Is Integrated with Its Context.
    It provides the value of a special relationship of critical unity.
    It implies that the object cannot be taken out of its context nor appropriately placed in another context.
    The ideal is to have the object and its space created by the same mind.

2. The Designer Is Both the User and the Owner.
    It provides for a maximum of free will, experimentation and development, regardless of cost and time.
    It implies that there is no conflict between the maker and the user.
    The ideal is to minimize externally imposed constraints and moral issues.

3. **The Designer Produces and Makes the Object Himself.**
    It provides continuity between thinking and making.
    It implies that there is no boundary between the conceptual form and the technical form-making. The making of the form/object can contribute to, support or discredit the form. During the production phase, the conceptual phase is restated or revised. Ideally, the object should be made under the observation of, or by the hand of, the designer.
    The ideal is in committing oneself to the full process.

4. **The Totality of the Object's Experiential Powers Is Encompassed.**
    It provides a medium for the mind's formal, rational and conceptual domains in addition to the common emphasis on the functional, structural and technical domains.
    It implies that art and philosophy are inseparable from science and nature.
    The ideal is to comprehend the power of the object as a medium for symbolic representation and aspiration.

Plan

5. **The Eye and the Mind Are Linked in One Cognitive Moment.**
    It provides a comprehensive sense of apprehension, inspection and critical judgement.
    It is a fusion of mind and eye that gives structure and force to the appearance of the object.
    The ideal is in the eloquence of visualization as a moment of integrity, combining sense evocation with cognitive engagement.

6. **The Force of Self-Expression Is Endowed.**
    It provides essential character to the object.
    It implies the structuring of creative form, inventive relationships and discriminating appearance.
    The ideal is in the identification of one's own distinctive idiosyncratic import.

7. **The Priorities of Physical Comfort Are Balanced with the Other Conditions.**
    It provides the critical measure that satisfies both anthropometric, ergonomic standards and geometric integrity.
    It implies integrative and manipulative adjustments without compromise.
    The ideal is to accommodate both the physical and the metaphysical necessities.

Section

Formal Description

Formally the chair contains two concepts combined as a clear strategy. The first concept, which I refer to as the "Ernst Mach Moment," fulfills the physiological and anthropomorphic requirements. In *Space and Geometry*, Ernst Mach wrote:

> The sensible space of our immediate perception, which we find ready at hand on awakening to full consciousness, is considerably different from geometrical space. Our geometrical concepts have been reached for the most part by purposeful experience. The space of the Euclidean geometry is everywhere and in all directions constituted alike; it is unbounded and it is infinite in extent. On the other hand, the space of sight, or 'visual space,' as it has been termed by Johannes Muller and Hering, is found to be neither constituted everywhere and in all directions alike, nor infinite in extent, nor unbounded. The facts relating to the vision of forms . . . show that entirely different feelings are associated with 'upness' and 'downness,' as well as with 'nearness' and 'farness.' [p.5]
>
> Our notions of space are rooted in our physiological organism. Geometric concepts are the product of the idealization of physical experiences of space. Systems of geometry, finally, originate in the logical classification of the conceptual materials so obtained. All three factors have left their indubitable traces in modern geometry. [p. 94]
>
> The results to which the. . .discussion has led may be summarized as follows:
> 1. The source of our geometric concepts has been found to be experience.
> 2. The character of the concepts satisfying the same geometrical facts has been shown to be many and varied.
> 3. By the comparison of space with other manifolds, more general concepts have been reached, of which the geometric represents a special case. Geometric thought has thus been freed from conventional limitations, heretofore imagined insuperable.
> 4. By the demonstration of the existence of manifolds allied to but different from space, entirely new questions have been suggested. What is space physiologically, physically, geometrically? To what are its specific properties to be attributed, since others are also conceivable? Why is space three-dimensional, etc.? [pp. 142-143]

With regard to the morphological structure of relationships, Mach's discussion legitimized my interest in the fundamental geometry of the referential coordinates of the three cardinal axes in space as the initial moment to be recognized. Moreover, I have extended the same interest to the object.

Elevation

All references from Ernst Mach, *Space and Geometry*,
Open Court Publishing Co.,Chicago, 1906.

By referring to the three-dimensional axes in space vis-a-vis the observer as the "Ernst Mach Moment," I am emphasizing the necessity for anthropomorphic experience – physiologically, psychologically and geometrically – as the mental device to awaken the observer, to provide the sense of space in the immediate perception.

The second concept — the artistic gesture — embraces the universal concept of form through analogy. In nature, the seashell provides enclosure, containment and support of an organic being. The thick walls and C-shape of the chair relate to this analogical aspiration and create a stable visual and mental field. This field is necessary in order to comprehend the differences measured in the unstable elements as dynamic behavior, and where random qualities can take place while maintaining the legibility of apprehension. The representational strategy of the restricted C-shaped walled enclosure around the horizontal and vertical planes within the two sides and the back, as an absolutely literal boundary of spatial reference against which everything else can take place, satisfies this particular basic moment of legibility. The other three sides are open and free: top, bottom and front.

The human body in the sitting position fulfills the irregular element in free postures which compositionally complete the formal essence of the chair. The back shoulder blade rests on a cushion plane that is free to open out and extend beyond the enclosure's top in its angle skewed to the vertical. The pelvis and thigh rest on a cushion panel that is free to extend beyond the front walled enclosure in its angle skewed to the horizontal. The bottom is completely restricted by the floor. The other three restricted sides have expressive articulations in the form of recesses, slits and cut-outs permitted by the layered wall thicknesses.

Diagram

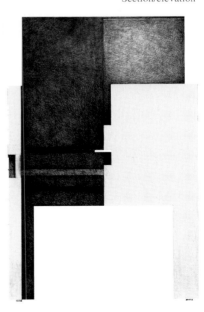

Section/elevation

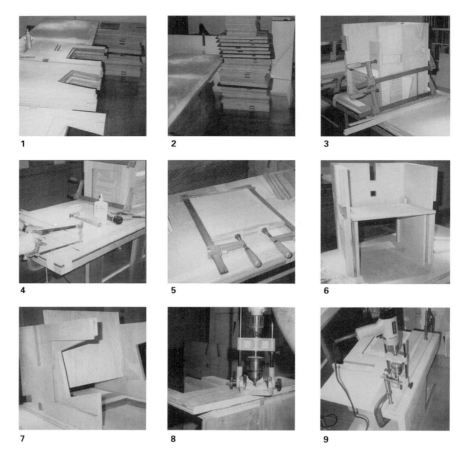

1 2 3
4 5 6
7 8 9

The Sequential Method of Making

1. A full-scale prototype was built to use as a pattern for the cut-outs on the panels. After adjustments to the dimensions were made, the panels were cut from 3/4" birch plywood in a local shop. The accuracy of the shopwork was disappointing.

2. The outer and inner layers of the sides and backs were glued and clamped. Small, temporary wire nails helped to prevent lateral shifting of the panels while the glue dried.

3. The double-thick sides and back were glued and clamped. The seat panel was used as a guide at top and bottom to square the interior angles.

4. For strength, four 1/2" dowels, 3" long, were glued and inserted on each side through the back to the side wall edge. Two chairs per day were assembled; the glue was allowed to dry for 24 hours.

5. Oak edging was glued and clamped to the seat and back panels.

6. Next, the seat panel was installed. The seat was glued along the edges and screwed through the walls. The 5-degree incline of the seat required temporary supports during installation.

7. The edges of the double-thick walls were sanded with a 3" belt sander. The notches and cutouts in the walls were hand-sanded, as was the seat.

8. The hidden, pivoted hinge was installed after the interior walls were glazed but prior to exterior lamination. The installation of the hinge required precise location and drilling of four holes for each chair.

9. Each hole was fitted with a 3/8" ×3/4" brass tube that contains a 1/4" ×1-1/2" stainless steel rod.

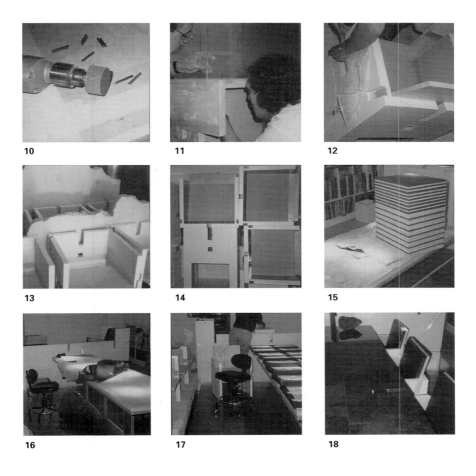

10 11 12

13 14 15

16 17 18

10. The ends of the 1-1/2" stainless steel rods were held in position by a counter–top vise and ground down using a drill with a stone grinding bit.

11. All the surfaces were prepared for finishing, the color was applied, and the interior surfaces were sprayed with polyurethane. The pivoted hinge was then installed, and the hole was plugged with a dowel – hiding the hinge permanently.

12. The exterior plastic laminate was installed, requiring touch-up of finished interior surfaces to remove router marks.

13. The finished, laminated, polyurethaned chairs arrived from the shop.

14. The chairs awaiting upholstery.

15. For the seat and back cushions, felt and foam were attached to 1/2" birch plywood backing panels.

16. Leather was cut to size, then wrapped around the felt and backboard and glued using a natural adhesive.

17. Velcro strips – each 2" wide ×6"long – were laminated to the cushion panels and to the back and seat of the chair, thus securing the two cushions to the chair with no mechanical elements.

18. Four 1/4" neoprene pins were hammered to the bottom of each chair, making the armrest height 26".

A R T H U R   A N D   C Y N T H I A   W O O D

Arthur Wood bought this building in 1979, and he
and his wife Cynthia have been working on its
construction ever since. The excerpts here are
from a conversation taped during a tour that Arthur
Wood gave the editors of the *Pratt Journal of
Architecture* in May 1991.

Broken Angel, brick and tile, 3-1/2 feet by 10 feet

Broken Angel

4 Downing Street
Brooklyn, N.Y.
Block 1969, Lot 79

View of top of the
building, south wall

This is our house and constant changes are always being made, all construction is being carried out by me and my wife.

When I bought the building there were ten apartments. And each apartment had six rooms, so that's sixty rooms. And each room had two inches of plaster all around, ceilings, walls, etc. This was about 100 tons of rubble, and I cleaned it all out. I mean, this is a low-budget building. I bought about 3,000 bricks and the rest of the bricks I just moved around.

People ask me why I didn't finish the building in two years, right? This is not a building, this is a health project for the mind and especially for the body – to keep in shape. I'm over sixty, and I'm in better shape than the firemen who had difficulty getting up here. When you spend years going up and down, you keep in shape. You keep alert, and that's the whole point of it.

When I had men working for me, I learned fast ways to do things, and I learned from my men. The best worker is a lazy worker. I have a test for workers. I'll have two workers come to work for me. I'll say, "Now you bring these bricks to the top of the building, and tell the other one to bring the bricks from the top of the building downstairs." Now, if they diligently go up and down the stairs, and keep working, I won't hire them. But if at some point, they both sit down and say they're accomplishing the same thing by sitting down, I'll hire them because they're intelligent.

Interior west wall

View from north

View into dome

Outer support complex with corbeled brick wall and triple arch

Nothing in the building code covers that because it's not exactly what they where thinking of. It's sort of a way around it. In fact, when I first started building the building, I went to Pratt. They said they couldn't help me much. But they did help me a lot, by answering one question. They said you could do anything you wanted to do, as long as you did it right. So, therefore, I read the building code to get the theory, and then do it my way.

Center support complex showing floor beams

This is still a four-story building, which you'll see on the plans. It's ninety-three feet tall, but it's four stories because the building department and the building regulations go by stories. They don't tell you how high to make the ceilings. I actually reduced the floor area. If you add anything, you need a building code variance. But if you take stuff away you don't. Actually the building is bigger and smaller at the same time. It's kind of an optical illusion that way.

Looking down at brick center structure with side bracing beams

There was a building that I liked around the corner. So I bought the entire facade of the building for sixty-five dollars and a bottle of vodka. I have it in the basement. It's all stacked up and some day I want to use that.

Concrete window showing clay dams

Detail of stained-glass window, cast in concrete, 12" × 18", reinforced with 3/4" steel

Rear wall showing stained-glass windows

This I picked up from Wright. Wright always built the roof first to keep everything dry. And, since I'm spending thirteen years building a building, it's going to rot downstairs unless I get the roof on first. And there's another reason, which I can show you upstairs. I'm a self-taught engineer, and I only believe in making the structure strong enough – alright, it's overly strong – but I want the strength where it should be. So the best way to do this is to build your structure on top, then go down below and see where the stresses are coming, where stuff is starting to bend, and add your strength there. It's a logical way of building.

Site-cast concrete window; blocks are designed to accept glass

Exterior view showing interplay between structure and glazing.

This was made for a car, of course, but just consider it as if you've just arrived from another planet and you found this and didn't know what it was. There's a thousand things this could be — so just because it was made for a car doesn't mean you have to use it for a car. It's a hubcap for a car. Not to me. That's a security window for the basement area. Put it in cement, it will weather well, and just put a Plexi window behind it. You've got a high-security window that's free and it looks nice outside. They take a direct hit from a Coke bottle without breaking. They're very good for this neighborhood.

I think architects should have to build at least one of the buildings they design, and they will rethink a lot of the things they do.

Floating air-
craft seen from
a distance.

Once noticed, it continued to occupy one's mind. It even persisted, as it were, in going about its own business.... The striking thing was that it was neither simple nor really complex, initially or intentionally complex, or constructed according to a complicated plan. Instead, it had been desimplified in the course of its carpentering.... As it stood, it was a table of additions, much like certain schizophrenics' drawings, described as overstuffed, and if finished it was only insofar as there was no way of adding anything more to it, the table having become more and more an accumulation, less

and less a table.... It was not intended for any specific purposes, for anything one expects of a table. Heavy, cumbersome, it was virtually immovable. One didn't know how to handle it (mentally or physically)... the thing did not strike one as a table, but as some freak piece of furniture, an unfamiliar instrument... for which there was no purpose. A table which lent itself to no function, self-protective, denying itself to service and communication alike. There was something stunned about it, something petrified. Perhaps it suggested a stalled engine.

Gilles Deleuze and Felix Guattari, *Anti-Oedipus, Captitalism and Schizophrenia,* Helen R. Lane, Robert Hurley and Mark Seem, trans., Viking Penguin, New York, 1977.

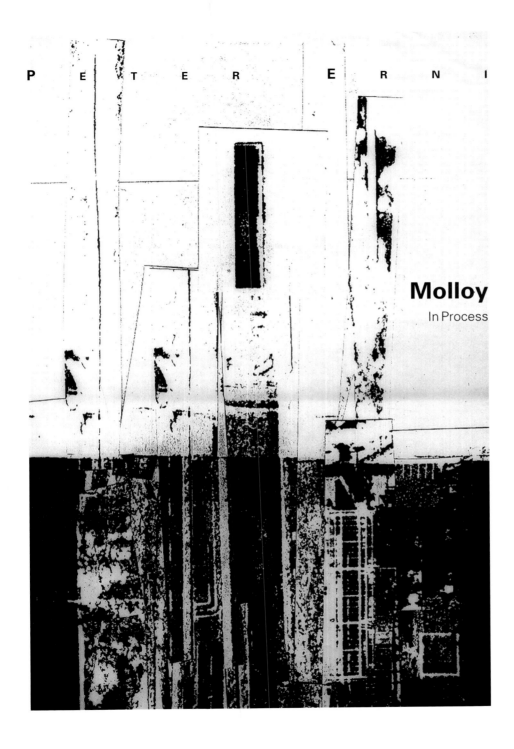

P E T E R   E R N I

Molloy

In Process

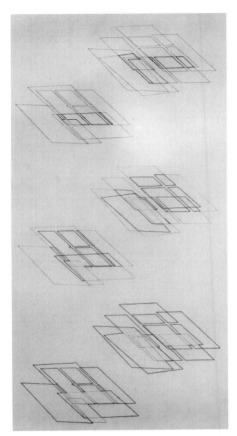

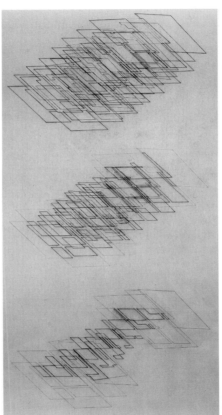

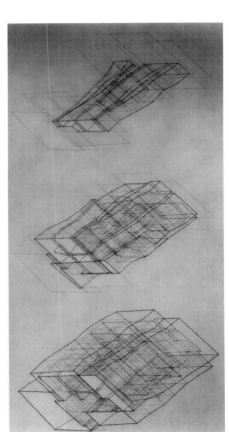

Chunk edges   Chunk fills   Chunks

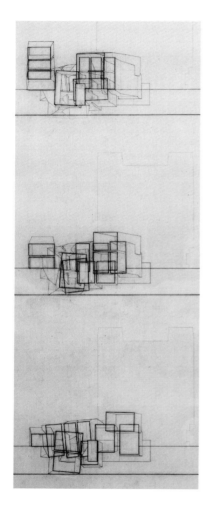

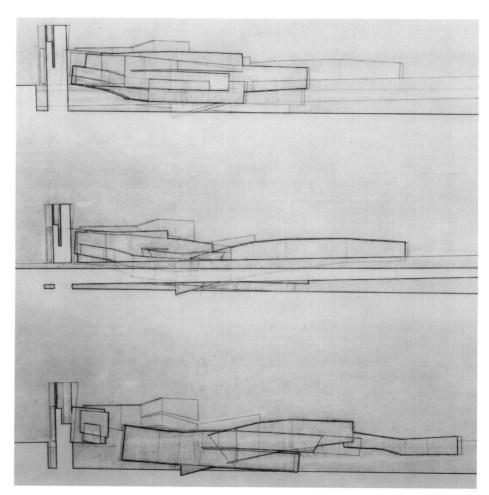

Sections

Sections

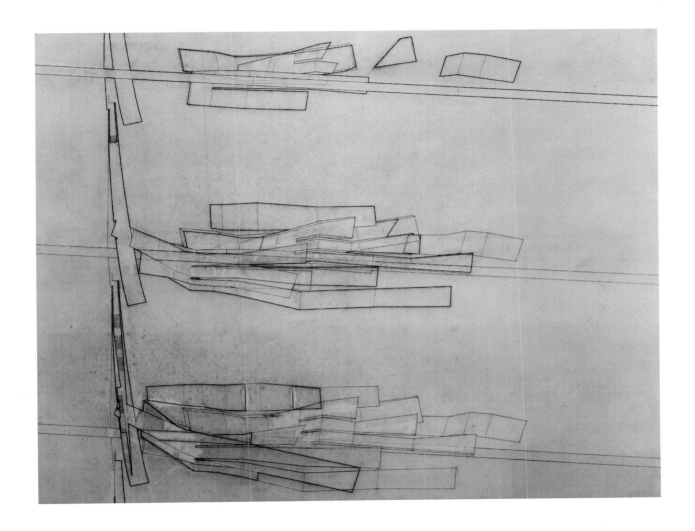

Plans

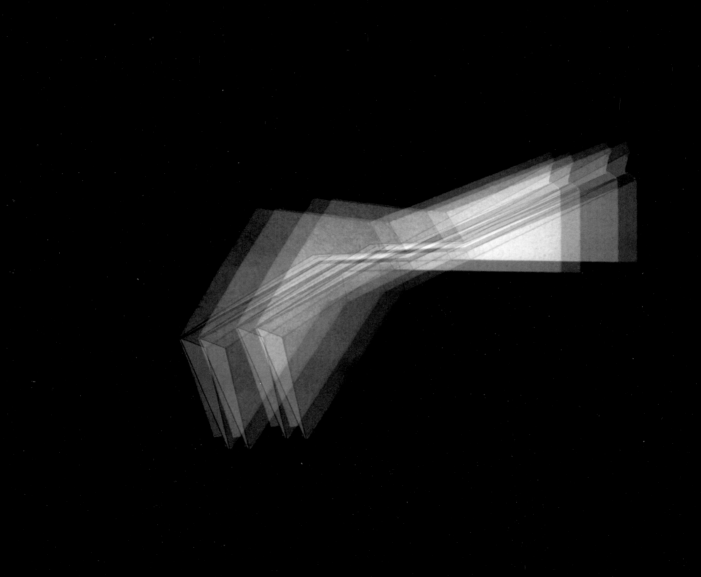

T H O M A S   L E E S E R

The Experiment of the Inverted (or Falling) House

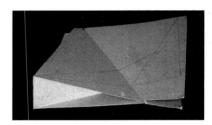

The clients for this house are twin brothers, a neurosurgeon and an eye sur-
geon. It is based on the principal of twinness, inversion, doubling and mirroring.
An inversion diagram of a convex spherical mirror served as a model for spatial
inversion, its physical realization as the possibility of having the mirrored, virtual
image be a real image, in real space: the condition of twins. Each end of the building represents an inverse of the other, any point of these two images projected
forms a line, and any line will eventually form two points, which define the extent of
the previously described line. Therefore, a line is not seen in the tradition of
Western thinking as a linear continuum, but rather as a constantly changing condition of inversion. The house can be read as such in any scale – the line is scale-less.
The images which are being inverted through this conoid projection undergo a similar transition from the "real" to a "virtual" condition, from the vertical to a horizontal and back to an inverted vertical position. What is upside down can be seen as
the real, what is right side up therefore becomes the image of the virtual. The house
contains a "zero-space," a space of no dimension, which is precisely the point
where that inversion or translation takes place. This "zero-space" can be described
as a one-dimensional space of no depth, as a line and two points. All parts of any
image, through which the house is produced, will eventually have to pass through
this "zero-space" of translation and will generate a distorted reflection. Through
this process, the two brothers programatically occupying opposite ends of the
house, at any given time each standing on the same plane that forms the other
brother's ceiling, are irrevocably entwined with each other, even though they are
physically apart. This embodiment of the brothers' twin-ness is spatially inscribed
in the building and creates a condition of inseparability in absentia.

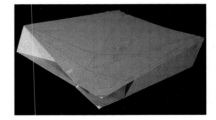

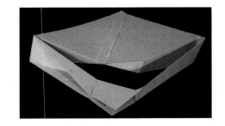

This house is located in the western region of New York state, in a heavily wooded area next to a sixty-foot
waterfall. The program contains the residential space for two brothers. The building is approximately 3300
square feet and is scheduled for completion in the spring of 1993.

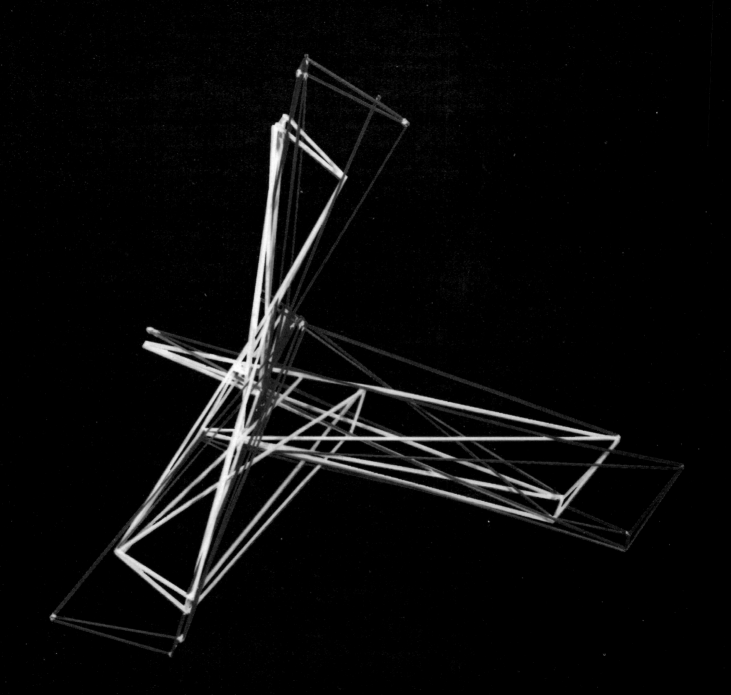

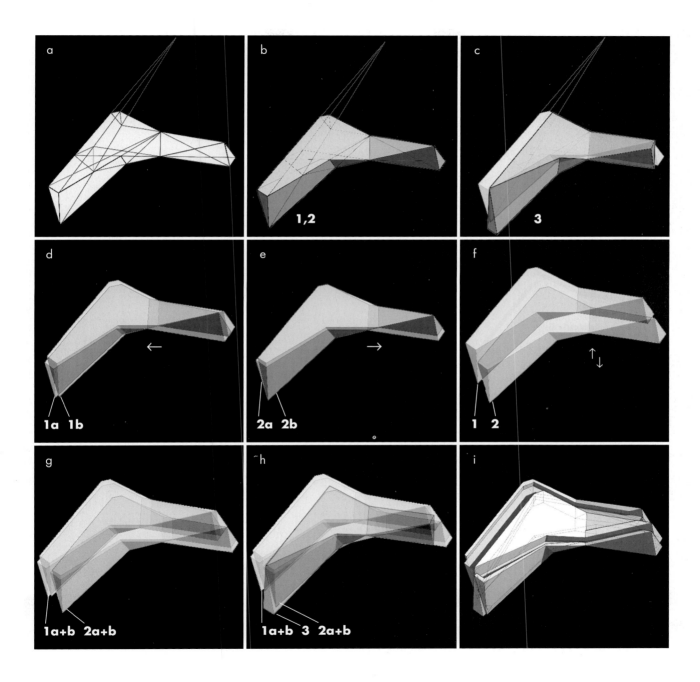

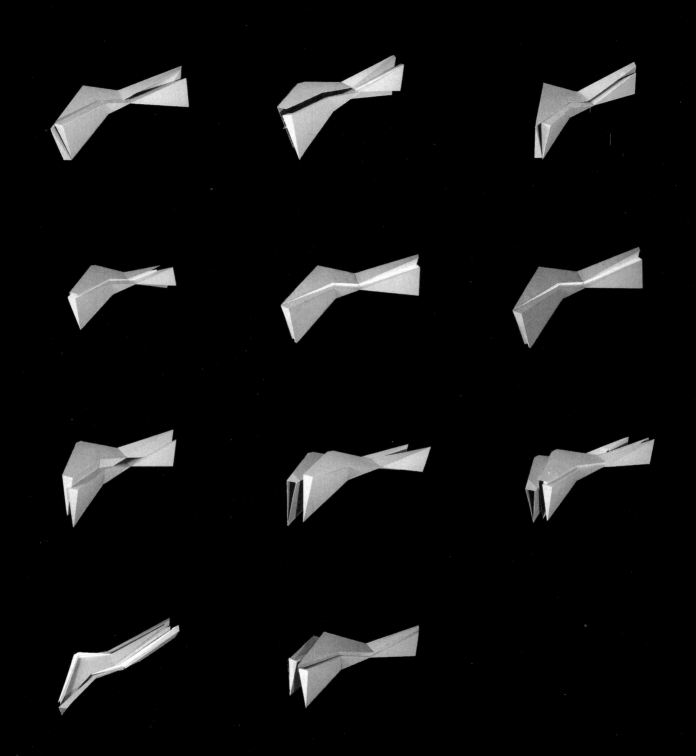

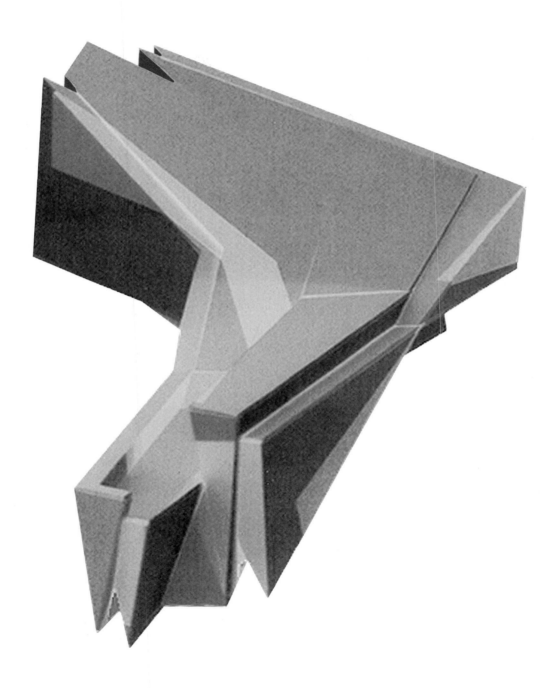

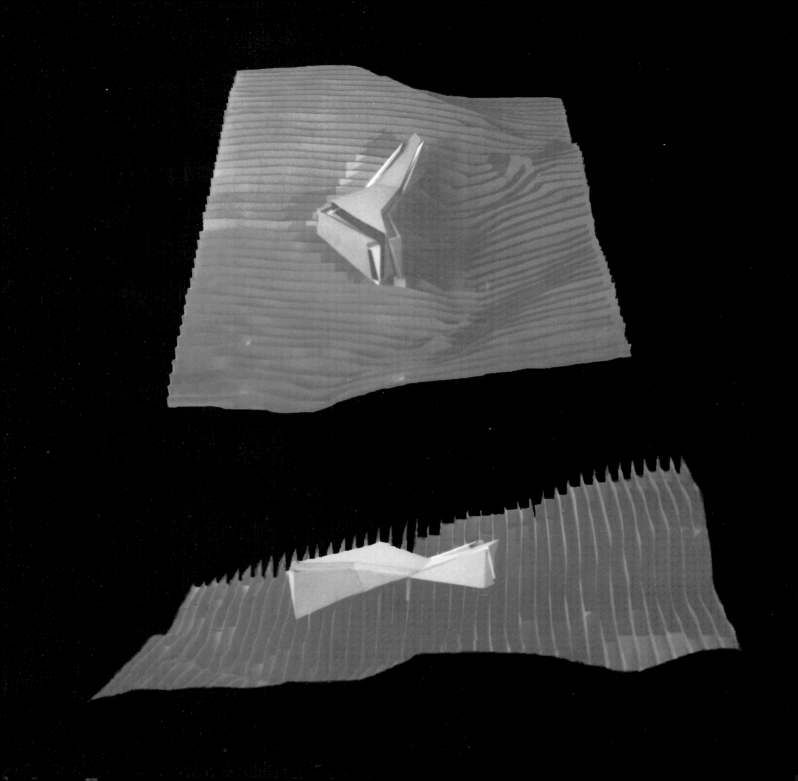

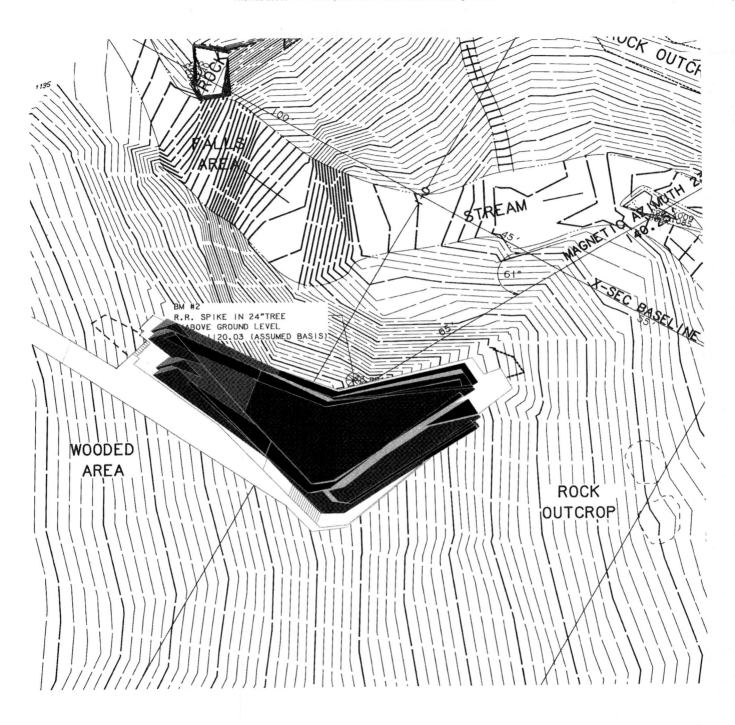

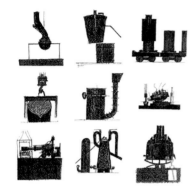

Steel Organs

Crossings: Golf Course × Steel Works

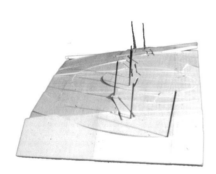

Golf Course

In objective terms, like those of analytical science, program describes the factual and the useful. First, it delineates relationships of object to object – codified as formal and tectonic relations among parts. Second, it encloses the dynamics between object and person – understood as useful, aesthetic and symbolic exchanges. And finally, it stabilizes associations of person to person – communications measured as political, economic and intimate. These three dimensions construct a space – a space of architecture – which delimits the relations among an architect, a public and a work.

The brief by Bernard Tschumi for the 1989 Shinkenchiku House competition requested new programs. From a recognition of the idiosyncratic overlays and superimpositions of programs for leisure and production in today's cities, Tschumi suggested that strategies of cross-programming, hybridization and dis-programming be explored within an urban area of one square mile.

Crossing (X as an action is marked by a geometric point of intersection and, in a biological sense, is a genetic meeting of two, perhaps even dissimilar, organisms. Cross-fertilization is a physical act: the genetic material of one organism moves to the other and, if the mating is propitious, a third results. The offspring, hybrids, "may show various combinations of the characters of the two parents; or exhibit new characters or reversion to ancestral ones. Sometimes they resemble one parent, but contain in a latent condition characters of the other." * At maturity, the offspring is capable of mating with another and continuing the expansion and contraction of the genetic field; it is fertile or potent.

In artificial crossings of plants, interpreting the genetic code remains the plant's project. The breeder may choose the parents in an effort to select for desired qualities, but his control of the crossing ends at that choice. The offspring may be supported or allowed to wither.

An architectural program is already a crossing of materials and motives; it does not exclusively describe one use, form or communication, but is a specific moment and measure of the constellations of human and object. Dimensions, for example, of tectonic, symbolic, useful and political activity are implicated in one another and form a space of conflict, negotiation and compromise. In the acts of programming – reading, drawing and writing – the architect does not stand at an analytical distance, but is drawn into the spaces of architecture. Geometrically, the space of a program resembles an assembly of the cross curve: "the locus of points in a complex-variable plane that have each two coincident correspondent points in a correspondent plane." *

But these planes are not so pure; they are cast as the images of the mirror, window and shadow. In the space of the crossing the analytical lines of the mirror, window and shadow are intertwined; lines and senses of projection, transparency and reflection multiply one another. The trampoline is a figure for the limit of this multiplication; it defines a boundary as it demonstrates the resonance of architectural space.

The trampoline moves with and against its collaborator. It is a surface of dynamic resistance – containing, supporting and propelling; not yielding insight to another side. The trampoline provokes a dynamic – attempts at balance, inversion, twisting, rotation and resonance – within its player. It is opaque to light, now is the only time that matters, and its space is explicitly determined in participation. The exchange between the player and the diaphragm is dependent upon gravity for activity – arabesques, changes in orientation and momentary weightlessness. This diaphragm supports the resonant actions of its player, it does not yield to a beyond; its surface tension binds activity within the dynamic space made by the energy, motion and attitude of the player. The player rhythmically extends and distorts the resistant surface. The trampoline is distinguished from the shadow of projection by the absence of a field of reception; from the mirror by the lack of an external image for repetition, and from the window by its opacity.

The trampoline's webbing is made of the abundance of the mirror, window and shadow; and its participants depend upon this excess. The programs are dependent upon the abundance of golf course and steel works.

Project assistant: Scott Vanzo

* Definitions from *Webster's New International Dictionary*, 2nd ed.

Golf collage

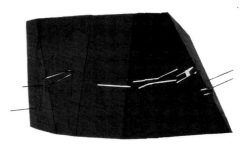

Golf Course

Originating in Scotland, the game of golf is played throughout the world today. Because it was seen as mere play, the king's archers in fifteenth-century Scotland were forbidden to play it. Although even today golf is seen as a nonproductive diversion, a real loss of productivity, it is an integral part of business life.

Golf is a form of mapping in which the player charts a course between two points, avoiding hazards along the way. The chart is drawn by following the projectile and keeping a record – the scorecard – of the number of shots for each pair of points within the course. Related to this scoring, but unwritten, is a narrative made as a consequence of where the ball landed and the territory the player traverses on the course. On many courses, these places are identified with symbolic titles; the most extreme version of this identification is found on the miniature course where the holes and hazards are given images such as windmill, maze and vortex.

The Royal and Ancient course in St. Andrews, Scotland, used in this project, names the hazards and greens based on their apparent shape: *The Scholar's Nose*, *The Pulpit*, *The Elysian Fields*, and other titles related to academics and the church. In this implied game, the golfer moves through the course connecting different references; significance is given to one's path rather than to a numerical accounting of the shots made. In the hidden narrative game, the trajectory of the ball delineates a path for the player's movement through the artifice of maintained nature. A walk in this country is not simply a walk, but a movement predirected by strategy, skill, exigency, and error; and this country is not nature separated from production or art. The game is a narrative play, a physical challenge, a symbolization of nature and the measuring of the player's powers. The golf object – an enfolding surface – engenders.

Golf object

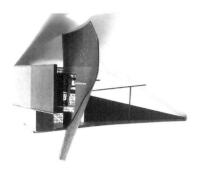

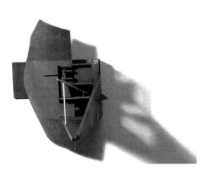

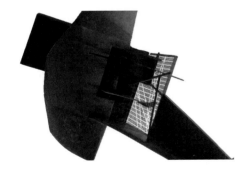

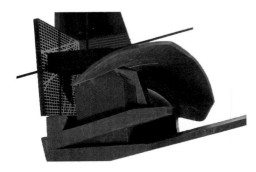

Steel object

Steel collage

Steel Works

The steel works as an image of production has become an icon for the mechanical age; less obvious, but evident, is the human figure embedded within the works and its processes. The steel works is mechanical technology embodied and the human body mechanized. This body is assembled in different orientations relative to the ground, the figure is at once in prone and vertical positions. The organs of the steel works perform very specific and isolated functions; their forms possess the geometric qualities of anatomical parts. In the coal-gas fired hearth, the gaseous fuel and exhaust alternate moving through brick chambers caged in steel frames; they resemble human lungs in both their form and literal uses. The chambers, called checkers, are heated by exhaust and breathe in the coal-gas, raising its temperature before the gas in turn burns in the open hearth and liquifies the ore. The steelworker is at the fire, in the laboratory, in the union hall, and operating the overhead cranes.

Modern steelmaking is a precisely measured and controlled activity. Exact quantities of ore, scrap, coal and gases are prescribed and recorded for each heat of the furnace. The sequential processes of steelmaking, from mining to finishing and fabricating, are intertwined in a simple rhythm of digging, melting, pouring, cooling, heating, stretching, rolling, fabricating and recycling. Arnold Palmer worked in a steel works.

Site

The site chosen in Cincinnati, Ohio, is an area of approximately one square mile east of the downtown, and west of the Mt. Adams prominence, with the Ohio River on the southern edge and Liberty Street on the north. Within this site are the courthouse, post office, barge canal, houses, office buildings, concert hall, light manufacturing, highway interchanges, vineyards, scrapyards and parks. Nine locations within the site articulate specific urban instances whose characters are analogous to the hazards, endpoints and organs of the golf course and steel works. They are publicly accessible. The six sites crossed with Golf Course and Steel Works lie at the intersections of three lines of hazards.

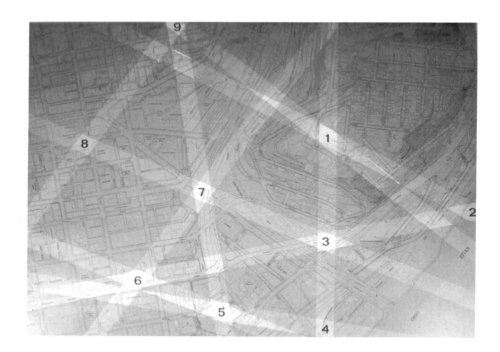

1:	observatory, monastery and office building		digging
2:	river's edge, in the river	measuring	
3:	highway ramps, skateboarder's dream		melting
4:	park at river's edge with train track and bridge	pouring	
5:	park with a statue of Lincoln and highway below		cooling
6:	corporate headquarters and gardens	heating	
7:	boulevard with canal below and highway above		rolling
8:	courthouse and jail	fabricating	
9:	residential block intersected by highway ramp		recycling

1: Observatory, monastery, office building

Digging

From the pool located at mid-section, the participants – office workers – can play the green granite slabs above and below them. During the day, the stones' movements vary the heat and light entering the structure through its metal surface. In different stages of closure, the slabs define spaces of intimacy and distance. When the slabs are fully extended day or night, they form an artificial ground which defines the back of the body's space and is inscribed with the names of lovers and hometowns. A shallow space is defined between this ground and the incised metallic shield. Brick chambers are excavated into the hillside behind the stone surface and a diving board projects beyond the shield toward the city and river below.

3: Skateboarder's dream – cartographic hysteria

Melting

The horizontal beam is pivoted from an earthen wedge allowing it to touch the production port at its lower end and control the orientations of nine hinged leaves. The mechanisms attached along the beam measure, block and open the reader's movements. The participant's mass and movement energize the machinery and extend its physical dimensions. Visual passage through the leaves is formed by steel tubes, and sound is reflected through a flesh-colored steel resonator.

5: Park with a statue of Abraham Lincoln and a tunnel below for Interstate 71

Cooling

The structure is used for memory, traffic control and ventilation of the tunnel below. The tunnel is formed in the shape of a human chest in a prone position and perpendicular to the line of traffic; it is sheathed in green and red stone where it intersects the observation structure above. Dark red stone inscribed with the writings of Lincoln is cut into and through the surface of the park to the highway below, allowing light to enter and air to escape. The observation structure is made of grey steel and has a clear view down into the tunnel and across the park to the statue of Lincoln and the highway beyond.

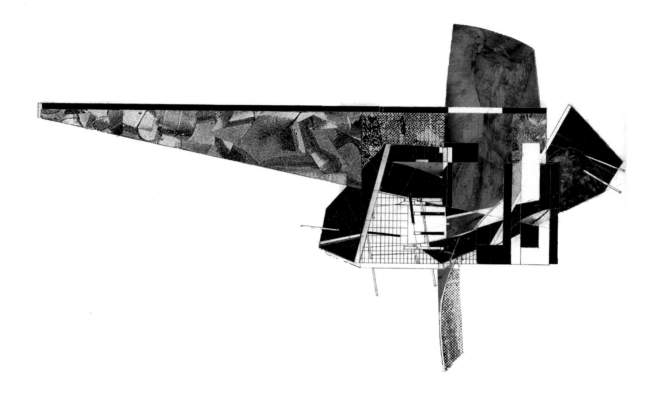

6: Corporate headquarters

Heating

An armor triangle extends the boundary horizontally as an arrow moving across the surface of the garden. It provides cover overhead. The bowed surface, which is flesh-colored steel, conceals productive spaces within containing projection equipment of many kinds. This surface intersects the garden's
green surface which is carried down into the earth. A public meeting room with a table for four people is formed between the green floors and the armor.
Entry is made by walking down the sloped green surface and through the projective spaces. The foundations of the cantilevered armor are visible.

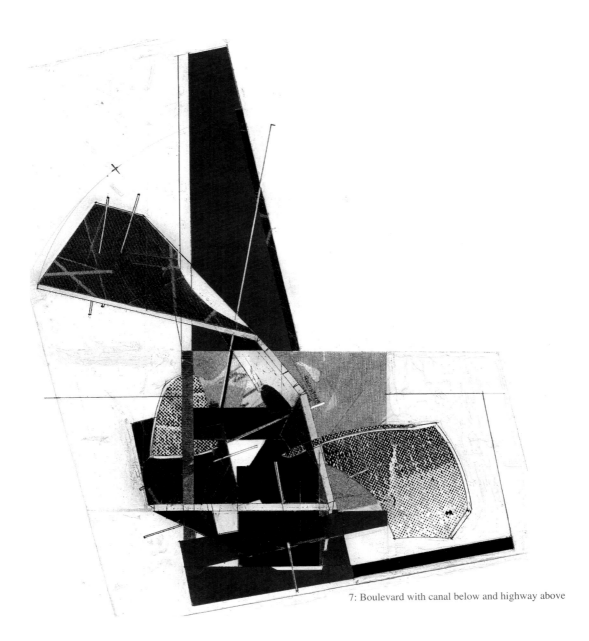

7: Boulevard with canal below and highway above

Rolling

The structure occupies the central and conventionally planted space of Eggleston Avenue, formerly a canal, leading to the Ohio River. A hidden mechanism moves a surface of green metal supporting a scorecard between a subterranean level and the highway above. The games union prints posters on an offset press at ground level. Access into the lower spaces from ground and highway levels is provided by the grey tower. Below, at canal level, in brick chambers are spaces for playing billiards, ping-pong, cards, miniature golf, and other games with green surfaces. Men and women play their games separately. The structure is anchored to the earth at the lowest level within the visible space of the canal and below.

9: Residential block intersected by highway ramp

Recycling

The house is enclosed on the north by the embankment of the roadway with the lowest level set into the hillside. The south-facing building's skin is green metal; it provides an outer layer of protection separate from the internal construction. Other boundaries are made by plants. The space within is constructed of earthen materials and steel. In the house, production and loss are nearly identical with one another; they often exchange places. Productive aspects of the residence are centrally located, and leisure activities occur at the periphery; production and leisure intersect at places of maximum external exposure. Separation between the occupants is made by the orientations of surfaces: the house has no rooms. Views from within are directed upward to the sky and south to the city below. The ceiling is gridded in the form of a calendar, but does not contain specific dates; a scale is suspended from the calendar. The house is leasable by two people from the city for a period of nine months.

ust Im
that the
you now
is only
its dime
folded
paper ai
And if yo
to un
this pap

B R I A N   B O I G O N

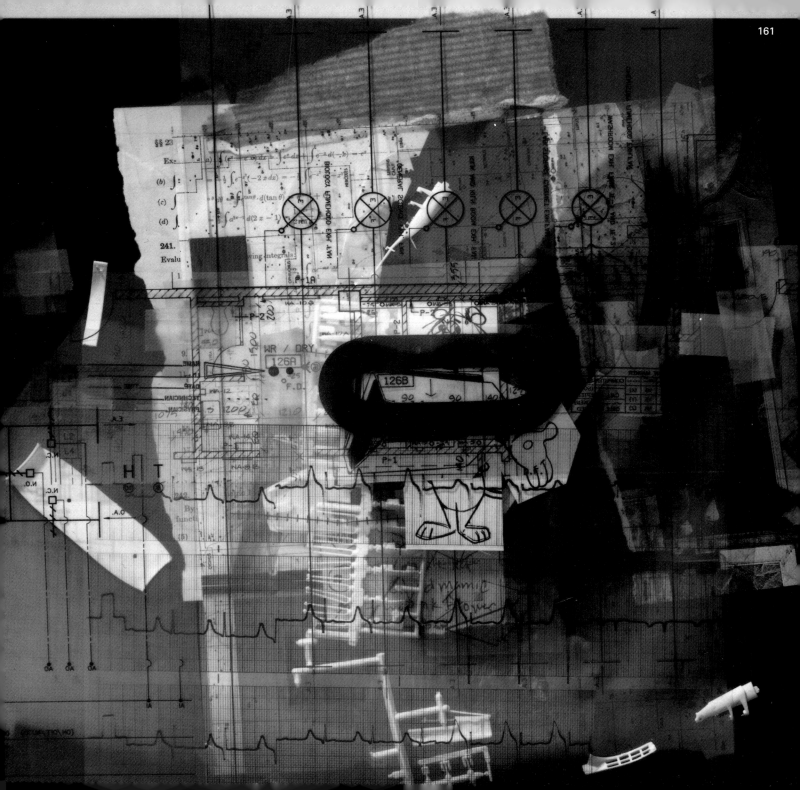

agine

space

occupy

one of

sions

ike a

plane.

u were

old

er . . .

Notes on the titles

All titles are renditions of gage-like machine instrumentations.

Each related work is an excerpt from a larger picture display. The picture plane itself acts as a segment of a potentially larger configuration, which is excluded and yet monitored by the frame. As the titles suggest, each collage is functioning in time (regulated) and presented as the result of an experiment.

Notes on the fabrication of the works

After each collage is assembled and photographically enlarged, it is dismantled. All collage works are circulated back into the collage machine. The studio supports a recycling system that transforms the copy into an original and disperses the original back into an image field of copies.

Notes on the theory shared by the works

1.   All the diagrams (architectural, art historical, biological, etc.) are considered diagrammatic realities. The diagram here is used not only as an information servicepart for reality, but an effect vehicle for it. When the monitor at the airport displays that your lover's plane has *ARR*, reality at that very instant is as diagrammatically real as its gonna get.

2.   The screen as a receiver surface for the projected images has been surpassed by the emergence of electronic pixelated surfaces. These new surfaces accumulate depth, or stretch depth out as if it were an elastic field. In particular it is the depth of this very surface which houses the viewer and its cartoon animation that allows the viewer to travel along it.

P A T R I C K   H E E L A N

The editors of the *Pratt Journal of Architecture* spoke with Dean Patrick Heelan at SUNY/StonyBrook on October 25, 1991. His book, *Space Perception and the Philosophy of Science,* and a set of questions from the editors served as the basis for the discussion.

Remarks on the Rivalry Between Science and Perception

Patrick Heelan

Deconstruction is about symbols. We live in symbols – linguistic, artistic, architectural – but symbols don't mean anything of themselves. They need to be interpreted, and they can be interpreted in a variety of ways. Deconstruction tells us that there is no one way of interpreting symbols. But deconstruction does not explain the fact that we live in a world in which people actually do understand one another, actually do get unique meanings from signs and texts. Take the LIRR timetable, for example. If everything is a misreading, how is that most people catch the trains that they go for? It's not that there's something missing in the analysis offered by deconstruction, it is only that the analysis is at a level which does not reach real life. That is, the analysis does not reach the dimension in which people grapple with "reality," meaning by reality the environment in which people attempt to fulfill their goals. The dimension I am interested in, the phenomenological, is the dimension of "real" experience and its description of this kind of "real" experience. Phenomenology is the attempt to understand the structures that operate within that experience. Husserl called them essences. Phenomenology is an attempt to get at them and, therefore, phenomenology itself is a theoretical attitude, not just an attitude of attention to experience. It's an attempt to be attentive to experience in order to find the underlying essential struc-

The Marriage at Cana,
Giotto di Bordone

tures. These essential structures are basically theoretical and don't have to be known for experience to take place. Consider, for example, the space that we experience visually. Our language tells us that we should deal with it as if it were a Euclidean space. This principle has become so ingrained in our language, in our thinking, in our philosophy (that is, in philosophy since Descartes), that we are at first shocked, and should be shocked, by the discovery that our daily experience of our environment does not in fact follow Euclidean laws. There are only two possible conclusions from this. One is that our daily experience is false, an illusion. The other is that the theoretical attitude incorporated in our language and description of the world is either false or relative to some set of conditions which are not always fulfilled. It's the latter view that I take; the world becomes Euclidean only when we approach it with measuring rods.

The spatial structure that underlies our everyday experience belongs to a family of geometries that are not Euclidean. I now call that space Aristotelian because it agrees with the description of the world that Aristotle gave in the *Physics*. For example, Aristotle speaks about the heavens as being finite; beyond the heavens, he says, there is no space. The notion that beyond the heavens could be empty space is a modern notion. Around the fifteenth century, for the first time, people like Nicholas of Cusa and Giordano Bruno began to think in terms of empty space beyond the stars, in which other worlds could be, where other things could happen. But Aristotle was quite explicit that the world was unique, finite and that beyond the stars there was no "beyond" in the sense of there being any space beyond. Now, such a world, evidently, could not have an overall Euclidean geometry. Aristotle took his paradigm of space from ordinary experience, not from measurement. The geometries for ordinary experience are Riemannian.

One of the questions you asked was, "Is such a space real?" I would say yes if the world of things ('res' comes from the Latin for thing, dealing with things) in which we move turns out to be a world that relates itself to human projects, and that emerges as a structured world, made up of objects of certain kinds, that respond to human needs and interests. That kind of world is described very well in James Gibson's book, *The Ecological Approach to Visual Perception*.[1] This book is an attempt to do for the psychology of perception much of what I have done in my book, *Space Perception and the Philosophy of Science,* for the philosophy of perception, which is to say that the world as visually perceived has a different structure from the scientific world. Science is concerned with one set of questions, vision is concerned with another set of questions. Vision is concerned with the needs of human life, and the world that emerges in our daily experience is a world of objects related to us, related to our projects, responding to our movements and needs. In the environment, we pick up clues to structures that tell us how to behave in order for the things in the world to show themselves as they are in relation to the projects in which we would recognize them to be what they are. So we have a notion of an environment which is defined humanly and of a humanity which is defined environmentally. That's the kind of reality I'm talking about here.

Question

You make a distinction between visual space and scientific space and/or the organization of these two spaces. Are you saying that these systems, these spaces, are irreconcilable?

Patrick Heelan

No, no. They're reconciled in two ways. The first way is simply that they respond to different human projects. The project of measurement is not the project of going out for a pizza. How far away the pizza parlor is, as a phenomenology of human estimation of lived distance, is not just a function of the Euclidean measures of distance to the pizza parlor. There are all kinds of conditions connected with the project of getting a pizza, other than simply distance as measured by the odome-

1. James J. Gibson, *The Ecological Approach to Visual Perception*, Erlbaum, Hillsdale, NJ, 1986.

ter of a car. The project of measurement is operating at one level, lived distance to the pizza parlor is operating at a different level. The former is a Euclidean project; the latter turns out to be a non-Euclidean project.

The second way is to say one project, the Euclidean, is inherent in the other project and is among its necessary conditions of possibilities. That the pizza parlor seems farther away on some days than on other days, makes sense only if there is a common Euclidean structure that keeps the measured distance to the pizza parlor constant. Science seems to find the conditions of possibility that underlie the variabilities of human experience, and in that sense, going back to space, one can even talk about it in a Husserlian way, as a condition of possibility of the variety of visual spaces defined by the family of negatively curved Riemannian geometries. That family makes sense because there is an underlying constancy in the Euclidean dimension reached by the measuring instruments of physics. What Husserl is always looking for are the variations that preserve an essence, an invariant structure. Both scientific laws and the objects produced by scientifically controlled processes are the constants, the invariants through which new dimensions of human experience can be lived. Science, then, is to human experience what linguistics is to language. Let us say language is how we use words in practice in order to get across practical meanings. Linguistics is the study of words and their structure, language is our use of those words and structures. Linguistics takes the language out of the culture, out of the moment, out of the look in the eye, out of bodily behavior, such as finger pointing, and focuses on the tools of language. That's the scientific turn of mind, the theoretical turn of mind. That's turning away from the world to focus on structures, in this case on the symbols we use to talk about the world, and more and more academic research is concerned with symbols and their structures rather than reality; it's concerned with the study of the symbols people use in their lives and careers, bracketing the lives and careers of real people who use these symbols in so many different ways. Once one is familiar with a significant set of symbols people use, one gets a false sense that one knows all about what they stand for.

People think they know all about science when they can work with the mathematical models of science, or when they can engage in sophisticated discourse about black holes and electrons and whatnot. To the contrary, science is known only to the expert scientific community that lives and does science, and invents the language of science. When, however, that language is exported by the expert community from the laboratory to the big wide world, a subtle, very significant and dangerous change takes place, which is characteristic of our culture. This change is the appropriation of the scientific word as the one and only true account of the world in which we live. If this table is "really" made up of mostly empty space and vibrating molecules, then it becomes a problem as to how and why anything can remain on top of it. Our culture then teaches us that the solidity of this table is a kind of illusion and that the reality of it is different from what we experience. In this way, a glass wall is set up between us and the table. To the extent that we fail to see the table as scientists see it, we must suspect that our knowledge of the table is illusionary and inadequate. But not being able to experience the table as the scientists describe it puts us at the disadvantage of having to say that we do not know the real table, only those experts in white coats know it. So any decisions about human life and human projects, or about political, social or religious life, which can be articulated in terms of the table as experienced in daily life, come to be undermined, because they are reduced to surface phenomena, appearances, illusions, overlying a reality that is inaccessible to ordinary people, and accessible only to scientific experts. This is the same problem we have with space. We are persuaded that the world is really Euclidean, and yet, in the real world, we never or rarely ever experience it as such.

Bedroom at Arles, Van Gogh

Question

Aristotle set out to describe the world as it is. It was not a question of finding the system that was most helpful to describe the world, but that there was in fact "a" system that described the way the world is.

Patrick Heelan

Aristotle was talking about the world that we live in and that we experience. Behind that project there is a theory and the theory is (as we now know) not Euclidean. Science as we know it today, however, has a different theoretical pro-

ject. It tries to find the underlying structures which are quantitative and can be expressed mathematically, which are the conditions of possibility of human experience, but which we cannot experience. In the origins of modern science in the sixteenth and seventeenth centuries, Newtonian science, for historical reasons, became natural theology. It became the new Christianity and was preached from the latitudinarian, or Low Church, pulpits in England around 1700. Natural science took on a role that was a rival to philosophical theology or

theological philosophy, which had been the name for knowledge up to about the sixteenth century. Part of this presentation of science was that science was God's own knowledge of the world. There were two revelations: the scriptural revelation, which was very difficult to interpret; and the natural revelation, given long ago to Trismagistus, and passed on to a whole tradition of people, to whom the mathematical wisdom of nature was revealed in primordial revelations. Science was believed by Newton to be part of a primordial revelation. The notion, therefore, that mathematical/natural science was in fact God's own idea of the world was very important because it enabled science to claim a legitimacy that made it a rival of the old theology. Thus, in the seventeenth century science came to be read as God's knowledge of the world, the truth about the world, and this obscured the fact that it was actually something else; science was about measurement, and it was about the conditions existing in the world that made possible the variety of human experiences.

Question

You talk about the Euclidean perception of the world as the product of a scientific framework. When did the change from a visual to a Euclidean perception take place?

Patrick Heelan

I think the change took place between 1300 and 1400. There's a good deal of evidence that it took place in the fourteenth century, in Italy. Giotto di Bordone (1266-1337), for example, decorated the Arena Chapel (Cappella Scrovegni) in Padua with narrative scenes from the Gospels and holy legends. Giotto was the first major painter to paint realistically since classical Greece and Rome. Giotto's own contemporaries spoke of him as painting scenes so real that they could picture events of the world around them. So we have the words of his contemporaries saying that they experienced these paintings as being the "real" world. Today they no longer seem realistic to us, since the floors curve up, the rooms are too shallow, and the carpentered right angles do not look right. We excuse Giotto because he didn't know the rules of perspective. That is a mistake. A skilled painter like Giotto, even without a technical knowledge of mathematical perspective could have done whatever he pleased, but it may not have pleased him to represent a Euclidean flat plane and right angles. He could have made the world look like the world as we described it – provided he was accustomed to seeing such a world. Instead he painted a different world that his contemporaries called realistic, one having rooms with sloping floors and curving walls that display the characteristics of Aristotelian or non-Euclidean space.

Question

Do you consider that way of perception privileged or natural?

Patrick Heelan

I see it as the natural way of perception for him in his place and time, one dependent on the structure and kinesthetically situated use of the human body. We, today, are different. We are the products of a scientific revolution that imposed the rule of measurement on the description of the world. Giotto's rooms, I'm sure, were just as boxlike as ours, but the viewers of his time, and Giotto himself, did not see the rooms as boxes. We, however, would have seen them first as boxes and would want to paint them as boxes. And that's the difference. He saw the room first as a lived environment in which things show themselves for the purposes of the scene. We are, according to our lights, more sophisticated, however, we see the room as an engineered product and we have to get the engineering straight first before we can tell the story of what is happening in the room. That's because we are modern. We have the Cartesian period inside of us that tells us that the engineering comes first and the human project comes second. By the early fifteenth century painters such as Brunelleschi wanted to paint rooms as boxes, and invented a technique for doing it. We call it mathematical perspective. The mathematical rules of perspective, however, didn't always work as evidenced by the problem of how to make a room look as if it were a closed boxlike space. Convergence points represent infinite distances; consequently if one such point falls within the picture of a room, the eye can be inexorably drawn beyond the closed room to an infinite distance. Given that a room is a closed box, convergence points have to be removed beyond the frame of the picture or hidden behind furniture so as not to distract the eye. Mathematical perspective

Bedroom at Arles, modified

in pictures generates a minefield of visual interpretations and confusions. In real life, however, we are rarely confused. The room we are in, for example, is closed and looks finite. Whether or not we are aware of an outside, whether or not there is room in our perceptual space for an outside depends on many factors – an open window with a view or a noise.

Take Van Gogh's *Bedroom at Arles,* for example. The genius of the artist is in his ability to make you see the room as he sees it: with the floor sloping up, and with a shallow depth. The shutters are closed and you see it as a space enclosed, not closed off from other spaces, but as if no other parts of space existed. The wall and the shutters seem to constitute the totality of the visual pictorial space of the painting. What now if I ask what's beyond those shutters? Merely by asking the question what you see has visually changed. The outside – an outside – has intruded into what you see and the room has changed its appearance to accommodate to this possibility. The walls and shutters that were the closure of space must now be imagined as dividing space into two parts, an inside and an outside. Let me open the shutters. The room immediatedly seems to be much bigger and deeper, the floor has become flatter, and the walls have straightened out. Vision has asked the question about inside/outside and has responded to it in its own practical way by enlarging the space so as to include within it the Cafe Terasse outside. In so doing, it converts the foreground, the room, into something more like a Euclidean box. Let me try a further experiment. Looking at the picture of the room with the Cafe Terasse in the open window, I now tell you that there is no open window, no Cafe Terasse, there is just a poster where the window seems to be. Immediately, space changes again and shrinks to what it was before. Which of these pictorial experiences gives you the "real" world? Is it the scientific Euclidean world? Science, instruments, technologies are necessary for the construction of architectural elements such as carpentered rooms. But rooms are sometimes not seen as carpentered, as structured by Euclidean geometry, but as constituting Aristotelian or non-Euclidean finite curved spaces. To use a Heideggerian example: a hammer is made to be used for hammering and becomes a hammer only to people who engage in hammering. It has, however, an invariant blueprint, a set of science-based instructions for its construction. Its mode of construction does not preclude it from being used as doorstop, as decoration for the room, for a variety of purposes.

Question

Our journal started as an attempt to get back to things themselves. How does Merleau-Ponty mean to return to "things themselves"? Is there a possibility to return to things themselves?

Patrick Heelan

Since Descartes our whole culture has moved away from (to use a phrase that both Husserl and Merleau-Ponty used) "things themselves" towards Cartesian representations of these things. Language became colonized by a scientific vocabulary comprising new and old terms, where the old terms are used in a new way emptied of their old meanings. All scientific terms have meanings normatively dependent on specialized science-based technologies. Some of these science-based technologies are readable, in the sense that ordinary people can learn from them. This is not always the case, but many modern technologies, such as equipment for metering or measuring quantities, are of this kind. Such equipment reveals things, new and old, as "things themselves," that is, as present and appearing to us under the character that relates to the interests served by metering and measuring. Merleau-Ponty called such technologies "detachable sensory organs." Where no such readable technologies exist or are not common or familiar, a glass wall is set up between us and the "things themselves" designated by the scientific vocabulary.

There's an interesting book in this regard, written by a German historian of medicine, Barbara Dudon. The English title is *The Woman's Body as a Public Place.*[2] The author studies the words used by physicians and women when describing their own bodily experiences in childbearing, for example.

These words are found in physicians' notebooks and diaries, in women's diaries and in novels written by women. Dudon's work covers the last 400 years. She compares the present-day vocabulary in Germany and America with that used before modern medicine. We now think of the reproductive process as a process of development of a fertilized ovum. At some point in its development a sonogram can pick it up and make a picture of it, at which point the doctor says to the woman "there is a child growing inside you," and looking at the image the woman says "there is my child." She does this even before she experiences the child within her. So the moment of experiencing the child doesn't come as a very significant moment. The older vocabulary about childbearing reflected solely and exclusively the woman's voice: its key word referred to quickening, the moment when the child was felt as a separate and living entity by the mother. Dudon points out that for better educated mothers the sonogram child is a thing itself, but comes laden with biomedical rather than cultural information. For less well educated mothers, the biomedical information is often misunderstood and the misunderstanding can do harm to both the mother and the child. Does "fetus" or "new life within" designate the same entity with the same cultural relations as was designated by the older words based on quickening? The

2. Barbara Dudon, *Der Frauenleib als Oeffenlicher Ort,* Luchterhand, Hamburg, 1991.

Bedroom at Arles, modified

more basic question, however, is: Which set of terms defines the child as a moral and cultural entity and the subject of human rights? There is confusion in the answers. The case is analogous to the question: How should we describe the space of Van Gogh's bedroom, redolent, as it is, of human intimacy? As carpentered or not-carpentered? As Aristotelian or Euclidean?

Question

I would agree that there is a glass wall between me and the things themselves, or between a particular thing and its "essence." Today the glass wall is primarily scientific. However, I wouldn't think that by simply eliminating scientific thinking I would necessarily be able to touch the thing itself, or be that much closer to it.

Patrick Heelan

Some equipment does bring the scientific thing close to us. The sonogram, for example, brings close the developing child in the womb, but only for a certain purpose – to visualize the developing child. It does not define for the mother the cultural and moral entity of the child that "talks" within her by the movements it makes. The child that is visualized via the sonogram is a "scientific" child, and this turns out to be strangely ambiguous: as such, has it moral rights? The television screen is a way of showing what electrons are and that they exist in an electron beam. The electron beam scans the television screen and causes small phosphor crystals to light up producing the picture on the screen. This is a perfectly good account to give to little Johnny. What it says is correct;

what it leaves out is enormous. But Johnny will learn more about the fundamental furniture of the world as he grows up. Scientific elements, as we see, do become citizens of the world, but they come to be citizens through specialized technologies, and therefore only within the context of specific social, historical and economic processes. Things that are satisfactory for a purpose might cease to be satisfactory later on, because the purposes have changed. It's not that the satisfactory character has changed, the purposes have changed.

Something that shows how deeply Cartesianism has colonized our thinking is that we talk about approximations, approximate solutions, that will give a more correct value. Such talk, deeply entrenched in modern language, supposes that quantities have a single transcendental value and that things are described best by the theories we have of them. To the contrary, a theory is a model to which the things themselves conform, not absolutely, but only to the degree that they are recognizable and reproducible entities in human experience.

And so the need to revisit an earlier period is an attempt at a historical recovery of the time when language was used differently, when Aristotle or Giotto used the language. Can we recover the experience that Giotto had before the world became Cartesian? What happens to the old meaning? Was it an illusion? Was it perhaps a superstition, a piece of medieval falsehood? This is where Cartesianism has been very abusive. The medievals weren't idiots, nor were the Greeks. The fact that they experienced the world differently and used language differently doesn't mean that they didn't use it intelligently, and that they weren't in contact with reality. But since we don't have the same contact with reality, or we may not recognize it any longer, or because we have agreed to use words differently, then we blackball them.

Can we recover older meanings of, say, spatial words that we presently use though with different normative meanings? We probably can, but only by taking a roundabout route through mathematical models, because we no longer know which among the illusions of our experience coheres into one thing itself and which belongs to other aberrations based, say, on neuropathology. These so-called perceptual distortions are just linked side by side as if they were all distortions relative to a Cartesian reality; among them, however, some are systematic and cohere because they belong to the old meaning of the term. But, among all these distortions, how do we know which ones cohere? We can only discover this by having a theory about the coherence, usually through a mathematical model, that determines the conditions for invariance, that is, conditions under which a thing itself can be constituted by a set of variable appearances. The route I followed in my book on space perception was based on such mathematical model building. I think that Merleau-Ponty would have approved of this method.

Still from *Brazil*

The symposium was held at Pratt Institute's Higgins Hall on April 11, 1991.

Moderator:

Dan Bucsescu

Panelists:

Michael Benedikt
Hani Rashid
Ken Kaplan
Ted Krueger
Dan Hoffman

In our effort not to privilege either subject or object, we chose to use **making** (a "neutral" word, for it is neither creation nor production) to describe an activity that we all engage in. We differ from the classical point of view where objects are external to us, static and circumscribable. Classical categorization is rivaled by a position of encompassment, conflict and multidimensional construction. This outlook has been partially shaped and is finding a parallel in the way electronic media operate. Our ability to tune in and work in the "infra/ultra," the "sub/super," is offering us a wider range of possibilities. The introduction of the computer (and all other electronic devices) is having as much an impact on our conception of ourselves and the things around us as did the invention of perspective, the printing press and the automobile.

However, we should be critical of the morality and seduction of "the more the better." Are we able to cope with an environment beyond our senses? Is the electronic world becoming another architecture accessible through some kind of interface? How is the speed of manipulating our environment changing the perception of it and ourselves?

S Y M P O S I U M

Between Digital Seduction and Salvation

Dan Bucsescu

It has been said that for the last twenty years, we have witnessed a "war" in the territory of architectural discourse between the formalists and the functionalists. This is, of course, just a local battle in a larger cultural war. Thomas Kuhn might have called it the "multi-paradigmatic" war in the field of architectural thought. But as of this moment, no dominant paradigm emerges. Tonight, we will look at tools, at the

new technology that contributes to this controversy.

Let me start by stating that the collective voice of the architectural community is in a state of confusion and hesitation, a kind of stuttering. While I am keenly aware of the pitfalls present in any attempt to define the mood of the times, it is impossible to avoid such definitions in any characterization of our information age.

The advent of the computer and, with it, the information revolution are often proposed as the cure, not only for all the schisms and biases of Western culture and society, but for the artistic stuttering of an architectural community uneasy with the culturally loaded and ambiguous free-play of relativist meaning that accompanies postmodern thought.

These symptoms have been pointed out before. According to Lewis Mumford:

> whenever man becomes unsure of himself, or whenever his creative powers seem inadequate, whenever his symbolisms breed confusion and conflict, his tendency is either to find refuge in blind Fate, or to concentrate upon the processes in which his own subjective interests are not directly involved....

In his chapter "Media as Translators," Marshal McLuhan wrote of the healing value of mechanical processes noting "the tendency of neurotic children to lose their stuttering when using the telephone."

Is this the electronic road architecture should journey in order to join the world it feels disconnected from? Is this the way to lose our artistic stuttering? What do these new technologies promise? mobility? speed? inclusiveness? exchange? universal codes? There has been much talk of the breakdown of all boundaries, a condition where the marginal takes priority over the center, the point of intersection over the grid. Implied is the loss of dialectical opposition such as human/animal, organism/machine, physical/spiritual realms, mind/body.... In this new world there would be no separation between authors and readers, maker and the tool, subject and object, no gender polarity, no private and public realms, no dominance and no control. It is our task here tonight to investigate some of the philosophical and operational implications of this new technology for architecture.

In order to locate myself in the ensuing discussion, I will choose a model of behavior from the following fictional models: Homo Faber, Donna Haraway's Cyborg and Neuromancer's Cowboy. The closest to my generation is Walter Faber, the protagonist of Max Frisch's novel, Homo Faber, man the maker. Hannah Arendt, in The Human Condition, also describes this modern hero. He is the human being for whom only the tangible, the calculable, and the verifiable exists: an engineer who devotes his life to the

service of a purely technological world. I am, I should say, much less at ease in the world of Donna Haraway's Cyborg, a cybernetic organism, a hybrid of machine and organism, intent on the reinvention of nature, or with William Gibson's Neuromancer Cowboy, the hero of the "informed society."

In Homo Faber, my hero, Walter Faber, travels from France to Italy to Greece, in search of truth. It is there on ancient grounds that he suddenly understands. By revisiting old questions, I hope tonight's discussion will do the same for me.

Michael Benedikt

First of all, what is cyberspace? It is not the same as virtual reality. Cyberspace is globally networked, computer-sustained, computer-accessed and computer-generated multidimensional, artificial or virtual reality. In this reality, through which every computer is a window, seen or heard objects are neither physical nor necessarily representations of physical objects, but are in form and character made up of data,

or pure information. This information derives in part from the operations of the natural physical world, but for the most part it derives from the immense traffic of information that constitutes human enterprise in science or art, business or culture. The dimensions, axes and coordinates of cyberspace are thus not necessarily the familiar ones of our natural gravitational environment. Although these dimensions may mirror our expectations of natural spaces, they have impressed upon them an informational value appropriate to optimal orientation and navigation in the data access. In cyberspace, information-intensive institutions and businesses have a form, identity and working reality, in a word, quite literally, an architecture that is counterpart and different to the form, identity and working reality that they have in the physical world. The ordinary physical reality of these institutions, businesses, etc., are now seen as surface phenomena, as husks, their true energy coursing in architectures unseen except in cyberspace. So, too, with individuals. Egos and multiple egos, roles and functions have a new existence in cyberspace. Here, no individual is appreciated by virtue, if at all, of a physical appearance, location or circumstances. New liquid and multiple associations between people are possible for both economic or noneconomic reasons, and new modes and levels of truly interpersonal communication can come into being.

Cyberspace. A word from the pen of William Gibson, science fiction writer, circa 1984. An unhappy word, perhaps, if it remains tied to the desperate and dystopic visions of the new future found in the pages of *Neuromancer* and *Count Zero*. Visions of corporate hegemony, urban decay, neural implants, life in paranoia and pain. But a word which gives a new name to a new stage, a new and irresistible development in the elaboration of human culture and business under the sign of technology.

Cyberspace. A new universe, a parallel universe, created and sustained by the world's computers and communication lines. A world in which the global traffic of knowledge, secrets, measurements, indicators, entertainments and altered human agency takes on a form. Sights, sounds, presences never seen on the surface of the earth, blossoming in the vast electronic night.

Cyberspace. A tablet, become a page, become a screen, become a world. Everywhere and nowhere. A place where nothing is forgotten and everything changes. A common mental geography built in turns by consensus and revolution, canon and experiment. A territory swarming with data and lies, with mind stuff and the memories of nature. With a million voices and two million eyes and a silent invisible concert requiring deal making, dream sharing, and simple beholding.

Cyberspace. Its corridors form wherever electricity runs with intelligence. Its chambers bloom wherever data gathers and is stored. Its depths increase with every addition and every contribution, fact and thought. Its horizons recede in every direction. It breeds larger and complexifies, it embraces and involves. Billowing, glittering, humming, coursing, a Borgesian library, a city, intimate and immense, firm and liquid, recognizable and unrecognizable at once.

Cyberspace. From simple economic survival through the establishment of security and legitimacy, from trade in tokens of approval, confidence and liberty to the pursuit of influence, knowledge and entertainment for its own sake, everything informative and important to the life of individuals and organizations will be found for sale or for the taking in cyberspace. The realm of pure information, filling like a lake, siphoning the jangle of messages transfiguring the physical world, decontaminating the natural and urban landscapes, redeeming them, saving them from the chain-dragging bulldozers of the paper industry, from the diesel smoke of the courier and post office trucks, from the jet fuel, fumes and clogged airports, from billboards, trashy and pretentious architecture, from hour-long freeway commutes, from ticket lines and choked subways, from all the inefficiencies, pollutions – chemical and informational – and corruptions attendant to the process of moving information attached to things – from paper to brains – across and over the vast and bumpy surface of the earth rather than letting it fly free in the soft hail of electrons that is cyberspace.

Marcos Novak, University of Texas at Austin, project, 1991

Hani Rashid

Recently, while embarking on a project, I hesitated before the empty space of "beginning" and contemplated the inks, adhesives, pigments and drawing equipment that lay spread across the work tables. I thought about the space that these archaic implements have always imparted on architecture. I thought about the mythopoetic moment when Brunelleschi sat before the Baptistry doors and aligned space using devices and tools similar to these. I began to construct a fictive architectural history ... pigments and the decorative tradition ... plaster and embellishment, plastics and modernity.... The realization that the weight of these anonymous artifacts was due to their being imbedded in the history of making itself lay as a critical burden on the work yet to emerge.

Beneath a discarded stockpile of Xerox copies, I discovered a camera. This weapon alone has been profoundly utilized in reconfiguring the very ground upon which we operate as architects. Could the works of Gustav Eiffel have been attempts to conceive of some infinitely static construct to rival the onslaught of photography? Was the cinematic and its ambiguous convoluted space a formidable influence on Gaudi's curious creations? And did television, with its liquid interior construed of rays and beams, have some ineffable impact on the works of Eero Saarinen and Naum Gabo?

Reaching for the camera, I realized that my meandering through time had reached a place akin to the vanishing point in a linear perspective. From here onward, I continued to negotiate the nebulous terrain with the keenness of an executioner abandoning the tangible and embracing the inevitable.

Televised space (a transmuted photographic space) has all but vanquished the architect's tools to obscure regions of the mundane and the habitual. As photographic images and cinematic phenomena dismantled space as we knew it this past century, computers and information technologies will undoubtedly contort the spatiality of the coming epoch. Even the studio space is rendered obsolete when one can draw through fiber-optic cables or model in electronic plasma.

This then is the dilemma of making architecture today: Here we stand steeped in history and tradition, surrounded by the provocative possibilities offered up by randomness and the digital. Our tattered tools have been exhausted by overuse and we stand ready to discard them, yet we hesitate as if we were caught in a deliriously nostalgic moment as the millennium draws to a close about us.

Asymptote

Ted Krueger

K/K Research and Development was organized in 1986 as an experimental laboratory that occupies the magnetic field between the institutions of academic and professional practice. We are particularly interested in experimental strategies in politics and culture that exploit telecommunications and information technologies.

Interactive telecommunications reduces the role of locality in the development of political systems. On the one hand, it enables small, but advanced, communities to develop in isolation, by engaging global communication infrastructures. As an alternative, it also facilitates the development of diffuse, errant networks that float free of Rand-McNally borderlines.

To explore the first of these features, the project Renegade Cities hypothesized the development of a series of aquatic cities off the Alaskan coast. These cities are conceived of as mobile communities of hybrid political composition pursuing one common objective: freedom from obsolete land-based ideologies. Local and national politics merge for these relatively small-scale developments. Politics becomes an experimental discipline where mutations are generated out of rapid iterations of short-term working hypotheses as the inhabitants explore new methods of human autonomy and social communication. Our model for this new type of mutated individual is the Alaskan mosquito, a hearty bug that is legendary in its ability to dodge the swatter of dogma. Ultimately the results of these experiments will generate advances in both architecture and politics. If they are truly experimental in spirit, they could generate nothing at all.

Communication hardware and software are increasingly controlled by multinational corporations. Many, in addition, are investing in information bases, recording and film production facilities, and as a "philanthropic" activity, support institutions of higher learning, exhibitions, musical and theatrical events, architectural commissions and so on. This concentrates the production, distribution and content of both scienific and cultural activity under the control of a limited number of players. And you are not one of them.

The long-overdue dissolution of Communism has effectively quenched the fires of ideological debate on the international scene. As large states fragment into bickering ethnicities, regional free-trade zones develop into another layer of bureaucracy in the techno-capitalist cake. The citizens of this new order

K/K Research and Development, computer power supplies under construction, Art Park project, 1990

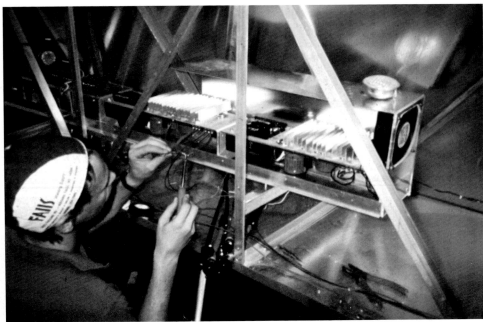

are not individuals, but corporate reps. If individuals are to survive this bureau-corpo pollution, they must outmaneuver this attack on their brains. The development of a diversity of diffuse networks may provide a viable counterstrategy by turning the products of the multinationals into tools of resistance that can operate from a bedroom, in the back of a pick-up, on the ocean floor and in orbit.

HYPOTHESES OF POLITICAL EXPERIMENTATION:

Every political and economic system suppresses competing ideas to ensure its own survival. Mosquitoes are the inevitable by-product of all ideologies. The mosquitoes will find their own way.

USING EVERY TECHNIQUE AT THEIR DISPOSAL, THE ENGINEERING TEAM HAD FINALLY SUCCEEDED IN ELIMINATING EVERY TRACE OF PERSISTENT NOISE FROM THE SIGNAL. IN ANOTHER LABORATORY, IT WAS THE SIGNAL THAT WAS BEING FILTERED OUT.

If you are not the lead husky, the view never changes.

A DIRECT-CURRENT MOTOR CAN BE USED AS AN ELECTRIC GENERATOR.

The electronic media is no longer centered in New York, Paris and Tokyo, but in Peekskill and Brooklyn, N.Y.

LIGHT-SPEED COMMUNICATIONS IN INSTANTANEOUSLY SHIFTING PATTERNS DO NOT CONSTITUTE THE DEVELOPMENT OF A GROUP MIND, BUT THE EXTENSION OF MANY INDIVIDUAL MINDS SIMULTANEOUSLY.

Read *Towards a Modem Architecture* by Le Moses-Quiteau, the great Franco-Zionist flatulist and pastischist.

THE ESSENCE OF THE MOSQUITOES IS RESISTANCE AND SURVIVAL. EXPERIMENTAL POLITICS IS NOT AN IDEOLOGY, BUT A METHODOLOGY.

Dan Hoffman

I would like to begin by talking about two possible devices in architecture, that of measurement, understood as geometry, and that of recording. Before I discuss these terms, I'd like to speak a bit about the word device. A device is a contrivance, something that acts upon the world. This contrivance is arrived at by devising a form of action that takes into account both the discursive conditions of the world and the specific manner in which the world is to be affected. This dual aspect can be considered a discourse towards a specific intent. The device is the means toward effecting the intent – take geometry, for example. Geometry is structured as a result of a discourse, a series of statements and a series of actions. You have the statement, the theorem, and then you have the proof of the theorem, given through a series of manipulations using the compass, the rule and the straightedge. The important thing about geometry, considered to be the prototypical architectural device, is that it has its end in mind. The end in geometry is really the beginning point. Everything proceeds from the point and ends at the point. The point is divided, split to make a line, rotated to make a circle, and so on and so forth. In geometry, the means are always understood in terms of their end and, equally true, the intent of geometry is to come back to the point, to return to this stable place as a beginning. Geometry has a very important and enduring legacy in architecture.

I would argue that architecture has been informed by Euclidean geometry up until this past century, and this influence continues in some way today. But we are entering a period where many of the initial propositions of the geometrical device are now in question. There are certain limitations; one of the primary limitations is that of time. Geometry occurs as the construction of space in terms of the absence of time. Geometry is not temporal. To make a very, very long story short, I think we've come to a place wherein architects (and others) are beginning to consider other devices that incorporate time.

This leads me to my second proposition, that of recording. As much as geometry and measurement refer back to a fixed point, recording is about a transference of a phenomenon from one location to another. There is no fixed point of reference in a recording, just a means of transference that remains stable relative to the phenomenon being transferred. Take a sound recording, for example. The phenomenon of sound is registered upon a surface and transferred back to another. The remarkable thing about the recording device – be it a sound on a tape recorder or an image on a camera – is that it becomes silent or invisible in the transfer. A recording device conceals itself. The ends are the reference of the means in geometry, while the ends in a recording device are obscured, the

end is simply to hear the recording. How do you fix that in a specific way? It is very difficult.

The limitation of geometry is that it occurs outside of time. The limitation of recording is that its means are invisible and, I would propose, invisible in an insidious way. The transference involved in every recording device is a form of interference, a form of friction, even a form of noise. What we hear through a recording in the end is not my voice, but the nature or structure of the interference between my voice speaking now and the recording you will hear later. As recording devices proliferate in our environment, they produce more and more noise, and more and more friction. Accountability for the noise and the friction is, to a large part, missing in the discourse surrounding recording. It's the hidden cost.

To conclude, measurement for

geometry is silent. Recording is noisy. Geometry is spatial. Recording is temporal.

Bucsescu

Allow me to address the first question to Michael Benedikt. Could you tell us how you traveled from a craving for a tangible reality, a craving many of us share, to an interest in virtual reality? How did you make that transition?

Benedikt

Some of you might know that some time ago I wrote a very short book about architecture and reality, in which I try to suggest that buildings have a very particular role to play as society becomes more and more influenced by media. A building should be a standard-bearer for our sense of reality. In *For an Architecture of Reality*, I also tried to reveal some of our intuitive notions about how buildings resist mediation. My position has not changed at all. I still think buildings are unique in their ability and capacity to serve us with what's real. I still have tremendous misgivings about various attempts to distort the nature of buildings – Disneyfication or virtualization of the structure, for example. Cyberspace could be the salvation of real buildings because it provides a way to siphon off the very natural creative urge to transcend the material. Virtual reality allows real buildings, if you will, to return to what real buildings are uniquely good at doing.

The advent of cyberspace can be

Francis Resendes, *Recording the Horizon of a Tank Filled with Water*, Cranbrook , 1991

seen in two ways; each can be regretted or welcomed. It's either a new stage in the etherealization of the world we live in, that is, the real world of people, places and things or, conversely, it is a new stage of concretization of the world we dream and think in, the world of abstractions, memory and knowledge. Which is it? Is the world becoming immaterial or is knowledge becoming "concrete"? Both views are useful, but both are misleading because they are modeled implicitly on the historical process of transformation, usurpation and replacement rather than a process of evolution, speciation and displacement. In other words, it seems to be that the proposition always placed before me is cyberspace *or* the real world. It's either cyber-architecture *or* regular architecture. I think that it is both. With the existence of cyberspace, the real world does not become etherealized or less real, nor does the mental world become concrete and less spiritual. Rather, with cyberspace, a whole new space has opened up. The new niche or realm lies between these worlds.

Bucsescu

Dan, is there a cost to using these new tools?

Hoffman

Well, I can't see how there couldn't be, but in this day and age one wonders who pays for it. I also read *Neuromancer* and found it a wonderful book, but half the book

occurs in the residue of cyberspace: the sprawl. My vision of cyberspace is the sprawl. Detroit has certain aspects of the sprawl, the New Jersey Turnpike is another image of the sprawl. Imagine endless abandoned K-Marts on the New Jersey Turnpike; this, in one sense, is the other side of cyberspace, and could be considered one of the costs. That's one short answer.

Another short answer is that cyberspace is about the mobility of information. There's a friction between the movement and the information. The mobility of capital today is in part indicative of the mobility of information. I think places like Detroit have become the residue of capital's mobility, which has to be examined by architects as much as the idealizing forms of cyber-architecture.

I might add one other thing: Michael spoke about real architecture in terms of its permanence. I regard permanence as another form of idealization. In speaking of the "real" as permanent, Michael betrays an idealizing desire in his architectural discourse whether it is in the form of so-called "real" architecture or cyberspace. As much as cyberspace portends to the infinite, you might say the permanence of architecture was a common ideal of a previous age. Today, we have the paradigm of permanence versus the paradigm of the infinite; to me they are two versions of the same thing. We are dealing with a very complex set of ideas that are served up to us

in an idealized form and I am suspicious of that. The other side, the cost as it were, is always present, but not always acknowledged. Media and media images are perspectivalized; they insist upon a certain point of view, ignoring other views, other considerations which are thereby treated as the residue, but they too must be examined and explored.

Bucsescu

Hani, you portray a happy realm where one could lose one's ego, embracing accident and merging with the tool. Is that possible when design is so often considered the willful imposition of order? Can you allow yourself to live with the accident implied by the tool?

Rashid

As far as we are concerned this isn't just about imposition of will with respect to cyberspace or virtual reality environments, rather it is about the very means by which these technologies allow us to comprehend space in unorthodox and unanticipated ways. I think these operations are very real and extremely pertinent in an image-laden, media-saturated reality. They are ultimately clues and sources for the architects to move towards and eventually through. I believe that we should embrace the advent of such technologies as an inevitable shift in the history of making architecture and architectural thought.

As for the tools and accidents, I

can't help but think that as architects we have always given over to, and ultimately allowed for, the tools to derail us from our most clinically perfect models of space making. We do not have to buy into the principles and phenomena of cyberspace to achieve this derailment, but we must try to understand its ramifications and possibilities for a potential consciousness, especially in terms of the use and misuse of such technologies that will soon be at hand.

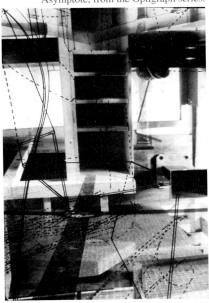

Asymptote, from the Optigraph series.

I purposely drew parallels between the computer, its spatiality, and the space imparted by the use of graphite or plaster because all of these things, as they coexist in our studios and workshops, will persevere. All of these tools must be resituated somehow in the realm of the accidental, at times even nonsensical.

Question

Almost everything all of you are saying is incredibly organic. Why, then, these mechanistic matrices? Why can't you say organic?

Benedikt

I am not proposing that with cyberspace we need to alter how we do buildings. I don't think cyberspace has a whole lot to say about how to do buildings, although there will always be feedback. I'm interested in architects stepping through the glass, so to speak, into whatever discipline cyberspace architecture itself becomes. In the virtual world of cyberspace, there is tremendous room for play, for organic forms, but they are harder to discern except under the aegis of art itself. Much of the audience for, and the people funding research in, cyberspace are hard-headed businessmen and computer professionals. For them, cyberspace is an extension of graphic user interfaces; it is simply a natural progression from a text-based to a graphic-based to a three-dimensional working universe. With that position, there is a certain discipline involved, a certain tightness between form and function.

Question

It does not seem to me that if you introduce a new tool, like a typewriter, gendered dualities, for instance, will disappear, or that if you write novels on a word processor you thereby fundamentally change the novel. How do you see the connection from this technology to the very particular current philosophical position espoused here today?

Hoffman

I think you are right to say that life goes on, but let me address the question of the impact of tools on the process of building today. Making a building used to involve putting a stake in the ground and taking a string and turning it around and bisecting an angle and so forth and so on. When you put up a wall, you had a string and a level and this operation of geometry continued throughout the making of a building. The string, the plumb, the stake, the level were important to the delivery and construction of the geometry of the building on the site. When you make a building today, there are some very different considerations. Much of the making has to do with adjustments of pieces that are fabricated off the site; much of the designing and making has to do with a continual process of adjusting pre-constructed pieces. It is a very different way of making a building than what was. The tools of adjustment – screws, neoprene gaskets, digital surveying instruments – demand a different approach to the building site, a process. Technology has a tremendous impact on how things are made and how things are organized. There are all sorts of other ramifications, all sorts of implications that affect not only building, but our daily lives.

Bucsescu

Ted, you bypass the computer, you make your own object. Is that correct?

Krueger

A lot of times when we make objects we put the computer inside rather than use it to make the piece. We feel that by having the kind of intimacy with the current technologies that we've created in our shop, we are able to see the possibilities and hopefully control them in a way that would not be possible if we were standard computer-phobic people. The possibility to create new social systems that link people in direct ways can enhance communication and lead to more direct political participation.

Rashid

There's something here that I tried to stress by showing you our projects (the work of Asymptote), that the constructs themselves are attempts to somehow enter into these uncertain realms [of cyberspace] following their own trajectories. As we were working on a project during the 100-day Gulf War, we were thinking about the space that CNN was constantly

carving out on our television screens. What kind of architecture does this media blitz compel? Could we somehow respond? Our inquiry was not only about virtual space but also about madness and technology. Another example is Times Square's latest addition, an enormous television screen that gets more attention than the road or the billboards. If a commercial for Sony is on the screen, it is much-more interesting than the Sony commercial that's on the wall. These very real, very pertinent and extremely potent fields in which we work as architects should be utilized, as events, without any facile means of exiting.

Kaplan

One important issue with computers is the phenomenon of cyberspace, a subject that is still somewhat unclear to me. However, this technology, even as we try to understand it, is still fundamentally a tool, something that you employ in architecture to do things. Implicit and explicit in this activity is the issue of the political. What do you do with this? How does it affect yourself and the people around you?

I disagree that cyberspace creates the sprawl. The sprawl has been here, will be here and it continues to be here. There are people who promote it, people who shop there and people who live there. To say that cyberspace creates the sprawl sidesteps the significant analysis of this technology. The politics of tech-

nology, how we use it, how it affects peoples' lives and how we participate in it is the real issue. If architects are

Renegade Cities, Bureau Dicto
K/K Research and Development, 1989

going to be a part of that, they have to understand this technology and how it is used. Ted and I experiment with technology, not the computer necessarily, for we haven't found one in the garbage bin yet, but we have found Xerox machines in the dumpsters. We take them apart, look at them and see how they work. Sometimes reassembly alone has introduced us to a number of aspects that make the machine usable and provocative in a different way. Looking at images of Xerox machines and cutting them up, reassembling them as a two-dimensional image is not as interesting to me as really understanding the technology, how it works how it operates, and what you can do with that as a political act.

Bucsescu

Poetic logic is defined as breaking of the code. Is this possible with the new technologies we are asked to embrace? Or is it, in fact, a freedom due to accident and randomness rather than purposefully breaking the code?

Are we left out of the process or can we merge with the machine as is suggested?

Benedikt

Virtual reality is a new medium, and I would like to talk about making in that new medium. Virtual reality is a very scary medium because as time goes by, less and less stands between what you can think of and what you can create. Much of the discipline of architecture is really the resistance offered by materials and the forces of gravity, wind and so on. Those engaged forces and materials give architecture the bulk of its meaning and its claim on reality. When you create a phenomenological sensorium, what else is there?

Getting into an office by flying clean through the roof and seeing the chair you are sitting on is really something, in spite of the fact that the image is grainy and wobbly. The crudeness you see today is equivalent to the crudeness with which people threw themselves off mountainsides with feathers tied to their wings.

I'll give you another example. In two dimensions it's very simple, we have all seen this on a computer screen. You have a window which is a panel basically, and inside of the panel, another panel. Now try to imagine this in three dimensions. Instead of a simple panel that you see through to information on another panel, you have a three-dimensional world. In that three-dimensional world is a three-dimensional object that contains a three-dimensional world whose dimensionality and behavior are not related to the first world that you're in. What is it like to look at a pocket of space imbedded in space? This is really almost inconceivable, and yet doable.

Question

Sounds like television, a pocket of space in space.

Benedikt

Not at all; television is not phenomenologically a pocket of space.

Question

I keep hearing only half the story. New techniques, new technology, new tools, whatever you want to call it; it's just not being produced out of thin air. It is produced by a set of circumstances and it is also producing a set of circumstances. You are talking about an increasingly privatized world. We can all get fascinated by these tools, we can all stay home and play with the computer, and we will increasingly do that at a

great cost to the other side of the private/collective. There is an increasing militarization that is both producing and being produced by it. All of us who were tuned into the Gulf War know very well the cyberspace of smart bombs. Let's talk about the effects of technology on privatization, cities, spacemaking – we're not yet rid of reality, no matter what you say about virtual reality.

Hoffman

Let's return to geometry, because I think its lessons are being lost. Michael Serres, in his essay "Mathematics and Philosophy. What Thales Saw," discusses the so-called invention of geometry by Thales. Serres relates the myth in the commentary on the theory of congruence in Euclid's *Elements*. In the commentary, Thales goes to Egypt and solves the problem of measuring the height of the pyramid by putting a stick into the ground and

Francis Resendes, *Recording the Horizon of a Tank Filled with Water*, Cranbrook , 1991

measuring its shadow at the moment that the sun is forty-five degrees, that is, when the length of the shadow equals the height of the stick. His invention is that the pyramid and its shadow are congruent to the stick and its shadow.

Serres makes the critical observation, however, that the sun had to stop for the geometrical relationship to be established. Time is therefore sacrificed for space. The lesson of the tale is that every discovery, every invention involves some kind of displacement. The understanding of this way of thinking can possibly constitute an ethical position towards the problem of "invention." The importance of myths such as those surrounding the "invention" of Thales is that they possess the human circumstance within the invention and thereby open the possibility for understanding, a condition that I find sorely lacking in much of today's discussion on technology.

Benedikt

I was a hi-fi enthusiast from way back, and I remember a turntable that I really, really lusted for. It was a gorgeous thing. It held the record up on three chrome platforms with little rubber legs and it had an arm of exquisite design. It was absolutely beautiful and was being produced and sold just when the CD was first coming out. I think a lot of technology is like that. The last gasp of a technology is always an exquisite attention to its making. There is

often regret when something is about to be lost, it becomes infinitely precious just as it goes over the brink. We often try to bring it back, invoking aesthetic justifications and nostalgic yearnings, but time and tide roll on. Architecture's current fascination with exquisitely cut pieces of metal seems to have this nostalgic quality, and it worries me, for it doesn't seem relevant and it is an expensive interest.

Question

I am not against what is going on with computers and so forth. I am not nostalgic, or asking that we historicize, but how do we explore the full implications of this new technology, this third computer revolution?

Benedikt

There's no technology that has ever come into the world innocent or guaranteed.

Stan George, University of Texas at Austin, project 1989

S A N F O R D　　K W I N T E R

The following interview was developed from a set of
questions submitted by the *Pratt Journal of Architecture*
and excerpts from a dialogue between Stephen Perrella
and Sanford Kwinter, January 1992.

On Vitalism and the Virtual

Question

Your interests now lie in the field of
architecture, yet your training is in
comparative literature. What is it that
drew you into architecture?

Sanford Kwinter

Having spent my student career
moving happily between countries,
universities and disciplines, always
with apparently genuine encouragement from my mentors, I marvel at how
systematically such questions are still
posed within the academy and the
amount of suspiciousness that they
still seem to harbor. All through the
1970s and 1980s one was told that
transdisciplinarity was the wave of the
future, that a significant transformation
in the organization of knowledge was
just around the bend – one, however,
that just kept on bending. In truth, I am
not really jumping disciplines at all –

given that my *topos* for nearly ten years
had been the study of the history of
space – but merely trying to fix my
enquiry within the domain of cultural
practice that ostensibly takes the question of space as its core problem or
defining object. My training is in the
Renaissance and the twentieth century,
in the two great epochs in Western culture that supposedly underwent systematic (not just episodic) processes of
modernization. I have always been oriented towards the problem of "the
modern," and my interest in working
within the field of architecture reflects a
conviction that this problem can no
longer be thought fruitfully within the
domain of language or even within its
broader analytical paradigm, but only
through the minute study of our physical, material and technical milieus – of
which language is little more than a
subset. This conviction, drawn primar-

ily from my studies of philosophy and literary theory (Nietzsche, Bakhtin, the pragmatists, Foucault), was reinforced while I was in graduate school, first by the sheer profusion, and often brilliance, of architectural invention during the last fifteen years (developments that in many ways continued minimalist and post-minimalist thought and practice by extending their inquiries directly into practical speculation) and second by the fact that, in contrast, scarcely a single work of "literature" had been produced since Thomas Pynchon's *Gravity's Rainbow* in 1974 that one actually felt was worth *studying*. Architecture was virtually the only area of cultural practice in North America that did not fall almost completely into retrograde mediocrity, commercialism or mannerism (or into mere triviality as in Europe), as did our cinema and art.

It would be unfair not to mention as well the long-term effects of that curious patina of worldliness or unparochialness, that attracts one to architecture faculties, at least from the outside; I am referring to a certain ecumenism that our overly professionalized humanities faculties no longer even dream of cultivating.

Of more concern today is the phase of intellectual provincialism that is deforming the architectural milieu from within: its resistance to anything but art-historical, narrowly deconstructivist or, at best, attenuated Marxist analytics (and even these are increasingly under siege). There seems to be a fear that intellectual invention, even of a type that would do little more than approach the formal invention of recent years, would somehow destabilize the field entirely.

Question

Recent theoretical approaches within the architecture world have suggested that architecture might yet be recast in a new way, that as a discipline it might yet take on a new status. What is your understanding of architecture as a discipline?

Sanford Kwinter

I can imagine no problem more pernicious, or one formulated with more bad faith, within architectural discourse today. These discussions, of architecture's status as a discipline, never amount to anything more than attempts by sterile academics illicitly to insinuate themselves into "priestly" discourse, in such a way that absolutely no one with any imagination will ever confront them, because those who produce new images, new ideas and concepts simply have no desire or need to legitimate themselves by defining a discipline. This petty paperwork is really the business of intellectual bureaucrats suffering from bad digestion.

On the other hand, I have always maintained that architects, more than any other educated group in our society, ought to serve as our society's real intellectual commandos. After all, who else may, and indeed must, deal with both economics and biology, human collectivities and geometry, history and matter? One mustn't understand this idea of commando in the classic macho sense. What is interesting about this manifold and promiscuous epistemological space I just described are the intricate patterns of interleaving, the faults and complex movements that continually destructure and restructure it, the "soft" or vague processes of partial and then violent emergence that drive it. In a milieu this rich, the synaptic trajectories, the passages and the fuzzy sets, the unforeseen mixtures, are where the truly new unfolds as an *unvarying law of nature*, as it were. This is clearly not the space of erection and creation *ex machina*, but rather of variation and immanence, stealth, subtlety and vigilance. Everything in such a space is hybrid and polyphonic and favors suppleness and intuition, not arrogant and impercipient strength. This new ethic has already begun to infiltrate the more adventurous areas of architectural production and I see it, albeit self-consciously, in the work of some of our women theorists. Forces like these will change our "discipline," not the ambitious operations of theoretical clerks.

Question

In your essay "La Città Nuova: Modernity and Continuity"[1] you use relativity theory as a paradigm that embodies many more general formal and cultural issues. Does scientific theory legitimize a proposition any more than philosophy, fiction or even religion? Isn't faith, in fact, involved in all of those systems?

1. Sanford Kwinter, "La Città Nuova: Modernity and Continuity," *Zone* 1 | 2, Urzone Inc., New York, 1986.

Sanford Kwinter

I am very happy that you asked that question. I was truly stunned – and have never entirely gotten over the shock – by the recoil of my dissertation sponsors from my desire to integrate scientific ideas into cultural history in anything more than an allegorical, analogical or literary way. The "more" that interested me then, as now, has to do with how scientific concepts represent actual working models of the imagination (one may think of these as little machines) whose criteria of acceptability are such that they must integrate and deploy massive quantities of adjacent information – greater quantities and in greater depth than are required of any other category of artifact in our culture. For a scientific concept even to be proposed within a given society, a simply colossal geometry of phenomena, events, images, ideas, experiences ... must be available – ordered and organized – and in potentially full and transparent agreement with it. In this sense scientific concepts are indeed very much like philosophical, literary and religious models, with one very important difference: these latter may be systematic and integrate entire "possible worlds," but scientific ideas need to. Science, most would admit, is clearly every bit a part of the historical process of the imagination – just like art and literature – yet why do so many find it flattering to their intelligence to deny this field of invention the same potential for creation, destabilization and freedom that they willingly accord to enterprises in the humanities? How long will our rapidly diminishing political options remain open if our intellectuals continue simplistically to demonize the scientific imagination as a priori corrupt and complicit with power? And this is not to say that in Western societies, the cliché of science as the "handmaiden of capital" is not frighteningly and depressingly true. My gripe, however, is with the new breed of self-appointed "sociological" critics and the clichés that they legitimate, not because they are wrong in what they do – they are often right, though rarely in a profound way – but because of their cheap form of intellectual satisfaction, which amounts to treating a topic only to give expression to a more deep-seated contempt for whole areas of human endeavor. We need to be a little more nuanced in our understanding of the historical dynamic of mutual implication and engenderment, more patient in mapping out the second- and third-order processes through which scientific innovations actually become subsumed by capital and more attentive to the powerful countermovements and remarkable richness that have always made Western science far less simple and monolithic and far more ambiguous than so many still consider it to be. In one's work, as in one's life, one should never lose sight of the fact that the potential of an innovation, scientific or otherwise, is never exhausted by the specific pathways of its subsumption by capital. That is why I have always argued that history and theory, not to mention design, must be creative and inventive, not only critical.

Finally, it is clearly easier today than it has been for a very long time to venture this type of commentary. We are currently undergoing a fundamental shift in scientific method and perspective, away from reductionism and towards complexity, away from fixed relations and precise values, towards general tendencies and evolutionary behavior. We are experiencing the waning of one of our most deeply embedded "classical" models. Whether this significant perturbation finds relays to, and within, other aspects of our culture depends largely on our collective and personal improvisatory skills and our ability to remain free from stylish cynicism and mindless prejudice. In that sense I myself am no enemy of what you call "faith."

Question

Transparency of technology, language and being seem to be tacit goals of humanity. How do you see this silent trajectory in relation to Merleau-Ponty's and Bataille's writings about the body as the most primeval, inescapable mode of being?

Sanford Kwinter

Though my colleagues and I at ZONE have published literally thousands of pages now on the subject of the body, I have never concealed my personal doubt that "the body" might well be a false problem when approached or formulated as such.

The huge book that I have just finished with Jonathan Crary, called *Incorporations*, explicitly addresses this doubt and attempts to engage the "body" as a merely hypothetical frame traversed in indeterminate ways by the more dynamic and unstable processes of "life," understood in the broadest possible way. In this sense our project is deeply and deliberately indebted to both Bataille and Merleau-Ponty. I agree with you that it is very important today to see the transparency myth – a central doctrine, for instance, of the cyberspace salesmen – as a nearly undisguised form of puritanical body hatred. If the mid-century philosophies of Merleau-Ponty and Bataille are important, and strange today, it is for their rejection of transcendence and their brilliant affirmations of the qualitative, the irreducible, the complex and the "wet" as the fundament of being. What we really have to fear now are the "narrow-bandwidth" systems, philosophies and architectures peddled to us like trinkets in exchange for renouncing our deep and polyphonic elemental and biological natures.

Question

The possibility exists that virtual reality will become a much larger issue in architecture than ever before. You have developed the notion of "real virtuality." How does this differ from virtual reality?

Sanford Kwinter

It is imperative to engage contemporary technological and social developments in the architectural curriculum, but it is even more important not to fall into slavish adulation and acquiescence of these processes. A very broad, and dangerous, tendency today is for architects and theorists to appear hip and on top of things, simply because they espouse modern cultural and technical developments, regardless of how impoverished and depriving these may be. In other words, I agree that every aspect of our debased cultural world is worthy, and in need, of serious study, but I am sufficiently snobbish to want to insist that these all must be judged from a historical and ethical standpoint – this first – and then to be thoroughly abused in the name of détournement or "resingularization."

The idea of "real virtuality" draws strongly on a visceral resistance to modern reality-engineering and its marketing. The premise in the studio I directed at the Harvard Graduate School of Design (GSD) was that no real space is ever univocal but always multiple and intertwined. The metaphysics of multiplicity, however, is obliged to account for the infinite generation of difference or information within a system in terms of the system itself, that is, in terms of what is immediately and concretely available to it right there. Difference, information and form simply cannot be explained purely in terms of spatial relations without recourse to a transcendent principle that lies outside the system and that introduces preexisting forms from without. But multiplicity can be understood in terms of time: as the result of a perpetual process of differentiation that occurs through the continuous, open-ended interaction of many elements. This gives way to an entirely new theory of structure based on "emergent properties," singularities, attractors, time series, and so on. The virtuality enters in because the space or the milieu in which forms arise is no longer seen as ideal but rather as rife with forces, tendencies and self-organizing pathways all straining to actualize themselves in morphogenetic events (forms). We design the space first and let the forms follow according to their own logic of regulation and encounter. These processes can be modeled very rigorously using quite simple topological methods.

In the GSD studio we were concerned with trying to understand technologically driven spaces from a historical and material perspective. Our express aim was to understand how an "old" space might be used to rupture a "new" one. We rejected from the outset the theory of technological development that focuses on units of hardware rather than on the social processes through which hardware innovations are integrated into working – that means productive – systems. Because we focused on the corollary processes of "subjectivation" that both accompany and forge the pathways of this economic-machinic integration, we were interested in the radical possibilities of hybridization in programming, and we rejected any primacy of high-tech over low. We tried to understand design as a blending of conflicting regimes, as a musical deployment of patterns and resonances, as a way of introducing entirely new mixtures of actions and affects into culture, like the homemade assembly of architectural genotypes that would spontaneously select unforeseen phenotypes of form and behavior – new forms of life and human subjectivity – from, and in coevolution with, the complex and evolving world around it.

One must understand dynamic structure as a type of *élan vital* or evolutionary dynamo that cycles real virtual relations deeper and deeper into the material world. These techniques are entirely in keeping with broader developments taking place around us. Our culture, it might be said, is in so many ways passing decisively beyond the classical epistemological framework of "representation" – a paradigm with its own historical specificity, problems and modalities – to one of "modeling," in which effects are no longer seen as mere reflections of more fundamental events occurring elsewhere (this is the great treason of the linguistic models in which so much of our culture still remains imprisoned), to one that engages by convergence the dynamic processes and incessant unfoldings of the real through emergent properties, not embedded structures. This new "framework" or paradigm comes to us equally from

economics, materials science, embryology, philosophy and popular sports and expresses, to put it very schematically, the momentary triumph of complexity and virtuality as determinant features of systems in which time functions as something creative, indeterminate and therefore **real**.

Question

Traditional modes of thinking have prevented both architects and philosophers from understanding the entwinedness of matter and events; rather, they have preferred to see these as belonging to entirely separate realms. Yet you have continued to insist on their inseparability. What does this have to do with the concept of vitalism that you have often discussed?

Sanford Kwinter

It is largely true that a metaphysics, or philosophy, of "events" has not existed in the West for many centuries and that its advent in relatively recent times might be seen as one of the characteristic and radical aspects of modernity. The problem was thought through very systematically by modernist philosophy – by Bergson and Whitehead, everywhere in Nietzsche, and in certain aspects of James. Vitalism played a major contestatory role in the life sciences for more than a century before it was put, in modified form, on a solid epistemological foundation in the early decades of the twentieth century. Vitalists argue that there are process-

es, activities and effects generated within complex systems that cannot be reduced to the properties of their parts, which brings us to the problem of the difference between "structure" and "organization." Most of our technological and aesthetic tradition has been oriented towards structure: stable, homeostatic arrangements of elements in apposition. But recently there has been an increasing interest in the large-scale, fluid and correlated, complex arrangements that fall under the category of pattern formation or organization. When a series of elements becomes "organized," it begins to manifest unexpected and unforeseeable activity. One could say that, from this point on, the system is more accurately defined by the events that it engenders and into which it enters, than by a mere description of the physical substrate in which these events take place. By seeing the concrete world in terms of organization as well as structure, one has no trouble attributing creative and even lifelike properties to what was classically seen as "inanimate" or inert. To say that a building, a town or a city is not alive or is reducible to the geometries of its physical parts, will soon be considered as silly and outdated a concept as the nineteenth- century mechanist assertion that an organism's behavior can be explained in purely physical and chemical terms. Whether this change in outlook can bear fruit at the design level is what makes speculation and experimentation so interesting today.

As he listened to the rise and fall of her voice, struggling to make out any word that connected the conversation to him, he began to disappear. Slowly at first, then progressively accelerating, he lost his place in the realm of things. He became a functioning absence. A shriek of laughter, through its sheer volume, would cause his reappearance, but then he would just as quickly fade again. In his absence, he imagined himself a cypher, unspoken, existing in the air between her mouth and the aperture of the telephone. He reverberated to the intake of her breath and the slight static of the Other sparking from the receiver. His absence was reclaimed as the site of diaphanous skin, coating the material absence of an Other. It wrapped itself around the sounding plastic seeking to deny this Other the right to physicality through speech. His body would reconstitute to delineate time. At these moments, he would find himself sitting at a desk, looking out of a window, facing an array of shops, located in a busy street, full of those going about their business. He felt, in these brief moments of seeming lucidity, that his time was absolutely distinct from theirs, just as much as it was materially distinct from the Other. As he raised his eyes to the digital clock illuminated in the office building opposite, he reflected on those moving below, momentarily. Then he was drawn back, back from the coherence of the being framed by the window. Anybody glancing up at that moment would be conscious of a shape, a colored blur, oscillating slowly behind a glass pane. There, in that glance, a consciousness connecting their space, the space between another's lips and the space in an Other's apartment five thousand miles away.

K **E** **I** **T** **H** **J** **A** **M** **E** **S**

A_O

Static...

"Mathematics is a domain," says Betrand Russell "where you never know (a) what you're talking about, nor (b) whether what you are saying is true".[1] As with mathematics, a work of art, or Art-object, is a being-in-contention. All you ever know is "about" the A_O, you can never know the object itself, as the Art-object in its totality can never exist. This is not a case of super-naturalism. The apparition Art-object falls in the interstices of a matrix of disciplines, and it is here, with the advent of digital reproductive technologies, that any surety in the realm of the actual has been vengefully undermined, and the disappearance of the Art-object is materialized.

1   G.H. Hardy at Cambridge professed his joy with pure mathematics by telling anyone who would listen that it was because it had no (practical) applications whatsoever.

Call Tracing...

For Plato the arts had a total mimetic character, thus it is possible, indeed obligatory, to judge their truth by their resemblance to actuality. Those who are to judge the success of the Art-object must have, "first, a knowledge of the nature of the original; next, a knowledge of the correctness of the copy; and thirdly, a knowledge of the excellence with which the copy is executed." [2]

Aristotle defined poiesis, a kind of aesthetic making, as imitation, the representation of objects or events. Aristotle further suggested that there is a need to imitate, and that imitation is used as a learning experience. Both Aristotle and Plato grounded the aesthetic experience in cognitive pleasure and this pleasure is most easily grasped in the term beauty.

Hutcheson, in his *Inquiry Concerning Beauty, Order, Harmony, and Design* (1725), showed that the sense of beauty does not depend on judgement or reflection and does not respond to intellectual or utilitarian features of the world. Beauty in an object is sensed when it presents "a compound ratio of uniformity and variety," therefore the object can be judged in and of itself, albeit within the framework of an aesthetic ordering.

David Hume wrote that, "beauty is such an order and construction of parts, as either by the primary constitution of our nature, by custom, or by caprice, is fitted to give pleasure and satisfaction to the soul." With Hume, at last, the Art-object is nearing autonomy and is severing its total representational relationship to the empirical world. That break takes place in the hands of Kant.

"A principle of taste would mean a fundamental premise under the conditions of which one might subsume the concept of an object, and then, by a syllogism, draw the inference that it is beautiful. That, however, is totally impossible. For I must feel the pleasure immediately in the perception of the object, and I cannot be talked into it by any grounds of proof." [3] Kant's aesthetic view of art sees the activity as simply an internal play of formal possibilities; in contrast, the ontological view of art sees it as the site of a privileged truth, the "truth of the work of art."

"What it begins by implying is that art – the word, the concept, the thing – has a unity and, what is more, an originary meaning, an etymon, a truth that is one and

2. Plato, *Laws*.

3. Immanuel Kant, *The Critique of Judgement*, J. C. Meredith, trans., Oxford University Press, 1952, p.141.

naked [une vérité une et nue], and that it would be sufficient to unveil it through history. It implies first of all that 'art' can be reached following the three ways of word, concept and thing, or again of signifier, signified, and referent, or even by some opposition between presence and representation." [4]

Interference on the Line...

I want to elaborate around a theory that the Art-object, in its thingness-in-the-world, has given way to the A$_O$, in that the A$_O$ is constituted by that which is *about* it, and which informs it in a matrixical manner. In this way, the A$_O$ is essentially an interdisciplinary (un)construct.[5] Shimmering, mirage-like in its tenuous and (un)essential reverberations, the Ao escapes any empirical totalism.

How do we know the Art-object? Basically, we know it because it is properly framed. Main-Framed. That frame is either actual or implicit, it delineates the Art-object from its surroundings.

> Take away from a painting all representation, all signification, any theme and any text-as-meaning, removing from it also all the material (canvas, paint) which according to Kant cannot be beautiful for itself, efface any design orient-ed by a determinable end, subtract the wall-background, its social, historical, economic, political supports, etc; what is left? The frame, the framing, plays of forms and lines which are structurally homogeneous with the frame structure.[6]

The frame, therefore, imposes boundaries, essentially (but not exclusively) boundaries of meaning. This is the simplest level of questioning concerning the frame; framework, to be framed, involved in a frame-up, etc. The notion of slippage here is very apparent as are the obvious questions of interior and exterior, front and back, with and without. The point here is simply to recognize the discourse of fram-ing and to realize that the boundaries are there to protect a prior discourse, a prior notion of perception, an essentially rational, phallocentric, point of view.

From the frame, we turn to Enframing (*Ge-stell*), the meaning of which immedi-ately escapes the limits of the frame. Heidegger's main thesis in *The Question Concerning Technology* is that Art is by necessity inscribed within the technological. This is developed in the context of the notion of Enframing which locates its essence in modern technology. According to Heidegger, there is a certain blindness to the potentialities that lie hidden in technology by the rigidity of its cause and effect. Heidegger uses the etymology of the word technology to find its hidden aesthetic:

---

4   Jacques Derrida, *The Truth in Painting*, Geoff Bennington and Ian McLeod, trans., The University of Chicago Press, 1987, p.21.

5.   The term, A$_O$ must be used but its use here exceeds its mean-ing.

6.   Derrida, *The Truth in Painting*, p.98.

The word stems from the Greek. Technikon means that which belongs to techne. We must observe two things with respect to the meaning of this word. One is that techne is the name not only for the activities and skills of the craftsman, but also for the arts of the mind and the fine arts. Techne belongs to bringing-forth, to poiesis; it is something poietic. [7]

So technology is a mode of revealing, but "the revealing that holds sway throughout modern technology does not unfold into a bringing-forth in the sense of poiesis. The revealing that rules in modern technology is a challenging." [8]

Enframing is not meant as a framework of any sort, it is an active term, a "challenging claim," a demanding summons, that "gathers" so as to reveal. It is continually restructuring itself. "Enframing means that way of revealing which holds sway in the essence of modern technology and which is itself nothing technological." A good description of what Enframing implies is given by Gregory L. Ulmer in *Applied Grammatology:* "Enframing, in short, concerns not any given form of technology, but the production and relaying of information by whatever means." [9]

When we come to contemplate the digital we find that Enframing, to use Heidegger's term, is seen as a mode of acting-in-(and on)-the-world. For the A$_O$ there is no Art and there is no Technology, the A$_O$ oscillates so fast that distinction becomes meaningless. The process of naming becomes irrelevant. This does not imply a necessary change in making, only a change in perceiving. It is possible that people will still paint pictures, will still produce sculpture, but the frame-up in which these works are produced is no longer subject to closure, except for the closure inherent within the particular chosen medium. It is no longer a case for rigid definitions. The work will not be subsumed under a directional signification, as signification itself will be seen as an impossibility. From here we can si(gh)t(e) the A$_O$.

The A$_O$ itself, in its self-containment, cannot be known as a totality, as in-and-of itself it does not exist. It has no essence and, therefore, essentially no form; it can only be approached from without and about. It might be argued that the A$_O$ can only be apprehended (with the concomitant connotations of fear, anxiety and dread). The real world exists at the end point of questioning the question of ontology. A convenient point to stop and to start, simultaneously. Yet another ending-beginning. The insertion of the A$_O$ into the real world (yet, it is always already there) must be in apprehension and it is that apprehension that mediates against the transcendental. [10] The A$_O$ is not a static, originary moment. To expand, the A$_O$ is not an object, but perhaps a constitutive sequence, a series of moments, of partial views, that are of infinite extension. What constitutes the A$_O$ is no-thing, but the continual return upon its moments.

7.   Martin Heidegger, *The Question Concerning Technology*, William Lovitt, trans., Harper & Row, New York, 1977, p.13.

8.   Heidegger, p.14.

9.   Gregory L. Ulmer, *Applied Grammatology*, The Johns Hopkins University Press, Baltimore, 1985.

10.   A notion briefly akin to this may be found in Theodor Adorno's *Aesthetic Theory*, "The concept of art balks at being defined, for it is a historically changing constellation of moments."

The Carrier Wave...

In retrospect, it all seems so obvious. Of course Claude Shannon had to leave meaning out of the question; otherwise how could he quantify the new concept that he called "information"? In effect, Shannon solved the problem...by defining it internally through relational differences between elements of a message ensemble, rather than externally through its relation to the context that invests it with a particular meaning. It is this inward turning definition that allows the information content of a message to be always the same, regardless of the context into which it is inserted. Thus, the first, and perhaps the most crucial, move in the information revolution was to separate text from context. Without this stratagem, information technology as we know it could not have come into being. [11]

Information theory can be viewed in a Kantian manner as a formalist systematic, yet it contains within itself elements that split it apart so completely that any notion of containment is dissolved. Here again, the question of the frame reappears. From its inception Information Theory contained the characteristics that were to define some of the most radical aspects of digital technology, that is the possibility to disassemble, manipulate and reconstitute in a totally transparent way, at will. This manipulation of all texts is, indeed, our context. The digital has made for the disappearance of any stable, universal, originary meaning in which to place ourselves and our products.

From panic art, panic astronomy, panic babies and panic shopping malls to panic sex, panic fashion, panic U.S.A. and panic advertising, this is the (panic) reader's guide to the fin-de-millennium. The *Panic Encyclopedia* begins with the fateful discovery in contemporary physics that ninety percent of the natural universe is missing matter, just disappeared and no one knows where it is gone (physicists most of all). Now, with the triumph of science and technology as the real language of power in postmodern culture, the *Panic Encyclopedia* argues that ninety percent of contemporary society is also missing matter, just vanished and that no one knows where it is gone (sociologists most of all). [12]

What is the practice of the A$_O$ under the signature of this coding, can the A$_O$ be seen as an information generator/generated-upon? It is tempting to view the A$_O$ as an infinite arrangement of ciphers, a constant switching of codes to avoid translation. Cipheric, or otherwise, it is here, here in this mesh of digital and informational techne that the A$_O$ absolves any material base and signals itself in absentia. The A$_O$ can no longer be postulated as existing outside of any-body, but must be seen

11. Katherine Hayles, "Text Out of Context: Situating Postmodernism Within an Information Society," *Diacritics 9*, Spring/Summer 1987. See also, by the same author, *The Cosmic Webb: Scientific Field Models & Literary Strategies in the 20th Century*, Cornell University Press, Ithaca, 1984.

12. See the Krokers' notion of a panic for a parallel shift. Arthur and Marilouise Kroker, David Cook, *Panic Encyclopedia*, St. Martins Press, New York, 1989. From the jacket blurb.

as threaded in as deep a structure as our DNA. If technology is inscribed techne, then our bodies are inscribed A_O.

> Once the informational nature of the genetic code was understood, information theory joined with genetics to create bio-technology. . . . If the body is considered as an informational text, this technique opens the body's interior space to a literal embodiment of intertextuality, for the foreign bacteria's DNA merges with the DNA that was the body's originary text to create an intertextual code that deconstructs the distinction between exterior and interior, text and context. [13]

By now, it appears to me, that the creation of the work of Art (in its Kantian sense) is becoming exceedingly superfluous. We have an arena with the realization of virtual reality, a space, a cyberspace, that is pure A_O.[14] It is a hyper-informatics, an informatique, that is beyond any definition of creativity, or making, or assemblage, beyond any of the traditional formulations that one would bring to a definition of the aesthetic experience.

As ghosts in the informatique, we are left with no definitions, no history and no meaning to accompany our no-body. When we just say *no* all is confusion, contradiction, fragmentation, catastrophe, discontinuity, speed, and implosion. All our making is referred elsewhere.

The picture hangs on the wall like a rifle or a hat.

Heidegger

In art, it is hard to say anything as good as nothing.

Wittgenstein

For videos and walkmans are reality in kit form: we use them not to watch films or listen to music, but to add vision and soundtracks to make us directors of our own reality.

Paul Virilio, War and Cinema.

13. Hayles.

14. A good outline is provided by Grant Fjermedal in *The Tomorrow Makers*, Macmillan Publishing Co., New York, 1986.

15. Fjermedal.

Tachi has succeeded with his vision system. It truly gives you the feeling that you are inside the robot, looking at the world from within its body, not your own. This is possible because the operator isn't just looking at a television monitor; his head is encased in a black-velvet lined box. Within this box are two televisions receivers, one for each eye. The receivers are gauged so that the image that is reflected against the retina of each eye is exactly the same as if you were looking at the world unaided. Further, every movement of your head is duplicated on the robot, where two precisely placed video cameras transmit a human range of what is seen. The result of this is that when I went into the laboratory and strapped my head inside the black-velvet box, it was as if I were seeing with my own eyes. The depth and scope of human vision was so clear, that it was unsettling and a wild visual delight. The robot mounted cameras are then focused on the author. The walls spun during the maneuver, and then when the motion stopped and I was looking at myself, the out-of-body experience began. It was as if I were standing a few feet in another body looking at myself. I moved my head to look up and down and even to look away. And when I looked away from that person who was me, it was as if that body were just another passerby.... The scientists in the laboratory laughed. They knew what was going through my head, for it had also gone through theirs during their own encounters with their out-of-body-selves. "Are you here?" Tachi laughed. "Or are you there? Where is your body?"[15]

H A N I **R** A S H I D

As the photographic image and cinematic phenomena have already dismantled our traditional understanding of making space, virtual reality and cyberspace are bringing about yet another systematic breakdown of the parameters by which we comprehend space. Form and meaning, once comfortably embodied in a photographic plate or a strip of celluloid, are all but irrelevant in a computer-generated environment where we are confronted with a scaleless, disconcerting reality in constant flux. This is the dilemma in the era of digitalization and telecommunication. Emerging from the infinite possibilities of the random are abstract fields of unforeseen constructs made up of information and data. There now exists a vast discrepancy between making and the made where the outcome, be it image, media or architecture are all ambiguously linked, no longer tied to the very act of making itself. The intersection between creation and manifestation can be likened to a-theory as an autonomous trajectory to d-practice.

Architecture surfaces after the act of making is brought to completion, that is to say, once architecture stops becoming, and remains only as a residue of some forgotten method on the horizon.

Meditations on Architecture in a Media Field

Televised space (a sim-mutation of photographic space) is a liquid realm reshaping the last vestiges of Euclidean geometry. Architecture is now indisputably implicated in the highly charged sociopolitical arena which media has already forged out of propaganda, advertising and the immediate.

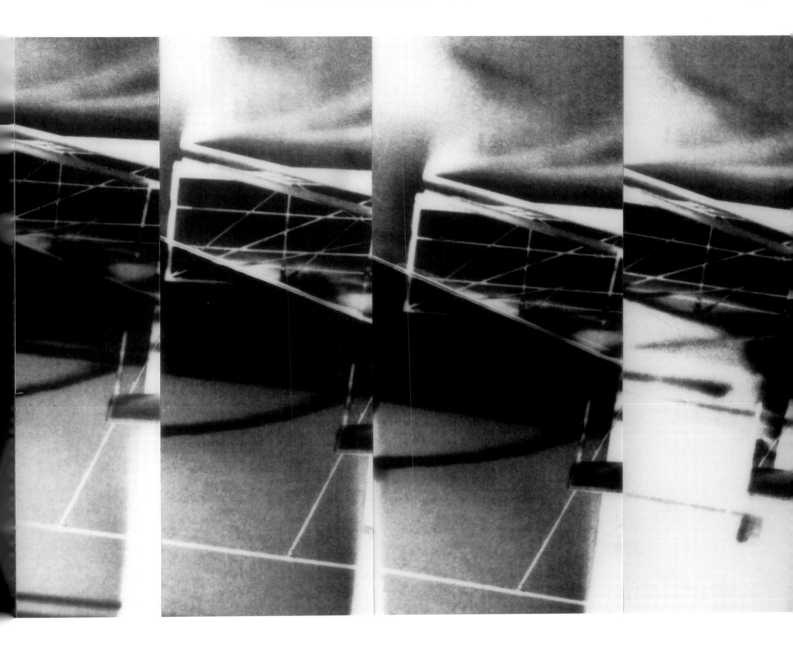

The space in which architecture moves is one of transience and extreme instability. The very "ground" it occupies is a slippery terrain constantly realigning itself with and against the technological.

In a global condition of blurred borders and the subsequent surfacing of indistinguishable cultures, there is a dissolution at work rendering history a meaningless pastime.

One cannot simply begin an architecture as tradition would have it, from the poetic, but rather end architecture from the pragmatic.

To draw is to deceive, to play a sort of game where one assumes control over a nebulous terrain of rupture.

A fluctuating reality of momentary relapses, split-second reasoning and "sound bite" policy making, is a space construed of the intangible and dominated by the immeasurable.

It is within this mechanism of comprehension (media) that we as architects attempt to make space out of a material dense with the irreconcilable. We operate as machinists manipulating reality in order to have it conform to some reasonable semblance of possibilities.

Making architecture now coincides with the unravelling of the already unravelled. The emergence of this all-pervasive uncertainty reveals a world caught up in the delirium of progress and a love of the instantaneous.

The constant disruption of method is in itself a kind of convoluted trajectory, problematic and yet noteworthy for its appeal to a delirious and hallucinatory euphoria.

A probable architecture is one liberated from the tedium of comprehension and knowing.

Within a charged electronic space, one is able to transform the tangible into the enigmatic, unfolding an architecture of dissonance, without hygiene, immune and spontaneous.

Imagine an architecture rising out of the deluge of fin-de-siècle eclecticism, an architecture that is an utterance, without language that anticipates the "necessary" decoding. This is the imaginary architecture that is beneath the weight of our culture.

Here then is an architecture liberated from nostalgia and the nausea of the trustworthy. Forged somewhere between the cacophonic and the uncertain, where the past is muted and the future suppressed.

This then can be a dictum to forget history; run amongst the ghosts and dine with the angels.

J O H N K N E S L

The Double Arrow

A Crisis of Making?

Asking questions about making unavoidably calls forth concomitant issues about the maker and the made, about intention and purpose, about modes of knowing and anticipating, and about values, desire and will. If there is a crisis of making, it is also a crisis of the subject and the object in our postmodern condition which, one might argue, follows fairly straightforwardly on the project of earlier modernity.

One could characterize the various critical diagnoses of our situation as aspects of two major topoi: A certain loss of *materiality* and of the *bodily,* and a loss of *foundation,* which brings a crisis of values, of authorship and subjecthood, of the very concept of order.

It now appears clear that the project of the Enlightenment, of modernity, as the extension of Western European classical thinking, had to undermine its foundations in metaphysics. Classical thinking is *representational* and is supported by Platonism, which represents the universe as a pyramidal ray of ideal forms at different levels of a *structure*. The individual subject takes its place in this pyramid and is organized internally in the same structural way. This model establishes and legitimizes perspectival optics as the proper mode of seeing and thinking: The tip of the pyramid is the eye of God. Through its self-closing structural order, classical architecture *represents* the path to the *One*, the great Identity to which the becoming of subject and object henceforth will be subjected.

To understand modernity, one had better focus not so much on its, after all, not-so-new "objectivity," but on the need to determine a purpose no longer guaranteed by God or even the natural light. Theory is called upon to give meanings and to assign functions. Conceiving itself as metalanguage, it surveys from above, reduces everything to its own objects, and then deduces from this arrogance a right to impose specific meanings and functions. While pre-World War II modernism still had trust in the substantiality of materiality and spirituality and in their ability to serve as foundational concepts, post-World War II existentialism and phenomenology began to undermine the classical concept of the subject and the object. From this vantage point, structuralism (also materialist structuralism) appears as the last effort to reestablish the classical model in formulas without a God presiding over them. Such progressive disembodiment may have readied us for the fleeting subject of post–structural consumption that finds itself reflected in the edible chunks of eclectic historicism and contextualism or in architecture as filmic sequences of images or representations of formal transformations. Structuralist thinking cannot cope with the slipperiness of the bodily/material and tends to condemn the bodily to opposition – that is, to a position where it can be held in check.

It is the merit of deconstruction to have sensed the wormy movements of differe/ance[1] which are suppressed by structural order but which break in when the object and the real sneak up on the body and take the watchful mind by surprise. Deconstruction has taken on classical thinking by undermining its premises in structural order and representation as the mode of referring to the real and as holding its contents. In classical thinking identities are defined by inclusion and exclusion, opposed to one another, and change is reduced to lawful transformations secured by the supreme power of the principle of unity.

Deconstruction of the myth of the individual creator leaves the author as a reworker whose contributions to the play of textual strategies are unclear but certainly rather limited. Deconstruction catches making on the make; it is suspicious of notions of authorship and originality including its overt and covert goals, references and supports. But the making of deconstruction seems overly dependent on antecedent texts, and it seems undecidable in what way the re-made might affect

Differe/ance: This form of writing is to induce a reading of the word in both the conventional sense and in the ambiguous sense of "sliding away," "missing the mark" and "being deferred" that Derrida imparts to the word.

1. Jacques Derrida, *Writing and Difference*, University of Chicago Press, 1978.

the strategies for power which are at work in the preceding texts or to what extent it might generate new (and also undecidable) meanings, values and powers. The rejection of master code metalanguages can justify all manner of supposedly critical quotation and message, as exemplars of contextualist design demonstrate. Also, and perhaps most importantly, deconstructing the metaphysics of the living voice and the spoken word means according absolute primacy to the written sign. The all too easily cheapened tenet "nothing outside the text" can legitimize formalisms that protect the status quo and lead to a sense of unease or even horror when facing materiality and justify a turning away from social problems and programs. Under the cunning guise of reconquering what it claimed was its lost autonomy, architecture had first revived its own classical formalism with the structuralist rage of the "Third Typology."[2] Now it seems to have turned to follow the generally equally formalistic deconstruction of certain hand-picked structures. While deconstruction has demonstrated that identity and structural order inflict violence on the free production of differe/ance, it has not had the courage to break away to free construction or making, one *without structure* and *representation*. And so the current debate revolves around the question of how much and what kind of structural order is needed – only so that one can play with deconstructing it.[3] Instead, we must ask: What kinds of order, in space and in thinking, need to be invented to make a freer and more intensive life at the threshold of the twenty-first century?

We seem to like being trapped in our own invention: language. Representative language had permitted us to construct an "ideal" world. Since this world of ideas is sheltered from reality, from the great destroyer – time – it will soon seem superior to the ordinary world, it will belong to God. As language hovers above what it thus turns into a mere "world," it also creates a place, a name, a location and address for the "I." Language forms the subject that looks at this world from outside. Today's image-word hyperlanguages with their simulated worlds have magnified this superiority. Whenever and wherever reality finally does break in, simulation simply regroups to cover over again. This is a dangerous condition since it prevents the kind of direct, bottom-up learning that can warn implicitly of imminent or far-off catastrophic consequences.

Simulation, a representation without depth, has shed almost all references to a larger order of things so that it may assault us more forcefully with the otherwise empty assertion "I am real." Representation at least could be held somewhat accountable for the truths presumably contained in its referential systems. Simulation eliminates any extended references that would be open to a critical thinking-through. In fact, such references increasingly can no longer be made because

2. Anthony Vidler, "The Third Typology," in *Rational Architecture*, Archives d'architecture moderne, Brussels, 1978.

3. Jeffrey Kipnis, "Nolo contendere," in *Assemblage 11*, MIT Press, Cambridge, April 1990, pp. 55-58.

the subjects of this communication industry will not have had any remotely real contact with what comes from the screens.   What remains of references is foreshortened, accelerated, densified and thrown at the subject in chunks that keep the subject captive and fascinated with the task of synthesizing all this into a world.   This world is made up as an intricate weave of images and words which alternate in functioning as subtexts to images and as subimages to texted worlds.   Are we any better off having exchanged the repressive predominance in classical culture of the logos over bodily figuration for this magic play between image and word that fabricates simulated worlds in midair so to speak?

The subject of simulations is fractalized; the fragments of self-recognition in consumption succeed one another at ever-increasing speeds and intensities.   There is total powerlessness and absorption on the one side and simulated omnipotence on the other.[4]   Even though the organization of the fractal subject is extremely loose and its components are almost totally exchangeable, this subject constructed in and of simulations is still constituted by separation from the world.   This constitution-by-separation in fact tends to make exploitive the desire, thinking, feeling and "activities" that make up and animate this subject.   When the subject is constructed by separation, representation becomes the dominant mode of thinking and of knowing and, in turn, these will dominate life.   Representation builds up an increasingly complex viewer; it creates forms of distancing that legitimize the idea of a central self entitled to be empowered to total ingestion and totalizing creation – by excretion, so to speak.   In consumption the classical dialectic between subject and object has been reduced to amoebalike incorporation and excorporation.   In this childlike world , one ingests the "good" and expels the "bad" objects, leaving them to be destroyed.   Could one, however, argue that the fractalized subject of simulations is already a becoming, the becoming of the freer and more intensive life I have proposed here?   No, incorporations and excorporations are not becomings and the organization of the fractalized subject is nothing more than the expansion of sequences of incorporation and excorporation.

As the farthest recesses of the world are "translated" into the hyperreality of simulations, distance, space and body are lost.   Better stay in touch, or rather, on the lines, or be forgotten, so runs the threat enforcing the new social discipline that obliges us to pursue the ecstasies of a progressively *pervasive communication*.   This communication drives towards ever-farther-reaching control over meaning in maximal transparence.   Such a process must generate insanity since the more it enforces communication, in the form of an exchange of signs, the more it removes the potential for direct, bodily and "real" communication.

4. Jean Baudrillard, Subjekt und Objekt fraktal,
Lecture at Kunstmuseum, Bern, October 19, 1986.

This disembodiment has led to everything being made over into objects that ultimately only serve to carry meanings for a bodiless mind. This disembodiment is, I believe, what underlies contemporary impasses in such areas as social formation, ethics and morality, ecological problems and of the invention and social division of work and of leisure. The sharpest critiques have not been able to cope with the sheer attraction of consumption, however suicidal it quite patently may be. Forming critical concepts of the bodily might show us that consumption is so irresistible because it offers something seductively close to consummation in Bataille's sense, which is a becoming in the streaming-away of the body of libido.[5]

Is there a sense that something is missing in this floating existence? Nothing can really grab us any more, everything is diverting games and skirmishes about access to power and consumption. Only a freer and more intensive bodily life would expose the treacherous immaterialism of a life in simulations. Rather than trying to find a new order for yet another world out there, we must make something that is "in-between-subject-and-object"; we must construct without metaphysics; and we must then live this to taste it and test it. Today, the body is needed only so that when paralyzed by the hypnotic effects of the mirage of simulations, it will give its intensive sensations and feelings fully to the consumption of hallucinations, of an other, freer, more intensive life, the stuff of its dreams. And yet, even as the body is becoming the last frontier for exploitation, is it still key to a way out of the malaise?[6]

Paths to Bodily Thinking

The legacy of Merleau-Ponty: "The Flesh"
Merleau-Ponty's last works on perception and the body offer footholds for developing a new conception of subject and object as a *crossed becoming*. From conceiving the wholeness of the body as a structural "comportement"[7] in the world, Merleau-Ponty went on to look for the grounding of the life and materiality of the body in a new element, "the flesh." The body is given to the subject to go to the heart of things by "making myself a world and by making them flesh."[8] The flesh makes possible a "fundamental fission or segregation of the sentient and the sensible, ... which laterally makes the organs of my body communicate and founds

5. Georges Bataille, *Erotism Death and Sensuality*, City Lights Books, San Francisco, 1986.

6. Jean Francois F.Lyotard, "A Response to Kenneth Frampton," in *ICA Documents 4*, Lisa Appignanesi, ed., Free Association Books, London, 1989.

7. Maurice Merleau-Ponty, *The Structure of Behavior*, Beacon Press, Boston, 1967.

8. Maurice. Merleau-Ponty, *The Visible and the Invisible*, Northwestern University Press, Evanston, 1968.

transitivity from one body to another." There is not first a subject that has perception and comes to inhabit the world, but there is only an anonymous visibility, the flesh, which as the "formative medium of the object and the subject" inhabits both. (Knowing of Foucault's appreciation of Merleau-Ponty, it would be interesting to explore a genealogy of this "visibility" using Foucault's history of his equally pre- and post-subjective "see-able" and "say-able."[9]) This bodily perception founded in the flesh produces a realm of bodily ideas that are intrinsically hidden and hiding and which cannot be erected into a second positivity without being destroyed. Such bodily ideas are the doubles of lights and sounds, their other side or depth, and as such they are the invisible of this world but they are also the "being" that allows a visibility. As "...the fragments of the luminous field adhere to one another with a cohesion without concept, which is of the same type as the cohesion of the parts of my body or the cohesion of my body with the world," there must be a flesh, a kind of pre-subjective tendency towards the formation of bodies and life. Before subject and object, there is "serpentement," "being as winding." Path and traveller, which are but two aspects of being, do not inflict themselves but snake through a landscape in the form of an "ineinander," an into-one-another, which diagrams a form of otherness and difference which is not generated by separation, but rather by a chiasma in which two movements cross to segregate and to engage.

While one should question Merleau-Ponty's sense of a preharmonized totality between sentient and sensible and the persistence of a dialectic of subject and object, it is more important to take up more radical departures than critique old scaffolding. It is true that a romantic reharmonization cannot deal with the alienation by separation that has produced the disembodied mind and eye, whether in the classical panoptic central subject or in the rapid sequences of mini-subjects flashing on and off with the consumption of perceptual bullets – the imagiles, semantiles, conceptiles of the media. What is most critical is the absence in Merleau-Ponty of the sense that other forms of body-mind can be constructed "artificially." Nevertheless, more than any other idea, "serpentement" and "ineinander" could help to launch us into a radically different subjectivity and objectivity, and thus into an architecture that would no longer simply sit "out there" to be looked at but one that would be a pole in a terrific intertwining.

What will the architecture of becoming look like? Resist old habits: This is beyond the question of another visual style. Ask what may come out of a different dance of architectural thinking.

"Serpentement" is the term used by Merleau-Ponty translated as "winding," indicating a new conception of the subject-object relation, close, in my opinion, to "becoming" and "returning" as they are postulated in this text as a new departure.

"Ineinander" is Husserl's term for the spiritual and ideal realm (translatable as "inside-one-another"), which Merleau-Ponty refers to as contributory to his idea of the flesh, which I take as a bodily-material connectivity of the mutual becoming in-and-into-one-another of what was the subject and the object.

9. Gilles Deleuze, *Foucault*, Editions de Minuit, Paris, 1986.

The legacy of Bataille: Erotism

Long before there is sexuality, erotism constitutes and pervades bodies whose desire and machinic functions are irreducible to a set of functional organs or a technical object. Bataille sees this Eros at work in his images of a horrific defunctionalization of organs and in acts of destruction that seek to annihilate separative distance and replace it by continuity between the body and the world. The eye, therefore, is swallowed back into the body, or it explodes and literally projects itself out into the world, in this way becoming the world.[10]

To escape its imprisonment in organic functions, the body seeks death. This death is the self-sacrifice of life inflicted on the sacrificial victim or on oneself. But, one may add, while the death of the physical body is the ultimate event and is often used in a half-metaphoric manner, the body could also be said to drive towards a death that is the most *radical becoming-other*, the death that is a portal for the return of life through becoming another body, any and all other bodies. Instead of following the neatly dialecticized Freudian contradiction between Eros and Thanatos, Bataille shows us a contaminating mingling and interpenetrating and, in a doubling of these, a promiscuous commingling between *bodies and minds* that have again become bodily, a raw erotism of engagements between body-mind and architecture that are to be recovered. In Bataille's analyses all the body's functions are revealed to be machines that seek to bring about total expenditure, a totally self-abandoning flowing of a life force. The Bataillian erotism of a bodily thinking sees life as parodic, sees everything as a parody of another thing, as a song of itself that connects itself through the copula, as in copulation, with any "other":

> Ever since sentences started to circulate in brains devoted to reflection, an effort at total identification has been made, because with the aid of a copula each sentence ties one thing to another; all things would be visibly connected if one could discover at a single glance and in its totality the tracings of an Ariadne's thread leading thought into its own labyrinth.... And when I scream I AM THE SUN, an integral erection results, because the verb to be is the vehicle of amorous frenzy .... Love and life appear to be separate only because everything on earth is broken apart by vibrations of various amplitudes and durations.... Beings only die to be born, in the manner of phalluses that leave bodies in order to enter them.[11]

Even though I would argue that the copula is fixated on a philosophy of being, of structure and dialectic, and that it should be replaced by becoming, and even though poetic language relies on metaphor that feeds and serves the very spiritual

10. Georges Bataille, *Story of the Eye by Lord Auch*, Penguin Books Ltd., Harmondsworth, Middlesex, England, 1982.

11. Georges Bataille, *Visions of Excess. Selected Writings, 1927-1939*, The Solar Anus., University of Minnesota Press, 1985.

seemingly natural boundaries of a body, object or mind must be seen as the modes of operation of perception and thinking at a rather primitive stage serving the survival of the organism and of human society in a world where the threat to this survival could be identified by the perceptual mechanisms that constructed a "good gestalt" from the ground of what was of no currently pressing interest.[13] To develop the idea of a bodily becoming and a correspondingly bodily thinking, one has to conceive of thinking not as a framing, defining, representing or a building of syntactic and semantic power structures, but as itself a becoming (which is a becoming of the power to be – by becoming-and-returning in ever-wider and deeper extents) and which, thus, is also a perceiving. This cognition and perceiving must continually split and undo older figurations of itself so that it can form, construct and make new bodies of life.

The concept of becoming-returning postulates the formation of life, perception, bodies and thinking [cognition] in processes that extend from the physico-chemical to the consideration of ideas as macro-figurations of becoming and returns. Several forms of subjectivity and consciousness live in the regions of life, perception, body, cognition, constructing new forms of perception and, thus, new forms of life. For new subjectivities to form, one must cut through the codes that set up an idea as what stands for something other, as a convenient abbreviation of some complex goings-on: It means abandoning hierarchical-structural systems of representation where each layer carries information about a lower layer for an upper layer that synthesizes and commands. Conventional science constructs hierarchical-structural models that concentrate information by using codes (representation) so as to have power to make things or people do things at a distance in space and time. Is it correct to speak of shallow and deep codes and of transcription and translation, of a genetic code? This is correct only if one already has adopted the viewpoint of *structural power* and *information/representation.* These molecules do not read their environment according to a set of interpretive signs or Göedel sets of codifying numbers. Should one instead speak of sensitivity? Should one say that DNA becomes in engagements or returns what is called messenger RNA which, in turn, becomes proteins in engagements with ribosomes, and so on? The point made by Varela[14] is that consciousness, knowledge and a certain subjectivity are *in* the body in a dispersed, direct, immanent, bodily way; they *are* the body as a kind of bodily becoming-returning that is a perceiving.

While it is true that the ideas of becoming and of the return have been abused, one should think of them in relation to Heraklitos and to Nietzsche who

13. K. Holzkamp, *Sinnliche Erkenntnis: Historischer Ursprung und gesellschaftliche Funktion der Wahrnehmung,* Athanaum Verlag, Frankfurt am Main, 1973.

14. F.J. Varela and A. Coutinho, "Immuknowledge: The Immune System as a Learning Process of Somatic Individuation," in *Doing Science, The Reality Club,* J. Brockman, ed., Prentice-Hall, New York, 1988.

changed the conventional concept of return by yoking it together with the idea of the will to (become) power (as the power to become a form of life distinguishing itself from an other, that is, the will to become other which, in turn, requires engaging an other).

If there is distinctory power to the idea of "making," it would be that making involves the participation of all bodily chains of becoming-returning in building extended becomings of bodies whereas "constructing" might refer to a structural and mechanical extension that provides for extended transmission of information.

Even if one wished to eschew speculative ontologies, this tendency that is coming to us from the body, this tendency to a wild deconstruction – understood as free-forming construction without superior principle – should be given a chance to try to make all the world become alive as entities *engaging one another in cleaving bonds of perception*. This should be done if only to see whether this freedom will get us out from under the tyranny of dialectical structure and power understood as information manipulation, allowing us to form ourselves as freer and more alive subjectivities who, now more directly engaged with the "all-that-is," would live a different rationality and morality.   In an order of bodily becoming-returning, desire and joy are not hostile or contradictory to consciousness, knowing and rationality: Is this recognized in the biblical "to know the other" which refers to the erotic act?

Bodily thinking

Bodily thinking is not an exercising of power through information transmission but a region in and through which subjectivities and objectivities are becoming and returning. It identifies entities not by framing but in a *mutually sustaining engagement – a return*.

Bodily thinking retains biological and linguistic dimensions, but it views congealed and frozen ideas and meanings as indexical machines and events of internal perception and thinking, some of which have become very strongly established in the biological core of the individual body. Such returns are, for instance, reflexes and instinctual behaviors (avoidance, escape, turning to, aggressions...).

Bodily thinking is both objective and subjective: *It* thinks, yet there is subjectivity in the form of reflective returns of becoming which have special powers as special alignments of becoming and returning to induce other becomings and returnings, to make some history.

Bodily thinking replaces representation by *maps* or *diagrams*; it is a *doubling*, not a copying. While representation seduces its subject to appropriate itself as a separated one through representations, bodily thinking becomes a map as a free form that *becomes action*. As a *perceiving* of sorts, it could make perceivable the strategic order that drives a text by following it out through the hidden molecular processes in it. In this way, it brings linguistic thinking into contact with other forms of thinking and feeling.

Bodily thinking is immanent: It is situated and concrete but never bound by situatedness and concreteness. As immanent thinking, it posits as superior over the model of a centralizing intelligence and consciousness, the model of a dispersed and diffusive intelligence and consciousness – and, therefore, a corresponding architecture as an extended intelligence and consciousness.

Bodily thinking as diagrammatic or maplike doubling of becoming generates different concepts of space, time, object, measure, scale and so on.

Bodily thinking does not carry content or meaning, but is the *form of matter* that can lead to the becoming of a new body of life. Bodily thinking as machinic engagement is not only thought but also "felt" and lived because the personal and other bodies are directly involved. Through this thinking, eye, hand, things, others, are brought together into an engagement intensive enough to undo their preordering, intensive enough to build with the machines of bodily thinking, different bodies, quicker and freer ones. It follows the logic of a machinic consistency immanent in the bodies which it forms. This consistency, therefore, depends on the reach of these bodies: There is a different consistency for the thinking of a microbe and for a life that seeks to expand beyond the "natural" human body.

The fact that representational language has lorded over bodily thinking for so long should not prevent us from realizing that a-representational thinking is essential for the construction of new bodies. One might say that language is an invention intended to open up spaces through which to make new bodies. Language makes a sort of body with artificial senses operating between its formations, that is, the words and sentences. The problem arises when this body is used as a representation of something, which use precisely prevents it from entering into *direct chains of becoming* with other bodies. Representational language constructs a subject that is seduced to contemplating something as if the personal body had already been given it and as if it could actually perceive what does not exist. Through the use of perceptual and thinking machines that fuse it with bodily events, language becomes flesh and body. But such becoming is, of course, nothing like the idea of a "translation" of word and program into architectural form which is no more than an overcoding of spatial form by linguistic formulations.

Bodily thinking does not represent the future as an image but in remaining situated and immanent it indicates, like an empty *glove*, the outlines of the desired and of the possible by *reaffirmatively repeating the present* so as to open up the holes or doors which pull into new becoming. In this sense, a bodily "sign" means what it can do. Thinking is a negative form that calls up what life could fill it. Architectural drawings or models do not represent but become "machines" that pull us into a process of becoming and making precisely by not representing what is missing but by addressing it. Bodily thinking operates with free similitudes or freed abstracted memories that can function as machines that bring about new or repeated becomings and returnings.

Bodily thinking, since it is a becoming, is also a *perceiving*; it is made up of engagements in and through sensitivity.

Bodily thinking is *pervasive* and *transgressive*: It goes down to the micro-levels, to the smallest elements so that the actual flows are re-lived together with those superimposed structurations or figurations, which we call "ideas."

Because this thinking is bodily, its rules of engagement (of itself and of all it can reach) do not follow a formalized and structural logic and a semantics that serve such a logic. It follows rules of consistency, that is, of *constructibility* in processes and figurations of engagement which are machinic and direct. The basic block or elemental construction is the *return – the crossed becoming in engagement* as that which makes something become an entity *for as far and as long as the return reaches*. Physical laws and laws for thinking are nothing more than internal constructions which are subjected to the overall flows of becomings and returnings of all-that-is. Their validity is tested internally against memory, that is, against the whole potentiality of internal returns, and externally when thinking becomes acting.

Other internal returns to be subjected to the constructive action of bodily thinking include "ingrained" tropes of thinking that repeat a certain structural logic of syntactic-formal order or of semantic order, or the type of consciousness and subject that is constructed by a framing performed by some internal viewer/perceiver/thinker.

Bodily thinking is erotic since it is a becoming that is being returned. As erotic thinking, it is also poetic, that is, it "makes." To be able to do so, it has to reach the subcognitional level. There words do not just call up meanings but form direct and wild figurations and so violate the codes and through them one is forced to become more intense. In this context, one may refer to Ricoeur's observations on the metaphor[15] in which a code is violated to establish new links and to shift meaning fields somewhat. This shift requires that the violation be read through the expected "right" semantics. Thus, it can be argued that the metaphor always also reinforces the previously established semantic structure while it may engender only minor local shifts in meaning.

While the metaphoric operation is a transposition of a relation that has been made into a formal construct, a quasi-body, from one level or area to another, metonymy is far more violent and more truly transversal: A word or expression irrupts into an unrelated context and sets off a dissemination, wild flows of becoming and figurations of engagements between hitherto unrelated meaning complexes. These rhetoric ruses force to some extent a bodily re-living of what otherwise would be left to an automatic reading through an automated code. In this sense, the poetic quality of bodily thinking turns the code against itself to take its subject down to the level of molecular bodily becomings from where it has to make anew its own world and its own "itself."

New bodies – perception/conscious

As a becoming, bodily thinking itself is also a perceiving, which means a witnessed and constructed becoming of otherness, difference, quality, power and bodies.

Instead of the order of structural/representative/ informational systems that conceive of a thetic erect subject opposed to its object across a plane of inscription: Subject and object are only the *traces left of a becoming* which is (at least) double, multiplicitous, and of crossing directions.

Bodily thinking assumes that it is *perception* (that is, sensitivity and consciousness in the form of a doubling of the crossed becoming) *which makes life* – in the form of *bodies*. Perception is the thread, the line, along which bodies are assembled, because it is a door for the becoming in-between other bodily becomings and because it reaches into the "negative" of the bodily, into thinking which initiates the opening up spacings for bodies to become in. (When a chemical becoming between two neurons is doubled – "perceived" – by another between other neurons, one has a chemical description of a perception.)

The becoming into-one-another inaugurates the idea of a different perceiving that is mutual immersion, crossed flowing away, enjoying itself in its return.

15. Paul Ricoeur, "The Metaphorical Process as Cognition, Imagination, and Feeling," in *On Metaphor*, S. Sacks, ed., Univesity of Chicago Press, 1978.

Perception is thinking that is *closest to material becoming* and as such it is critical for the making of machines in space that would *expand life into new dimensions* and intensify it by weaving a web of new engagements. After the reign of representation, architecture should become food for the building through perception of "superbodies." Classical sacred architecture's representational myths made such "body-building" into spirit-building. One might argue that making freer and stronger bodies of life requires pervading the universe with *finer (stronger and freer) modes of becoming*, which means, in other words, with more powerful "consciousness," with more powerful doublings of returns of becoming. Such doublings would no longer be the meaningful "signs" and "forms" that are provided for and by the subject of signification and with which it identifies itself, but they would be nonsignifying forms that would intervene in a bodily way to form the new sense surfaces that would call for new becomings and returns.

The environmental perceptual constructs, for instance, that Gibson[16] has termed "affordances," afford a normalized subject a perception of its normalized world and keep on reconstructing normalized bodies. These affordances are a list of returns of becoming that have been framed in the service of a certain normalized mode of functioning. From the more elemental to the more complex, they read like the history of types of order as elaborated by classical architecture: obstruction, behindness, ground, supporting, holding, verticality, horizontality, inside-outside, object quality, direction, centrality, closure, passage, faciality, dislocation as manifestation of movement, surface qualities and, most importantly, constancies of form, size, color and order. Since normalizing perception prevents the forming of other bodies, radical philosophies and arts have invented shocks to frighten the complacent normal subject out of its constraining wits in order to open the doors of perception to all-affirmation of that-which-is. This is necessary whether this subject is of the older hierarchically structured variety or formed as a flat succession of simulative perceptiles and conceptiles.

Consciousness forms when additional transversal engagements spark between different lines of becoming-returning and *double back*. Normal contemporary consciousness is dominated by an internalized dialog of representations addressing themselves to an "I" made up of representations. For the model of becoming-returning, linguistic forms are only relatively privileged extra vectors of becoming which can form additional transversal returns with other "bodily" processes of becoming-and-returning. Forming a sentence then means to form a complex becoming across sensitive word surfaces and through such formation, other life processes can be engaged immanently, transversally and directly. In this

16. E. Reed and R. Jones ed.,
*Reasons for Realism: Selected Essays of
James J. Gibson,*
L. Erlbaum and Associates,
Hillsdale, NJ, 1982.

way, thinking can become action and new bodies. When consciousness is conceived as the forming of returns in-between returns, it becomes the webbing that
constructs a palpable present and, as its constructions become more powerful, it
will eventually reach into all possible pasts and futures of the hyperspace/time of
becoming-returning; it will truly become "all that is."

A body is an order of life forming in cross-weaving, reflective, returning
becomings, building up in direct sensitive/machinic engagements in which entities
become "parts" only by virtue of engaging one another directly as an other.
Following such a concept of a body of life, attention, will, desire and action will be
thought of as *alignments* of processes of becoming-returning with multiple loop-
ings that produce new bodies. As life extends and intends itself through the
becoming-returning of new bodies, might unfolding movements be associated
with Nietzsche's "reactive" or resistant vectors, which would release implicate
orderings and might enfolding movements, the creation of new bodies of life be
associated with his "active" force?[17]

One can argue that this our body still has primacy because other, "quicker"
bodies must become *through* it by using it to form bodies of life in the farther
reaches of materiality. (Simply adding mechanical prosthetic information-pro-
cessing devices to the body will not produce a wider, more powerful becoming-
returning.) Perception, in turn, has primacy because perception is the moment
and the place of the crossing of the arrows, that is reachable to "us," where *life
recaptures itself "through itself"* (as the Latin says). In this sense, perception,
occurring as a becoming-returning through the surfaces of sensitivity, may be said
to be what forms bodies. To form other bodies, other subjectivities, other life, one
must construct new senses and open up new spacings by inserting the perceiving
machines of a new architecture to split open and re-engage the rigidified, informa-
tion- and code-bound, normalized perceptual becomings. This means a new view
of culture: The old "affirmative" culture (in Marcuse's sense[18]) had made us
believe that we might attain the life of gods in the bloody wars of a history that is
but an aberrant representation of the real war of culture: There life would build its
new bodies.

We should be able to learn from our bodies since they live this becoming-
returning and since they *are* a bodily form of consciousness; yet they must not be
elevated to models for future, more complex forms of life. The individual body
immerses "us" into this becoming-and-returning on one side while on its other
side it opens up spaces of thinking, of a bodily abstractness. Abstraction then no
longer means ever more remote and inclusive signification but a bodily pulling

17. Gilles Deleuze,
"Active and Reactive," in
The New Nietzsche,
D.B. Allison, ed.,
Dell, New York, 1977.

18. Herbert Marcuse, "Über den
affirmativen Charakter der Kultur,"
in *Kultur und Gesellschaft, I*,
Suhrkamp Verlag,
Frankfurt am Main, 1968.

away into an other dimension from which a free abstract form may return to affect that from which it had escaped, in offering its formal/material body not to "mean" but directly to conduct the birth of a new line of becoming-returning.

Art is bodily, diagrammatic and machinic thinking when it follows its instinct to make doors for becoming-returning through which life comes as other, renewed, invigorated, freer, and farther- and deeper-reaching. Representational thinking imitates so as to tame, freeze and possess wild becoming. It is imposed on art to press it into serving structural and representational power. In best Nietzschean forgetfulness, strong and liberating art has driven towards unmaking, towards "de-differentiation" of the classical subject and object by weaving bodily-machinic masks, the surfaces that would attract and strengthen the will of life to enter into a new becoming.[19]

Diagramming becoming–returning

The *crossed* movement of *becoming* is a *bodily segregating/engaging* in which, one might say, life *cleaves* itself into ever freer and stronger forms of subjectivity and objectivity. The universe needs life, since this becoming must go through the forming of ever new sensitivity, which means forms of engagement, the traces of which manifest as limits, boundaries, skins, surfaces, masks and marks. These latter are the senses for becoming to occur through them and to be conducted by them into further segregating/engaging, into now more multiplicitous becomings. In this sense, a form in general is a *sense between "things"* that allows a becoming to occur and makes them into bodies of life. In such an erotism of becoming, the other is not reduced to an object but becomes an attracting but also frightening irreducible otherness that both threatens and entices and enables life to construct itself anew.

Bodily thinking conformed to this concept of becoming, itself consists of lines of becoming which can transversally engage other lines of becoming. Certain figurations of such transversal engagements are what we call perception which here is conceived as a witnessed and constructed becoming of otherness, difference, quality, power and bodies. The subject and the object have their nature and their dwelling neither in themselves nor in some larger reality but their life, consciousness and identity are forms of the return of becoming, be it instantaneous and parallel or through time.

The double arrow diagrams becoming as always necessarily a *return*, namely the simplest return of becoming as an engaging from the other and to the other.

Cleaving is the term introduced by Arakawa and Madeline Gins for the forming of perceptioned consciousness[20].

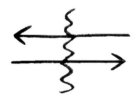

19. A. Ehrenzweig, *The Hidden Order of Art,* University of California Press, 1971.

20. Arakawa and Madeline Gins, "The tentative constructed plan as intervening device (for a reversible destiny)," A+U, December 1991.

This return is not a feedback loop, which is the transmission of information understood as a difference coded to carry a certain meaning. The feedback loop focuses on a rigidified pattern of material flows of becoming and seeks to control and command by manipulating only that level of suprastructural and molar forms which it has linked more or less rigidly to the actual flows through the mechanisms of coding and meaning. Becoming needs to be *answered*, it needs to be returned because it needs engagement to occur and recur. The return of becoming is not to be misconceived as mechanical recurrence of the same; it is, if one insists, at best the return of difference. The returning is an engaging-answering coming from an other desiring to become other, and this answering can be diachronic or instantaneous, it can create a "this" that may live a nanosecond, a year, or a million years.

Through the crossing, folding or knotting of the lines of becoming, there occurs the event of the return – instantaneous or diachronic. As lines of becoming form ever-longer, multiply intersecting returning chains, they form bodies. The crossed becoming replaces the centered or decentered subject by subjectivities formed from reflectively returning lines of becoming that can encompass ever-wider spaces and times. Of special importance for architecture, the return of crossing becomings produces a new kind of wholeness and closure which permits an other, an open kind of *perfection* and *completion* with and in *otherness* and *multiplicity*.

As the crossing vectors of becoming go on engaging and disengaging, connecting and disconnecting, bending and unbending, folding and unfolding, knotting and unknotting, splitting up and splicing together, they form, in-between one another, a multiplicity of spaces and times for perception to go into and for life to live in. Each double vector of this cleaving opens up a dimensionality of life in which intensionalities (intensity, duration) and extensionalities (measured spaces and times) are no longer opposites but aspects of a becoming that appear intensive or extensive, depending on through which traces left by this becoming they will have been thought.

When the return is postulated as that which forms any "thing" and any body, Eros and Thanatos no longer appear as dialectical foes but as crossing/ed becoming-return. This relieves death of the negativity and morbidity which have justified the classical conception of architecture as monument. Only becoming-returning can generate a radically affirmative ontology and epistemology. Support may come from new physics, for instance, where the separation of object and subject and of information and matter is becoming untenable. This could support positing a double becoming-returning between sign/form and content/matter in which becoming-returning would manifest alternately as one or the other. And, on the other side, one could argue that deconstruction could be pushed to arrive at a bodily textuality in which differe/ance is the engagement that makes linguistic forms become new bodies which, in turn, engage other forms of thinking, feeling, acting.

Architecture as Body-Building: A New Animism

Bodily thinking in architecture would lead to a truly radical deconstruction of what constitutes it – that is, the modes in which it thinks spatial-material order and form, and the modes in which it thinks its values and purposes and its relations to the world. On the former point, this would mean moving to thinking and making form as a free and freeing *extending-and-intending*, as multiplicitous figurations made from *self-engaging othernesses*. On the latter, this would mean making new values via a *remaking of client and program*.

When consciousness and life are conceived as doublings of returns of becoming, there is life in stones insofar as they can maintain such returns or become part of more complex and extensive bodies of life. One can argue that the oldest function of art is magic, the art of marshalling any means available and necessary (including destructive ones) to *make life*, employing representational material only as a ruse to trigger becoming. Such an architecture inserts machines into the processes of internal perception and/or into the material environment, and so forms new senses or modes of perception which build new bodies of life (as returns upon returns of becoming), which may live in more intensive and extensive dimensions and thus develop some independence from existing individual and social bodies. An architecture for such animistic becoming needs to open up to science and art but on the other side, it itself becomes a necessary field for not only the humanities and ecology, biology, sociology but also physics and mathematics to engage their knowledge.

In an architecture of becoming, an object is not a lump but a *nodal complex of returns* (of thinking, remembering, feeling, imagining, sensing, doing), where these engagements are seen from the viewpoint of a subjectivity as a node with self-involving returns perceiving a becoming going out from or coming in to itself. So is the "place." While the idea of place has somewhat shifted the emphasis from the object at least to a mediated subject-object relation, perhaps even to a little contamination, it seems almost invariably to end up as an expression of the spirit of a collective subject. "Place" and "site" now become *surfaces, in-betweens* that offer tentacles and gates for cleaving engagements and reengagements that would form new kinds of subjectivity and objectivity. Place and site are privileged because they offer the power directly to address and reach the personal body which is the primary gate for the weaving, knotting and folding of doubled crossing arrows of engagement that can be constructed with/against the place.

As bodily thinking espouses a radical affirmation of becoming-returning, the subjectivities it forms inhabit as they are being inhabited; they open up and fill all the spaces through which they are becoming and returning as subjectivities. What is outside is that which has not been engaged, or that which can only be engaged indirectly after detours in space and time. This architecture is not about making a home but about making ever-wider and deeper returns that are both subjectivity and objectivity and at-home and off-home all together in the engagement of one and an other.

To make an architecture of becoming requires rethinking notions of program and spatial order. To give direction and strength to bodily design thinking we still need theory. This theory will not explain but will *diagram* and *conduct* the making of an ever-unfolding manifold of thinking/feeling/doing that reach from the most spiritual bodiliness to the most material doing. This theory is the art and science of dance, of engagement, and despite its lowly position it is more, far more, than tunes to whistle in the forest or a little story to make us tick that Johnson, speaking perhaps for a substantial part of the profession, has recently postulated as the proper role for theory.[21] This theory will have to engage many "outside" sciences and arts, especially as related to the bodily as a kind of consistency, of thinking, and of consciousness. It must operate at all levels of program, situation and building, beginning with intensifying the doubled crossed becoming where it has been congealed into static and infertile roles, and it must concern itself with the tacit programs imposed by the larger societal organization and the prevalent modes of thinking. Also at this level theory would begin with intensifying "reactive" becomings so as to form a different subject and object, not as a *"weak"* subject, object or form (they already are), but as returns of crossed becomings: This will bring about other forms of social association, of work, of culture, of economy, of politics. A theory that constitutes itself as re-doublings in thinking of concrete bodily connections quickly shows who or what actually makes architecture and, in turn, what architecture makes: Program, client, forms of professionalized practice,

21. Philip Johnson, "Preface." in J. Kipnis.
In the Manor of Nietzsche.

law, fashion, theory, personal preoccupation. All of these factors point to the need critically to assess and re-form the classical ideology of the dialectical subject-object relation that underlies all these roles and practices.

In bodily thinking, space is no longer a preexisting gaping emptiness to be occupied by objects, but is an *opening made in* and *for becoming-returning*. Space is a conditionality of becoming and returning. It is a tensional "spacing" arising as the in-betweens of segregating/engaging becomings. And, correspondingly, time is no longer a succession of atomic moments but a "timing" arising from the same movement of crossed/ing becoming-returning. Space is freed from being a representation of closure, time is freed from representing the schema of origin/beginning-telos/end. Both become pulsations, the *breathing in and out of becoming-returning*, the building elements of bodies forming in the dance of becoming that returns from ever-wider and deeper rounds at ever-higher speeds and with ever-more freedom.

Consequently the place is not a center established in space and the present is not an elusive section through the flow of time: They are specific crossings of becoming that open to a situated perception. More importantly, these localities of becoming can become the openings through which transversally other becomings can run. In this sense the situation, the present and the place, can now reach anywhere and anytime in space-time through concatenations of becoming-returning. This gives a new ontological foundation to architecture in the form of a carpet of connectivity between all-that-is rather than as a representation of structural Being.

What bounds an object or subject is not what has been cut out or framed by an imposed expressive and meaningful container. On the one hand, a boundary is established by the extent of the *reflectiveness of the becomings-returnings* that open an *"internal"* space-time for an object. On the other hand, the intensity of penetration of new engagements can push the bounding surface deep into the object or far out beyond the outline that is constructed in normal perception. Before art became craft, it had been magic, that is, the making of new life for which it needed to open up bodies, spaces, time flows, so as to rebuild them. Such an art would make diagrams or maps which form the mutual surfaces of sensitivity or masks for the spacing-and-timing of the engagement of the new becoming. The surface of both the classical and of the modern object is conceived as an emitter of messages decoded by a viewing subject who reads (unconsciously) a message establishing the presumed unicity of the object as part of a structural system of objects and subjects. The surfaces of an object in crossed becoming are *sites* or *doors*, outgoing *tentacles* and inbound *gates* and *paths* producing new crossing/ed becomings-returnings. These surfaces enfold or unfold multiplicitous space-times for the becoming of subjectivities and objectivities which are always multiple in themselves with as many intensities and extensionalities as there can be becomings.

Plans, sections, elevations or models of a building can be made in a manner that seeks to represent an absent goal or they can be made and used as machines, as bodily forms that participate in a process of becoming and making. Drawings, models and linguistic formulations all join to set off becomings that lead towards the becoming of a building. The working methods of Loos, Scarpa or Siza demonstrate their tendency to such a machinic bodily thinking. The use of "external" material forms for thinking is necessary because perceiving these forms makes our bodies participate intensively and directly in the process of becoming/making.

Even verbal or pictorial "descriptions" are not representational when they function by inserting themselves as little machines that give memories of bodily perception and thus specific direction, quality and scale to a process of making life. Drawings, scaled or free, and the models are ambivalent: On the one hand, we allow ourselves to be fascinated in seeing them as representations; on the other, their formal power is needed to engender a becoming of new thought-perception. In bodily thinking, drawings are liberated from the burden to represent a content according to the extraneous logic of a trained perception, and their lines and planes serve to permit the eye and attached processes to become a new objectivity-and-subjectivity to enter into lines of other becomings which will lead to building a building. The forms bring back memories and offer their bodies to a new perception and thus a construction of a different body. These little becomings *repeat* – in the sense of bringing back – certain characteristics that have been *abstracted* – in the bodily sense of having been *pulled away* from a becoming that has been experienced. Memory is what performs such repetition by forming abstracted bodily returns of becomings as little building blocks for new bodies. These forms must cross out their tendency to become representations by declaring themselves insistently as free similitudes, as free abstractions. Instead of perfecting illusionistic means, architectural thinking needs to invent bodily-machinic forms with diagrammatic qualities that have the power to pull in whole complexes of becomings that may exist as memories, knowledge, desire, be they individual or collective. (This concept of abstract diagrammatic form was proposed by Deleuze and Guattari and has been presented more recently with Guattari's "partial enunciators," animating perceivings that bring about an intensive re-living of memory in a bodily event.[22])

22. Félix Guattari, presentation at symposium "The Caged Body," in honor of Paul Nelson's work, Graduate School of Architecture, Planning, and Preservation, Columbia University, April 1990.

Since model and drawing heavily favor the eye that commands a scene by being in a position to survey it, a-representational models and drawings should offer diagrammatic qualities that permit partial – in the sense of abstract – returns of experiences that are more strongly "bodily." This would include, for instance, moving along or across or into or out, being arrested, uplifted, being surrounded, touching and being touched, living a partial aspect of the effort and time that something takes, having a repeated, more quotidian experience of the projected space. In this way the absent qualities in relation to the personal body of a building that does not exist yet would not be represented, but the body would be subjected to perceptual travails which would construct qualities of scale in a becoming-palpable.

Making bodies of life means first instituting the segregating/engaging cleaving, the opening up, the making of senses for crossed becomings between what otherwise are only brute mechanical encounters. This requires techniques to undo the normalized constructions of perception and to suck the normalized senses away into new opened-up worlds: to become the stone and the tree as they become the perceiving subjectivity. Overaffirmation that overloads the active or passive movements of normalized becoming can take the form of repeating, luring, interrupting, splitting, frustrating, speeding up, suspending. While overloading may be the first step in extending perception in order to extend life through and beyond the individual body, what are the machines and weapons to build an other body for life, how do they ally themselves with parts of the individual body, how does the older body split, what inserts itself into it and propels it into multiplicitous forms of life with higher "speeds"? Once new sense has extended the body and enabled it to penetrate and become more of the universe, how is it sustained and nourished until it becomes capable of forming its own return, its own body, life, and consciousness? As a horde of warriors or dancers engage one another, they are empowering one another temporarily to perceive and function as a new body. For new, more complex and "faster" bodies of life to endure, they must be able to nourish themselves through perception in a broad sense, that is, through redoublings of crossed becoming at their boundaries. Can such bodies become independent of the individual body? The "economies" of other bodies of life can only be invented by trial and error utilizing any available experience, whether currently deemed scientific or not.

As the dimensions and boundaries of perceiving and thus of bodies in becoming shift, perceiving appears more like an internal feeling/knowing or a bodily thinking going through a multiplicity of surfaces of ever-more intensive and more extensive bodies of returns of becoming – and, correspondingly, thinking becomes an "internal" perceiving. While in classical architecture interiority had been the concept that permitted construction of unitary objects that frame and symbolize a content, an architecture of becoming should speak only of the coherence of bodies as a measure of the returns of becoming of which they are made and of the intensity with which these multiple coordinated returns are intertwining and redoubling one another. Architecture is no longer all out there, our bodies are no longer all in here: The returns of becoming form complex bodies of life wherein one can speak of subjectivity whenever there are reflective redoublings of becoming which perceive themselves as a subject of a movement of becoming while they perceive as objects what they see in the other direction of becoming.

Yet, this architecture is still primarily about inhabiting and only secondarily about looking at. But this inhabiting is no longer the classical seeking to return to the Mother/Father, to find a place to be accepted in the greatest return run by a power that we can never become. This longing to be allowed inside, this longing to belong, this longing to be comforted and have comfort, is what classical architecture and humanism and their postmodern revivals are about.

Such an architecture belongs with an ontological schema that postulates an increasing penetration of the universe of possible life forms through constructing bodies of life with the aid of abstract thinking machines that build new sense and perception to form bodies as new forms for life. Historically, the state, the region and the city, with their monuments and their spatial fabric, have served as the *symbolically represented* versions of this moving-out of life into new bodies and have provided *vicarious satisfaction* to life's drive to become hotter, *more intensive* and *extensive*, and *immortal*. Since it is the unperceived that kills, one can argue that to prevent our self-destruction, perception must be made more a penetrating becoming that intensively and extensively cleaves to every corner of the universe.

We seem to be entering an era of cold and deadening unkindness in comparison to which even the fascination with the self of the 1980s seems almost endearing. Society is fast losing all remaining social bonds and is, therefore, incapable of developing an ethic or of generating vision since both of these require a sufficiently well-functioning bodily connectivity between people: My vision means nothing to you if we are not connected into a shared becoming through/with or even against this vision. If we make architecture together, we will also make our personal bodies and the bodies which they form with one another into new bodies. Forget the fascinating representational image and the power it conveys, work with bodily engagements: Architecture could yet become an important discipline.

There is no fate but what you make.

Terminator II

When one has emerged from the circle
of errors and illusions within which actions
are performed, taking a position is virtually
an impossibility. A minimum of silliness is
essential for everything, for affirming and
even for denying.

E. M. Cioran

C O N T R I B U T O R S

Michael Benedikt, professor of architecture at the University of Texas at Austin, is the author of *For an Architecture of Reality.* He also edited and contributed to *Cyberspace: First Steps.* In addition to practicing architecture in Austin, he has lectured widely and published numerous articles that cross the boundaries of architecture, science and literature.

Brian Boigon is an artist and architecture theoretician living and working in Toronto. In addition to exhibiting his work internationally, he has published several articles in the genre of ficto-theory. He is currently assistant professor at the University of Toronto School of Architecture, editor of *Impulse* magazine and director of the Culture Lab in Toronto.

Lee Breuer is a theater director and one of the founders of the Mabou Mines theater group.

Dan Bucsescu, a native of Romania, studied architecture in Bucharest and New York City. In the early 1970s, he spent several years working and studying in Europe, completing his graduate degree in England. Upon his return to New York in 1976, he continued his academic and architectural activities, dividing his time between teaching and architectural practice. He has lectured and written about architectural education with a focus on grounding the pedagogical experience in theories of knowledge and philosophy of art. He teaches at Pratt Institute.

Lucinda E. Dip received a B. Arch. from Pratt Institute.

Keller Easterling is a playwright and architect living in New York City. Her plays have been performed in New York, Los Angeles and Edinburgh. After having acted and directed for many years, she began writing serial pieces for the theater. One series, for example, explores rooms, spaces and houses; another is a series of behavior demonstrations. She also teaches at Parsons School of Design and Pratt Institute. She is currently making an NEA-sponsored videotape/videodisc documentary entitled *Call It Home,* which focuses on suburbia in America from 1934 to 1960. She also recently received a Graham Foundation grant to publish a volume of essays on the comparative taxonomy of small towns and suburbs in America.

Gamal El-Zoghby, a native of Egypt, is a professor at Pratt Institute.

Peter Erni wishes he had been born in one of the dark Eastern European backwater countries whose linguistic melancholy would have predisposed him to thick sophisticated stuttering in American English. He is currently in his fifth year of entertaining the possibility of an undergraduate degree in architecture at various institutions in New York City. His latest essay is *ee neem e any mykn ee mo: Possibilities of Cathartic Play in an Architectural Rendezvous with the Shoehorn.*

Kenneth Frampton is currently the W.A.R.E. Professor of Architecture at Columbia University. He is author of the acclaimed *Modern Architecture: A Critical History.* His most recent book, *Studies in Tectonic Culture,* will be published at the end of the year by MIT Press.

Tom Finkelpearl is an artist and director of the Percent for Art Program for the Department of Cultural Affairs, City of New York.

Deborah Gans is an associate professor at Pratt Institute and a principal of PATH Architecture. She is the author of *The Le Corbusier Guide* and managing editor for Building Arts Forum/New York (BAF/NY) of *Bridging the Gap: Rethinking the Relation of Architect and Engineer.*

Bolleck Greczynski is an installation artist living and working in New York City.

Patrick Heelan is a professor of philosophy and dean of Humanities and Fine Arts at State University of New York at Stony Brook. He holds Ph.D.'s in theoretical geophysics and the philosophy of science, and does philosophy in a post-Husserlian hermeneutical vein, specializing in three interrelated topics: the logic of contextual discourse, characteristic (he says) of both quantum mechanics and the social sciences; the phenomenological transformation of theoretical terms into perceptual ones during the course of laboratory performances (so that the data comes under suspicion); and the geometrical structure of visual space which, even as Aristotle testified, is not Euclidean (even though its measures are Euclidean).

Dan Hoffman, a graduate of Cooper Union, has taught at several schools of architecture including the University of Detroit, Carleton University and the University of Toronto. He currently heads the Architecture Studio at the Cranbrook Academy of Art. He is also a practicing architect who has worked with William Kessler in Detroit and Edward Larrabee Barnes in New York.

Keith James teaches at Pratt Institute.

John Johansen, professor of architecture at Pratt Institute, is a practicing architect who trained under Walter Gropius and Marcel Breuer. Some of his built projects include the U.S. Embassy in Dublin, the Charles Center Theater in Baltimore, the Goddard Library at Clark University, the Oklahoma Theater Center, parts of the Roosevelt Island neighborhood, and numerous houses – some forty buildiings to date. He lectures widely and is currently involved in experimental architecture and the research and development of building technologies. His work and writings have been exhibited and published in the U.S. and abroad.

Andrea Kahn is a New York architect engaged in a practice of theory and criticism. She has taught at numerous schools on the East Coast and in the Midwest and is currently the Cass Gilbert Visiting Professor of Architecture at the University of Minnesota School of Architecture. She is the editor of *Drawing/Building/Text,* and her writings have appeared in various journals, including *Design Book Review, Midgard, Harvard Architectural Review* and *Journal of Architectural Education.*

Tibor Kalman, a childhood Hungarian emigré, first came in contact with design problems when employed as a women's shoe salesman. He launched his design career by filling in for an ill window display artist, and in 1979 he founded M&Co., a multidisciplinary firm that tries to reinvent the wheel for clients ranging from Knoll International to Talking Heads. Among M&Co.'s many projects is their award-winning watch design, which occupies a permanent place in the design collection of the Museum of Modern Art.

Ken Kaplan and Ted Krueger are co-founders of K&K Research and Development, a prototyping laboratory for the recombination of architecture, technology and politics. Their current minimum security facilities are split between Peekskill and Brooklyn, New

York. Recent investigations include *Renegade Cities* (a traveling exhibition) and *Buffalo Analog* (commissioned by Art Park in Lewistown, New York). Their forthcoming publication, *Mosquitoes*, will be issued by the Pamphlet Architecture Limited Series.

John Knesl was born and educated in Vienna, Austria. He has worked as an architect and planner in Austria, the United Kingdom and the U.S. and has also taught in Austria and the U.S. He is the author of numerous articles and essays on architectural theory and criticism and is currently chief urban designer at the Department of Transportation, New York City.

Sanford Kwinter is an editor of ZONE Books. He earned his doctorate in comparative literature at Columbia University and has taught at Harvard University Graduate School of Design, and Ohio State University. He is the author of the forthcoming, *Immanence and Event.*

Thomas Leeser practices architecture in New York City and teaches at Princeton University.

Ed Levine, sculptor and director of the Visual Arts Program, Department of Architecture at Massachusetts Institute of Technology, writes "born in Brooklyn and can't forget it...."

Adrian Luchini teaches at Washington University School of Architecture and is one of the principals of Schwetye Luchini Maritz Architects. Located in St. Louis, the firm considers itself a place where theory and practice, in all their implications and virtues, are not seen as two independent or mutually exclusive ways to produce architecture, but as two fundamental components in a profession that faces a pressing challenge from the multiple demands of today's society. Their work has appeared in publications from the U.S., Italy and Japan and has been exhibited in Seattle, Chicago, Kansas, Arkansas, New York City and St. Louis.

Brian McGrath teaches at Parsons School of Design and is a principal of PATH Architecture. His forthcoming book, *Transparent Cities*, will be published by SITE Books.

Alvaro Malo is a practicing architect currently on the faculty of the University of Pennsylvania School of Architecture. He has also taught at Columbia University.

Taeg Nishimoto, principal of Taeg Nishimoto + ALLIED ARCHITECTS, received his B.Arch. from Waseda University and M.Arch. from Cornell University. He is on the faculty at Columbia University and Pratt Institute and has taught at New Jersey Institute of Technology. Recent awards include a 1991 NYC/AIA Project Award, as well as grants and fellowships from the New York Council on the Arts and the New York Foundation for the Arts.

Philip Parker teaches at Rhode Island School of Design and practices in Providence.

Stephen Perella, an intern architect, is editor and designer of *Newsline* for Columbia University Graduate School of Architecture, Planning and Preservation. He was an editor of *Pratt Journal*, Volume 1 and the editor and designer of Volume 2, *Form; Being; Absence.*

Pascal Quintard-Hofstein is a practicing architect with projects in New York City and Paris. He is on the faculty at New York Institute of Technology and Columbia University, and teaches at Pratt Institute.

Hani Rashid was born in 1958 and received his B.Arch. from Carleton University and M.Arch. from Cranbrook Academy of Art. He and his partner, Liseanne Couture, founded Asymptote in New York City in 1987 as an alternative architectural practice. He has been teaching at Columbia University since 1989.

Robert Rogers is principal of Rogers Marble Architects in New York City. He is currently visiting assistant professor at Pratt Institute.

Michael Silver received a B.Arch. from Pratt Institute and M.Arch. from Columbia University. He lives in Brooklyn where he is completing *Of Milk in Violet*, a project which examines the exteriority of space in terms of the central nervous system. *Brooklyn-Cycle* appeared in Volume 2 of the *Pratt Journal.*

Kim Tanzer teaches at the University of Florida School of Architecture and practices in Gainesville.

John L. Veikos was born in New York City on May 28, 1968.

Peter Wilson was born in 1950 in Melbourne, Australia, and completed his architectural studies at the Architecture Association in London in 1974. He taught at the AA from 1978 to 1988. He is currently a principal of Architekturbüro Bolles Wilson & Partner. Recent projects include Blackburn House (London, 1988), Munster Library (1993), Frankfurt Kundergarten (1992) and Folly (Osaka, 1990).

Arthur Wood has had a varied career as architect (Pratt '53), painter, inventor (with several patents in process for drawing instruments, cameras and artist's easel), sculptor and artisan. His monumental work, an ongoing building project undertaken with his wife, Cynthia, is the environmental sculpture and home, *Broken Angel.*

Christian Xatrec is an artist presently living in New York City.

Sol Yurick is author of several novels and essays including *Metatron*, The Auction, The King of Malaputa and The Gerontomat. His novel, *The Warriors*, was made into a movie.

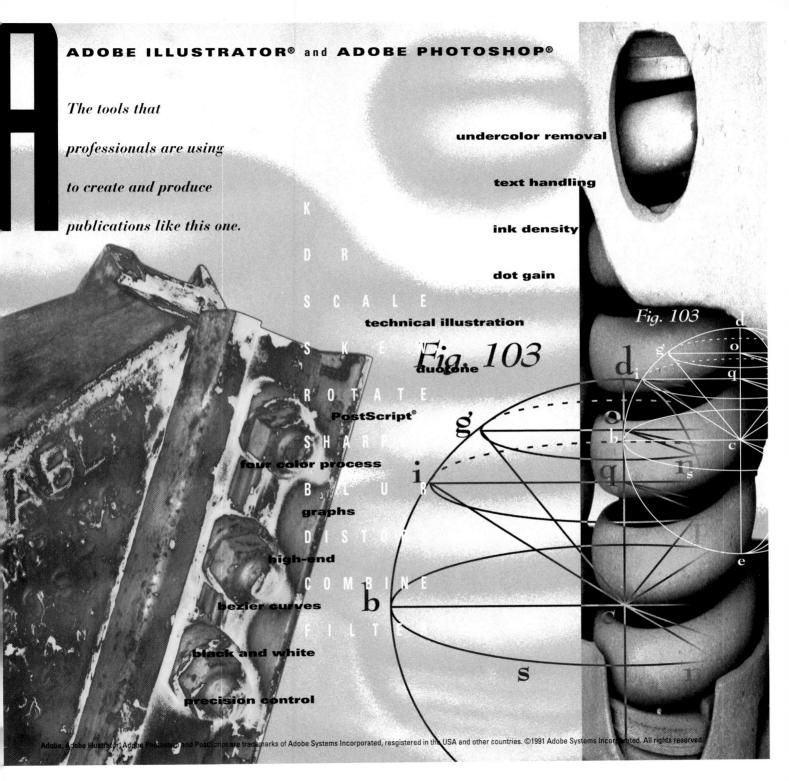

ADOBE ILLUSTRATOR® and ADOBE PHOTOSHOP®

The tools that professionals are using to create and produce publications like this one.

undercolor removal

text handling

ink density

dot gain

technical illustration

duotone

Fig. 103

PostScript®

four color process

graphs

high-end

bezier curves

black and white

precision control

K D R SCALE S K E ROTATE SHARP B L U R DISTO COMBINE FILTE

Fig. 103